P9-CFN-401

THE
SUCCESSFUL
INVESTOR
TODAY

Also by Larry E. Swedroe

Rational Investing in Irrational Times
What Wall Street Doesn't Want You to Know
The Only Guide to a Winning Investment Strategy You'll Ever Need

THE SUCCESSFUL INVESTOR TODAY

14 Simple Truths
You Must Know When You Invest

◆

LARRY E. SWEDROE

◆

TRUMAN TALLEY BOOKS

ST. MARTIN'S PRESS

NEW YORK

www.stmartins.com

Library of Congress Cataloging-in-Publication Data

Swedroe, Larry E.
    The successful investor today : 14 simple truths you must know when you invest / Larry E. Swedroe.—1st U.S. ed.
        p. cm.
    Includes bibliographical references (p. 299).
    ISBN 0-312-30979-1
        1. Investments—Handbooks, manuals, etc.   I. Title.
HG4527.S94 2003
332.6—dc21

2003047145

First Edition: September 2003

10 9 8 7 6 5 4 3 2 1

This book is dedicated to the love of my life,
my wife, Mona. Thank you for all your
support, patience, and most of all your love.
No man could ask for more.
Walking through life with you has
truly been a gracious experience

Contents

CONTENTS

Introduction

There is an ongoing war on Wall Street. Not a conventional one fought with armies, tanks, and planes, but a war nonetheless. It is a war being fought for control of the hearts, minds, and ultimately the wallets of individual investors. On one side are aligned the investment banking firms of Wall Street, the media, and the vast majority of the financial press. On the other side are aligned the academic community of financial economists, a relatively small community of fee-only registered investment advisors (RIAs) who have adopted passive asset class investing as their investment strategy, and a tiny minority of Wall Street's no-hype financial press. The tiny minority includes Scott Burns, Jonathan Clements, Humberto Cruz, Beverly Goodman, Jane Bryant Quinn, and Jason Zweig.

I wrote the book you now hold during the period of possibly the greatest bear market of the post–World War II era. To a great extent this bear market was a result of the inevitable bursting of the technology-led bubble of the late 1990s (what Federal Reserve Chairman Alan Greenspan called "irrational exuberance"). Millions of investors unnecessarily incurred trillions of dollars of losses because:

- They believed the investment myths of Wall Street, including "this time it's different" and "the price you pay for a great company doesn't matter."

- They were bamboozled by Wall Street's many conflicts of interest, such as between the investment banking arms of brokerage firms and the recommendations of their security analysts, ultimately leading to the destruction of their financial health.

- They were caught up in the hype and exuberance created by the media, particularly TV, which only wants to excite investors to grab their attention, not educate them.

- They wanted to believe there was easy money to be made.

- And, perhaps most important, most investors did not have the knowledge about how markets really work that would have allowed them to defend themselves against the heavily armed propaganda forces of the investment community.

It is important for investors today to understand that neither this bubble nor the ensuing devastating losses were anything new. Both the bubble and the "afterbath" have occurred many times before. It seems that while investors (and therefore markets) are rational most of the time, about every thirty to forty years they become irrationally exuberant. Forty years appears to be just long enough for those caught up in the last mania to forget its lessons and for a new generation of young sheep to come along to be sheared. There is always some new technology that galvanizes investors into a state of irrational exuberance. In the 1990s, it was the Internet and the dot.com revolution. In the 1960s, it was the electronics/computer revolution. That period was characterized by the Nifty Fifty—fifty great companies that investors were told they should buy regardless of how high the price became. That period of irrational exuberance was characterized by the same type of irrational valuations we had in the 1990s, with P/E (price-to-earnings) ratios in the hundreds; the same IPO boom and bust; the same collapse of prices by as much as 80 to 90 percent for the glamorous technology stocks; and interestingly enough, the same types of accounting scandals surrounding phony earnings. The 1920s bubble was fueled by the automobile age and the promise of the great new technologies of radio and, later, television. That bubble ended in the crash of 1929. Just a few years later, the president of the NYSE (New York Stock Exchange) was imprisoned. In the prior century, we had a similar bubble fueled by the mania created over railroads. And prior to that there were enough bubbles for Charles MacKay, in 1841, to write a book, *Extraordinary Popular Delusions and the Madness of Crowds*. MacKay noted: "Every age has its peculiar folly: some scheme, project, or fantasy into which it plunges, spurred on by the love of gain, the necessity of excitement or the force of imitation." Among the fourteen essential truths of investing you will learn about in this book is that knowledge of financial history is critical to investment success.

I hope after reading this book you will learn that if you had been armed with the knowledge of the *14 Simple Truths You Must Know When You Invest* and followed the commonsense advice contained within those truths, you would have been able to avoid the disastrous results that have devastated millions of investors in the past few years. For example, you would have avoided:

- Placing your faith (and assets) in hot active fund managers, such as those of the Janus family.
- Gambling your hard-earned assets on sector funds, such as those investing in Internet and telecom stocks.

- Having too many eggs in one basket, no matter how safe that basket looked (e.g., Enron, WorldCom, etc.).

- Strategies that the very best and brightest professionals had already tried and failed at, such as choosing actively managed mutual funds based on their historical track records.

- Taking more risk than you had the ability, willingness, and, perhaps most importantly, the need to take in order to achieve your financial goals.

Those investors who followed the fourteen simple truths outlined in this book, including the building of globally diversified portfolios using only passive investment vehicles, did not suffer the devastating losses experienced by millions of investors. For example, while the NASDAQ was losing over 75 percent of its value (and many tech stocks and tech funds experienced even greater losses) and the large-growth stocks of the S&P 500 Index lost almost 45 percent between January 2000 and the third quarter of 2002:

- Real estate investment trusts rose by almost 50 percent.
- Small-value stocks rose about 5 percent.
- Small-cap stocks remained virtually unchanged in value.
- Large-value stocks fell less than 10 percent.
- All government fixed-income funds provided healthy returns.

As you can readily see, the devastating losses could have been avoided, and it did not take any great stock picking or market-timing skills to achieve superior performance. What it did take was an understanding of how markets work and how to make them best work for you. As you will learn, the right strategy never changes, regardless of whether the bull is stampeding or the bear has emerged from hibernation. And you will learn the right strategy. While learning these fourteen simple truths cannot undo the damage already done, the knowledge gained can act just like an inoculation against a disease, providing immunization against future investment debacles.

This book explains fourteen simple and universal truths, each of which stands the tests of logic and time, about how the market really works, as opposed to how Wall Street and the media would have you believe it works. These truths are based on the views of the opposition to Wall Street, an opposition that has no biases. Its only objective is to seek the truth. To repeat, the opposition is comprised of the academic community of financial economists. Financial economists, along with their allies in the fight (fee-only advisors who have adopted passive asset class investing plus a few print media columnists), are in a battle over the minds and wallets of investors as to which investment approach is most likely to produce the best returns for the amount of risk taken.

There are two contrasting theories about how markets work. These theories compete for your investment dollars. The conventional wisdom is that smart people, working very diligently, can uncover stocks that are undervalued (mispriced) and can successfully time the market (be fully invested when the bull is raging, and sell just before the bear awakens from its hibernation). This is the art of active management. It is also the "wisdom" in which Wall Street and its allies want and need investors to believe because that is how they generate their sizable profits. Unfortunately, as you will learn, Wall Street's own profits come at the expense of investors. It is why in this battle I call the proponents of active management "the dark side," to use a *Star Wars* term.

It is important to remember that just because something is conventional wisdom does not make it correct. For example, believing that the Earth is flat was once conventional wisdom. And Galileo spent the last eight years of his life under house arrest for espousing the theory that the Earth was not the center of the universe. As author Anatole France warned: "If fifty million people say a foolish thing, it is still a foolish thing."

The other theory about how markets work is called the efficient markets hypothesis (EMH). The EMH is how financial economists explain how markets work, how assets are priced, and how the risks and rewards of investing are determined. There are investment firms that provide vehicles that allow investors to implement an investment plan based on the EMH. Among them are Barclays Global Advisors, DFA (Dimensional Fund Advisors), State Street, and Vanguard. They are the forces of good, the providers of light against "the dark side." At the core of the EMH is the insight that *new* information is disseminated to the public so rapidly and so fully that stock prices nowadays instantly adjust to the new data. A good analogy is that financial markets operate much like our body's central nervous system in that they receive and relay information in an extremely rapid fashion. The EMH theorizes that the market's price is always the best *estimate* of the correct price; otherwise the market would trade at a different price. If this is the case, an investor can consistently beat the market only with either the best of luck or with inside information (on which it is illegal to trade). Believers in the EMH adopt what is known as a passive investment strategy. They build portfolios using passive investment vehicles such as index/passive asset class funds and ETFs (exchange-traded funds), and they adhere over the long term to their desired allocations, engaging in no stock selection or market-timing activities.

As a principal, as well as the director of research, for both the investment advisory firm Buckingham Asset Management and its affiliated company BAM Advisor Services, one of my roles is to expose Wall Street's "investment propaganda" and conflicts of interests and to bring the light of truth about how markets really work to our clients, both individuals as well as other investment advisory firms. This knowledge is then used to help construct portfolios, using only passive investment vehicles that are based on each investor's unique ability, willingness, and need to take risk.

The purpose of this book is to lead you to the winning strategy. I hope to accomplish this by explaining the simple truths about investing and how markets really work. Being exposed to these truths will help investors learn:

- Why Wall Street and most of the financial media are not your friends.
- Why much of what Wall Street and the financial media and press put out is rightly called investment propaganda.
- Why active management is the loser's game.
- Why passive investing is the winner's game.

I hope that by providing you with this knowledge you will learn that disciplined, passive investing is the best way to avoid many of the most common and dangerous mistakes investors make. As author G. K. Chesterton stated: "Fallacies do not cease to be fallacies because they become fashions." The knowledge gained will also help protect you from being exploited by the wolves of Wall Street. Ultimately, the book is about making you a better and more informed investor, greatly increasing the chances of achieving your financial goals by increasing your wealth, gradually, over time. It is about inoculating you against the investment propaganda of "the dark side" of the investment community.

In summary, equity investing is an act of faith. It is a faith in the United States, and an increasingly global capitalist system.

(There are very few noncapitalist countries left in the world.) In the long run, equity markets reward investors for taking the risk of owning equities. But that is true *only* if investors have faith in the market and the discipline to ignore the noise and clutter of the market and the emotions stirred by the noise of the financial media. Having a well-thought-out plan is only a necessary condition for success, not a sufficient one. The sufficient condition is having the discipline and patience to stay the course, building *your* wealth, not Wall Street's. The key to discipline is knowledge, the knowledge provided in the *14 Simple Truths You Must Know When You Invest.*

Finally, investors should note this truth. At the end of 1999, investors were almost universally rushing into the stock market, in many, if not most cases, without regard to the risks involved. After all, there was easy money to be made. After experiencing the worst bear market in the post–World War II era, compounded by the related corporate-scandal fallout, many individuals have become shell-shocked when it comes to equity investing. In some cases, they have sworn off investing in stocks forever. In other cases, they are paralyzed into inaction. What these investors fail to understand is that the *expected* returns to individuals willing and able to take the risk of equity investing are now substantially greater than they were at the end of 1999 (although still lower than the historical average). The reason is simple: Prices are now much lower than they were in 1999 (although still higher than they have been historically). The environment for equity investing is thus much more favorable now than it was when most investors were throwing caution to the wind. The truth is that bull markets enrich those already invested, while, in effect, making poorer those who are not (because expected future returns are lower). Bear markets, on the other hand, while reducing the value

INTRODUCTION

of current assets, bring the promise of higher expected future returns. Keep this in mind as you develop your investment policy.

Readers of my other books should note that some of the material covered here is also covered in the other books. Where appropriate, data has been updated.

THE SUCCESSFUL INVESTOR TODAY

◆

Active Investing Is a Loser's Game: It Must Be So

Active management is a beauty contest in which the average contestant is kind of ugly.
—John Rekenthaler, *Wall Street Journal*

It is not easy to get rich in Las Vegas, at Churchill Downs, or at the local Merrill Lynch office.   —Paul Samuelson

We are not afraid to follow the truth wherever it may lead, nor to tolerate any error so long as reason is left free to combat it.   —Thomas Jefferson

Those whom the gods would destroy they first make active managers.   —Anonymous

There are widespread misunderstandings about asset allocation evident in its practice in portfolio management. These conceptions lead to error in its practice which would be comical, were they not so terribly costly. [Investors] shuffle their asset mix and churn portfolios in an emotional response to the markets.
—Robert D. Arnott, "Managing the Asset Mix: Decisions and Consequences," *Pension Fund Investment Management*

Probably the most contentious debate in the field of investing is whether active or passive management is the strategy most likely to prove to be the winning one. Believers in passive management as the winning investment approach generally use the EMH (efficient markets hypothesis) as the basis of their argument. The foundation of the EMH is that efforts to outperform the market are highly unlikely to produce returns in excess of the market's overall rate of return because everything currently knowable about a company is already incorporated into the stock price, and the next piece of available information will be random as to whether it will be better or worse than the market expects. Believers in active management believe that the market is inefficient—that the market not only misprices securities, but that new information is not incorporated instantly; it is, instead, incorporated into prices slowly, over time.

The vast body of evidence clearly falls in favor of the passive management camp. It can be summarized as follows:[1]

- The average actively managed fund has underperformed its appropriate passive benchmark on a pretax basis by about 1.8 percent per annum. On an after-tax basis, the performance is even worse.
- There is no persistence in performance beyond that which would be randomly expected—the past performance of an individual active manager is a very poor predictor of his/her future performance.
- Expenses reduce returns on a one-for-one basis.
- Turnover reduces pretax returns by almost 1 percent of the value of the trade.

Similar evidence has been found in international markets, including the emerging markets.

While the body of evidence in favor of passive investing is powerful, no such evidence is needed to draw a conclusion as to which is likely to be the winning strategy. Active management must, *in aggregate,* underperform passive management—the laws of mathematics cannot be denied.[2] This is true regardless of whether we are speaking of the market as a whole or a particular asset class. The reason is simple: All stocks must be owned by someone!

The Mathematics of Investing

A simple example will demonstrate conclusively that active investing, despite the claims of active investment managers, must, in aggregate, be a loser's game. The market is made up of only two types of investors, active and passive. For the purpose of this example, let's assume that 70 percent of investors are active and that 30 percent of investors are passive. (It does not matter what percentages are used, the outcome will be the same.) Let us assume that the market returns 15 percent per annum for the period in question. We know that on a preexpense basis a passive strategy (like owning Vanguard's Total Stock Market Fund) must earn 15 percent. What rate of return, before expenses, must the active managers have earned? The answer must also be 15 percent. The following equations show the math:

A = Total Stock Market, B = Active Investors,
C = Passive Investors
A = B + C
X = Rate of return earned by active investors
15% (100%) = X% (70%) + 15% (30%)
X must equal 15%

If one active investor outperforms because he overweighted the top-performing stocks, another active investor must have under-performed by underweighting those very same stocks. The investor who outperformed had to buy those winning securities from someone. Since passive investors simply buy and hold, the stock must have been sold by another active investor. In aggregate, on a preexpense basis, active investors earn the same market rate of return as do passive investors. Note that if we substituted the S&P 500 Index (or small-value stocks or REITs [real estate investment trusts] or emerging-market stocks) for the total stock market, we would come to exactly the same conclusion. It does not matter which asset class we are discussing, the math is exactly the same. The same thing is true for bull and bear markets. The math doesn't change if the bull is rampaging or the bear comes out of hibernation—active management must earn the same preexpense gross returns as passive management regardless of asset class or market condition. This is also true whether or not it is a so-called "stock-pickers' market" (there is no such thing, as you will see). Because of the investment propaganda put out by Wall Street's advertising machine and the coconspirators in the media, this is an extremely important issue for investors to under-stand. We will begin by examining returns in various asset classes, from the most efficient to the least. We will then turn to the issue of bear markets and the performance of active funds, and conclude with the issue of a "stock-picker's market."

The Efficiency of Markets

There has been a very persistent failure of active managers to out-perform in the asset class of large-cap stocks. For example, for the ten-year period 1982–91, only two of the seventy-one actively managed large-cap funds that even survived the period outperformed the Vanguard S&P 500 Index Fund on an after-tax and after-commission/load basis.[3] With evidence like this, it is becoming harder for active managers to claim they can outperform against a large-cap benchmark. Therefore, we now often hear claims that while the large-cap market may be efficient and thus hard to outperform, the small-cap and emerging markets are not as efficient, and thus active managers can add value. Notice that in the equation (A = B + C) we used to prove active management must lose, there was no mention of market efficiency. That is because it is irrelevant whether markets are efficient or not: Active management must, in aggregate, be a loser's game simply due to greater costs.

Let's look at some of the evidence, beginning with the asset classes of small-cap stocks and small-value stocks. Using Morningstar's database, we can compare the performance of actively managed funds to appropriate passive benchmarks. The passive asset class funds of DFA (Dimensional Fund Advisors) can be used for this purpose. While the data does contain survivorship bias (making the performance of actively managed funds appear better than the reality)—poorly performing funds are made to disappear by fund sponsors—the evidence is quite revealing. For the five-year period ending December 2002, the DFA Micro Cap Fund returned 4.3 percent per annum and the DFA Small Cap Fund returned 2.0 percent per annum. All actively managed small-cap funds returned just 1.9 percent. The DFA Small Value Fund returned 4.9 percent, while actively managed small-value funds returned just 2.6 percent. And these are pretax returns. The tax inefficiency of actively managed funds in all likelihood would have made their after-tax performance look even worse.

The asset class for which the active management argument is

made most strongly is the emerging markets—an "inefficient" asset class if there ever was one. Believers in active management have one problem: There isn't any evidence to support their claim. In fact, there is substantial evidence supporting the opposite position.

The sharp drop in emerging-market equities in 1998 brought down the reputations of many emerging-market fund managers. As Richard Oppel Jr. of the *New York Times* put it: "Another casualty of the [emerging markets] sell-off: the widely held notion that emerging markets are fertile ground for active fund managers."[4] The year 1998 was certainly one in which active managers had plenty of opportunity to add value, either by moving to cash or by choosing the winners (South Korea +110 percent, Greece +87 percent, Thailand +27 percent, and Portugal +26 percent) and avoiding the losers (Russia −87 percent, Turkey −51 percent, Indonesia −45 percent, Mexico −38 percent, and Brazil −38 percent).[5] Let's look at the facts. The 164 actively managed emerging-market funds tracked by Morningstar fell 26.9 percent in 1998, far more than the 18.2 percent loss by the Vanguard Emerging Markets Stock Index Fund, the third largest emerging-market fund. And the DFA passively managed Emerging Markets Fund fell just 9.4 percent.[6]

To show that 1998's poor performance by active managers was not a fluke, using the Morningstar database I examined the performance of all emerging-market funds for the nine-year period 1994–2002. The Morningstar database provides us with a list of just fourteen actively managed emerging-market funds with a nine-year track record. I then compared the performance of the actively managed funds with that of the passively managed DFA Emerging Markets Fund. (The nine-year period was chosen because that is the life of the DFA fund that we can use as a benchmark.) Even with survivorship bias in the data, the DFA fund outperformed 79 percent of the actively managed funds (all but three funds). Although the DFA Emerging Markets Fund fell 2.7 percent per annum, it outperformed the average active fund by 2 percent per annum. Only one actively managed fund beat its passive rival by more than one-half of 1 percent per annum. It is also worth noting that in addition to its Emerging Markets Fund (which is a large-cap fund), DFA also runs two other passively managed emerging-market funds, a small-cap fund and a value fund. The Emerging Markets Small Cap Fund returned a negative 0.6 percent per annum for the period, outperforming all but one fund. The Emerging Markets Value Fund returned a positive 1.4 percent per annum, outperforming all active funds. On the other hand, Fidelity's fund returned a negative 9.8 percent per annum. That is a high price to pay for belief in active management. Other well-known underachievers were the funds of Montgomery, Merrill Lynch, JPMorgan, Morgan Stanley, and Frank Russell. Consider this: If you managed to pick the top-performing fund, your belief in active management was rewarded with 3.2 percent per annum of pretax outperformance. On the other hand, if you were unlucky enough to choose Fidelity's fund, you underperformed by over 7 percent per annum. Does this sound like a game you want to play? What is perhaps most disheartening for believers in active management is that since the emerging-market returns for the entire period were negative, an active manager in this asset class would have outperformed a passive strategy by simply holding cash!

Why do active managers do so poorly in such markets? The reason is simple. There are really two issues surrounding the efficiency story. The first is information; the second is cost. And they are inversely related. For the largest cap stocks there is a great amount of liquidity in their shares. For example, using data provided by Bridge from November 8, 2001, the largest large-cap stocks traded over $277 million worth of shares each day, and the bid-offer spread (an estimate of trading costs) was just 0.12 percent. Thus while the trading costs are relatively low, the high degree of information efficiency surrounding these stocks (e.g., GE, Microsoft, etc.) makes it difficult to gain a competitive advantage that can be exploited. On the other hand, in the very smallest of the small-cap stocks, the average trading volume was only around $192,000, and the bid-offer spread was 4.03 percent.[7] Thus while it may be possible to gain a competitive advantage in terms of information (because fewer analysts and traders follow these stocks), the cost of exploiting any such advantage is much greater—almost 4 percent, or over thirty times, greater.

In the "inefficient" emerging markets, while it might be possible to gain an information advantage, the trading costs incurred in trying to exploit any such advantage are huge. According to Joshua Feuerman, manager of the SSgA (State Street Global Advisors) Emerging Markets Fund, a round-trip purchase and sale of a block of stock in a typical emerging market costs about 4.5 percent of the value of the stock. "It's a disgustingly expensive asset class to trade in."[8] Because turnover is much greater in actively managed funds, trading costs hit them harder than passively managed funds.

The Costs of Active Investing

The mathematical equation we began this section with to prove active investors must underperform represents preexpense, or gross returns. Unfortunately, investors don't earn gross returns; they earn returns net of expenses. To get to the net returns we must subtract all costs, including trading costs. The most obvious cost is a fund's operating-expense ratio. According to Lipper Inc., the median stock fund's operating expense for actively managed domestic funds as of 2003, is 1.46 percent.[9] This is much higher than the costs of the typical domestic index or passive asset class fund, the expense ratio of which is generally between 0.2 percent and 0.5 percent.

We have already touched on the issue of trading costs. However, it is important to note that the bid-offer spreads are just one of the trading costs incurred by a fund; commissions are another. An estimate of the negative impact of the trading (turnover) of active managers is provided by a Morningstar study. Morningstar divided mutual funds into two categories: those with an average holding period greater than five years (less than 20 percent turnover) and those with an average holding period of less than one year (turnover greater than 100 percent). Over a ten-year period, Morningstar found that low-turnover funds returned an average of 12.87 percent per annum, while high-turnover funds gained only 11.29 percent per annum on average. Trading costs and the impact on prices of trading activity reduced returns of the high-turnover funds by 1.58 percent per annum.[10]

One reason the trading costs of active management are so high is "market impact" costs. Market impact is what occurs when a mutual fund wants to buy or sell a large block of stock. The fund's purchases or sales will cause the stock to move beyond its current bid (lower) or offer (higher) price, increasing the cost of trading. Barra, a research organization, did an extensive study on market impact costs and found that while market impact costs will vary, depending on many factors (fund size, asset class, turnover, etc.), they can be quite substantial. Barra noted that a fairly typical case of a small- or mid-cap stock fund with $500 million in assets and an annual turnover rate of between 80 and 100 percent could lose 3 to 5 percent per annum to market impact costs—far more than the annual operating expenses of most funds. In another example, over a specified period the PBHG Emerging Growth Fund had the highest estimated market impact cost among small- or mid-cap funds at 5.73 percent per annum. Even large-cap funds can have large market impact costs, as illustrated by the 8.13 percent figure estimated for the Phoenix-Engemann Aggressive Growth Fund.[11] Without access to the specific data it is very hard to estimate a fund's market impact costs. However, you can at least consider high turnover as an indicator of the size of the impact. In addition, the smaller the market capitalization of the stocks the fund owns, the greater the market impact cost is likely to be.

For taxable accounts, taxes are unfortunately often the greatest expense of active management. The negative impact of the burden of taxes is a result of IRS form 1099 fund distributions. Take one example. For the fifteen-year period ending June 30, 1998, the Vanguard S&P 500 Index Fund provided pretax returns of 16.9 percent per annum. The fund lost 1.9 percent per annum to taxes. Its after-tax return of 15 percent per annum meant that the fund's tax efficiency was 89 percent. The average actively managed fund provided pretax returns of 13.6 percent and after-tax returns of just 10.8 percent. Losing 2.8 percent per annum to taxes resulted in a tax efficiency of just 79 percent.[12]

The least understood cost, because it is hidden, is the "cost of cash." The cost of cash is a result of a mutual fund holding cash instead of being fully invested in the market. A study by Russ Wermers found that nonequity holdings reduced returns for the average actively managed equity fund by seventy basis points per annum.[13] The greater the cash position held, the greater the impact.

In each of the above cases, the cost of implementing a passive strategy will be less than that of an active one. Thus, in aggregate, passive investors *must* earn higher net returns than do active investors. The mathematical facts cannot be denied. The result of all of these excessive costs (excessive because they have not proven to add value) is that investors believing in active management as the winning strategy are leaving tens of billions of dollars a year on the table. Those billions go into the pockets of investment firms, their employees, the media, and also Uncle Sam (in the form of unnecessarily higher taxes).

As stated earlier, the math of active management applies to all markets, including bear markets. Because behaviorists have found that for investors the pain of a loss is about twice as keenly felt as the good feelings generated by an equivalent gain, bear markets are when the claimed protective value of active management is needed most. Let's now examine the historical evidence of active managers in bear markets.

Active Management and Bear Markets

Theoretically anticipating bear markets, active managers can reduce their exposure to equities and protect their investors from the type of losses that index funds experience (since index funds are always virtually 100 percent invested). However, keep in mind that whenever a stock is sold, there is another buyer somewhere—all stocks must be owned by someone. Since passive investors are not altering their positions based on anticipated market conditions, if an active fund is a seller, in general another active fund is the buyer.

Let's look at the historical record to see if active managers actually provided the protection they claim they provide in bear markets.

- Just prior to the second worst (at the time it was the worst) bear market in the postwar era (1973–74), mutual fund cash reserves stood at only 4 percent. Cash positions reached about 12 percent at the ensuing low.

- In mid-1998, when the "Asian Contagion" bear market arrived, cash reserves were just 5 percent. Compare this to the 13 percent level reached at the market low in 1990, just prior to beginning the longest bull market in history.[14]

- During the bear market of 2000–01, cash reserves of actively managed mutual funds fell to an average of just 1.35 percent. In other words, they were basically fully invested at the worst time.[15]

It seems fund managers are very good at executing a buy high and sell low strategy.

A Lipper Analytical Services study provided further evidence on the failure of active managers to outperform in bear markets. Lipper studied the six market corrections (defined as a drop of at least 10 percent) from August 31, 1978, to October 11, 1990, and found that while the average loss for the S&P was 15.12 percent, the average loss for large-cap growth funds was 17.04 percent.[16]

Fund managers fared no better in the bear market of July–August 1998. During the decline between July 16 and August 31, the average equity fund lost 22.2 percent. This compares to losses of just 20.7 percent and 19.0 percent for a Wilshire 5000 Index fund and an S&P 500 Index fund, respectively.[17] Susan Dziubinski, editor of Morningstar's *FundInvestor* newsletter, put it this way: "The average fund can't keep up with its index when it's sunny or rainy."[18]

And finally, consider this evidence. Goldman Sachs studied mutual fund cash holdings from 1970 to 1989. The study found that mutual fund managers miscalled *all* nine major turning points.[19]

It is worth noting that the commercial success of indexing among institutional investors began in 1975 (a fund was built for New York Telephone's pension plan). The poor performance of most active managers during the bear market of 1973–74, the second worst since the 1930s, revealed just how hollow is their claim that their "expertise" in protecting capital is most valuable in difficult markets. While it may be coincidence, I suspect that the motivation to adopt indexed strategies was partly attributable to disappointment with the traditional active management approach, which failed to deliver when it was most needed. Let's now turn to examining the issue of "it's a stock-pickers' market."

It's a Stock-Pickers' Market

In 2000, 63 percent of active managers outperformed the S&P 500 Index. Active managers immediately declared that it was once again a stock-pickers' market and that active management would prove to be the winning strategy. Unfortunately, this is an old canard that is trotted out every so often in an attempt to both keep alive the myth that active management is the winning strategy and to keep investors paying high fees for poor, inconsistent, and tax-inefficient performance. However, when the proper light is shed on the subject, the canard is exposed.

Active managers point to their successes in years like 1977–79, when 85, 69, and 80 percent, respectively, of the actively managed funds outperformed the S&P 500, and 1991–93 when 55, 54, and 60 percent, respectively, did so, as "proof" of their ability to outperform the market. The claim is that those were stock-pickers' kind of years—as opposed to the years 1994–98 when no more than 22 percent of the active funds accomplished that feat. The problem with the claim of it being a stock-pickers' market is that it doesn't hold up to scrutiny. The reason is that the "defendants" are using an apples-to-oranges argument to make their case. The conclusions are drawn because of confusing indexing (or, more broadly, passive investing) with the exclusive use of the S&P 500.

For the twenty-eight-year period 1975 through 2002, there were eleven years when large-cap stocks outperformed small-cap stocks. In each of those eleven years fewer than 50 percent of the active managers beat the S&P 500 Index. In fact, in only one of those periods did more than 26 percent of the active managers outperform the S&P 500 Index. The one exception was 1990, when just 36 percent of the active managers beat that index.[20] In most years when small-cap stocks outperform large-cap stocks, a majority of active funds will generally outperform. The explanation for the seeming outperformance of active managers in those years is that the typical actively managed fund holds, on average, stocks with a smaller market cap than the weighted-average market cap of the S&P 500 Index. One obvious example of this is small-cap funds. Small-cap funds should be expected to outperform a large-cap index when small-cap stocks outperform. This, however, would have nothing to do with stock selection and everything to do with asset allocation. And it is asset allocation, not stock selection or market timing, that determines almost all returns. The S&P 500 Index is, therefore, not the correct benchmark for *all* actively managed funds. Actively managed funds should always be benchmarked in a way that ensures an apples-to-apples comparison.

Another explanation for the "outperformance" of active managers in 2000 is that value funds outperformed growth funds (like the S&P 500). Thus any actively managed value fund, or even an actively managed growth fund that had more exposure to the value asset class than does the S&P 500 Index, was highly likely to outperform that particular benchmark. For example, while the S&P 500 fell just over 9 percent, the DFA Large Value and Small Value Funds both rose more than 10 percent. Those funds would be more appropriate benchmarks for value-oriented funds than would the S&P 500 Index.

To gain further perspective on whether or not active management is the winner's game, let's take a longer term look at the performance against two benchmarks, the Wilshire 5000 and the Russell 3000, which are broader indices than the S&P 500 Index. For the five-, ten-, and fifteen-year periods ending in 2000, only 16, 16, and 17 percent, respectively, of actively managed funds outperformed the Wilshire 5000, and only 14, 14, and 15 percent, respectively, of actively managed funds outperformed the Russell 3000.[21]

Does Indexing Affect Stock Prices?

The S&P 500 Index returned almost 29 percent per annum in the second half of the 1990s, the greatest five-year run in history. This led to S&P 500 Index funds becoming villains of an investment soap opera. Active managers were blaming their underperformance on S&P 500 Index funds. The theory goes like this: Money pours into the index funds because of the dissatisfaction with the underperformance of active managers; the funds "blindly" buy the large-cap stocks and drive the market ever higher.

The problem is that this theory is based on a false premise, as Melissa Brown demonstrated in 1998. Brown, then head of quantitative research at Prudential Securities, found that while S&P

500 Index funds had grown in assets from $255 billion at the end of 1992 to $600 billion at the end of 1997, they represented only 6.1 percent of all stocks by the end of 1997, down from 6.7 percent at the end of 1992. Brown pointed out that since the total return (price appreciation plus dividends) of the S&P 500 Index was 152 percent, all of the gain in the amount of S&P 500 indexed assets was a result of price appreciation, not cash inflow. In fact, if the amount of funds in S&P 500 Index funds had grown as much as the 152 percent total return of the index itself, the amount of money invested in these funds would have grown to almost $650 billion. This is $50 billion more than they actually held. This indicates there were actually net cash outflows from these funds. This clearly suggests that the underperformance of active managers is not due to inflows into index funds.[22]

It is important to note that the net cash outflow from S&P 500 Index funds during this period should not be taken as an indication that investors were decreasing their commitment to passive investing. In fact, the contrary was true. Not all index funds are tied to the S&P 500. In recent years, index funds have been created to replicate the performance of the Russell 2000, the S&P/Barra Value Index, the EAFE (Europe, Australasia, and the Far East) Index, and many others. When all passive funds are considered, their market share was growing at a rapid pace.

Burton Malkiel and Aleksander Radisich took another look at the claim that indexing influences security prices.[23] Their study, "The Growth of Index Funds and the Pricing of Equity Securities," tested three hypotheses:

1. Index funds will tend to increase their advantage over actively managed funds during periods when the market rises.

2. S&P 500 Index funds will tend to increase their advantage over actively managed funds during periods when large-cap stocks outperform smaller firms.

3. S&P 500 Index funds will increase their advantage as the proportion of fund inflows into index funds increases.

The first hypothesis is logical in that in rising markets index funds have the advantage of always being virtually fully invested while actively managed funds typically carry cash positions of as much as 5 to 10 percent or more—for liquidity and trading purposes. The study found that the hypothesis is correct in that the excess performance of indexing increases when the market is rising. The t-stat, a measure of statistical significance, was very high at 4.9 (with 2.0 considered the hurdle for significance as it provides 95 percent confidence that the result was not a random outcome). It is important to remember that indexing has outperformed in bear markets as well. Thus while the size of the outperformance shrinks in bear markets, it never disappears.

The second hypothesis that S&P 500 Index funds will tend to increase their advantage over actively managed funds during periods when large-cap stocks outperform smaller firms is also logical in that not all actively managed funds hold only large-cap stocks, as does the S&P 500. As we discussed, in periods like 1977–79 and 1991–93, when small-cap stocks outperformed large-cap stocks, we should expect that not only will small-cap funds outperform a large-cap index fund but that some large-cap funds will also do so (as many are not style pure, holding smaller cap stocks than are in the S&P 500 Index). The study confirmed this hypothesis as well: When small companies outperform, the

17

advantage of indexing large-cap stocks shrinks. The t-stat again was very significant at a negative 3.2.

The third hypothesis that indexing influences prices is, however, rejected. They found that the flow of money into index funds was *totally unrelated* to the excess performance of index funds. Thus there is no support at all to the claim that the success of indexing has been self-fulfilling.

The authors also studied the impact of a stock's entry into the S&P 500 Index. There have been studies showing that a stock's entry bolsters demand and on average increases the price of the stock. The study examined the price action of all stocks entering the S&P 500 Index between July 1980 and July 1999. The authors found that while there is a statistically significant postentry "pop" lasting about one week, the excess performance is essentially reversed over the following year. This contradicts the notion that there is any permanent price impact for stocks that enter an index.

The authors also made another important observation that demonstrates the false nature of the claims that indexing influences prices and was responsible for the failure of active managers in the late 1990s. They note that the superior performance of the S&P 500 Index during this period was driven mostly by the returns of the very largest stocks in the index—the performance of the top 50 far surpassed the performance of the remaining 450. Because indexing purchases a proportional share (based on market capitalization) of each stock, it cannot be responsible for the outperformance of the top 50. Thus it must have been the actions of active managers who were, in fact, driving returns.

The evidence and the logic is that indexing does not drive prices. The advantage of indexing is based solely on the mathematics of investing: Despite this logic, there are two things of which we can be sure: The first is that the next time small caps outperform large caps we will hear once again that "it is a stock-pickers' market." Nothing of course could be further from the truth. It is simply an issue of understanding what is the proper benchmark to use. Small-cap fund managers, while outperform-ing the S&P 500 Index, will be underperforming the index against which they should always be benchmarked, the S&P 600 Index (a small-cap index). The second is that in periods when large-cap stocks outperform (thus the S&P 500 Index will outper-form the majority of active managers), the marketing machines of Wall Street will find a different excuse for their poor perfor-mance. Passive investing is the winner's game in all markets; the math dictates that it must be so.

The Triumph of Hope over Experience (and Wisdom)

Steve Galbraith teaches security analysis at Columbia University in its M.B.A. program. He is chief investment officer at Morgan Stanley and a coauthor of Morgan Stanley's *US Economic Perspectives.* In March 2002, Galbraith invited John Bogle, the for-mer chairman of the Vanguard Group and a strong advocate of passive investing, to speak to his class.

In the April 3, 2002, issue, Galbraith related the following about Bogle's presentation. "He laid out the case against active management and for indexing quite powerfully. My guess is that more than a few students left the class wondering just what the heck their hard-earned tuition dollars were doing going to a class devoted to the seemingly impossible—analyzing securities to achieve better-than-market returns." He added: "At least the students have the excuse of being early in their careers; what's mine for staying the course in my current role?" He also admitted: "We recognize that the odds are against active managers."

Galbraith went on to point out that the actual returns to investors in the greatest bull market ever ranged "from the sub-prime to the ridiculous." He also wondered what will happen now that returns are more likely to be in the neighborhood of just 7 to 8 percent, instead of the almost 18 percent per annum returns the S&P 500 provided in the twenty years from 1980 through 1999.

Galbraith closed his letter to investors on a very revealing note: "From our perspective, *perhaps in a triumph of hope over experience,* we continue to believe active managers can add value." Another perspective might be that, given the role of his employer, to believe otherwise would be committing economic suicide. The winning strategy for investors is simply to accept market returns. Unfortunately, that is not the winning strategy for Morgan Stanley in terms of profits. While active management does offer the potential for greater than market returns, it is far more likely that investors will end up with below benchmark returns. This is why Charles Ellis called active management the loser's game. The odds of winning are so low that a prudent investor would choose not to play—unless he or she placed a high entertainment value on the effort.

Active Management Is the Loser's Game

Does the math of investing mean that investors in actively managed funds are doomed to underperform? If we are talking as a group, the answer is a resounding yes. Does this mean that all active managers will underperform? No. In fact, given the thousands of fund managers (and individuals) playing the "game," randomly we would expect some to win. However, if outperformance was random, the number succeeding should not only be no greater than would be randomly expected but the number succeeding should decline as the investment horizon increases. The reason is that the burden of expenses increases over time due to compounding, making the task more difficult. The evidence, as can be seen in the chart below, is that the performance of active managers looks very much random in nature. The number of outperformers declines over time, and the graph shows performance to be to the left (underperformance) of the normal bell curve.

The only question then left for believers in active management

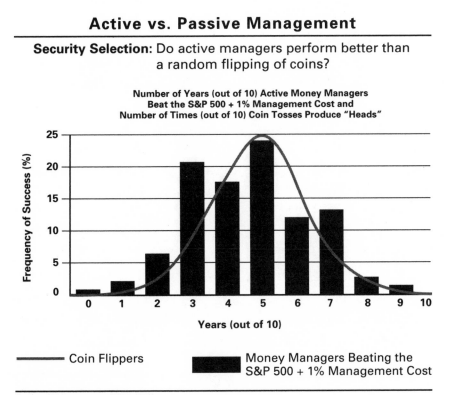

Active vs. Passive Management

Security Selection: Do active managers perform better than a random flipping of coins?

Number of Years (out of 10) Active Money Managers
Beat the S&P 500 + 1% Management Cost and
Number of Times (out of 10) Coin Tosses Produce "Heads"

Coin Flippers

Money Managers Beating the S&P 500 + 1% Management Cost

Source: SEI Investments (1984–1993)
Manager returns are calculated without subtracting fees.

is whether or not an investor can identify *ahead of time* the very few active managers who will outperform their passive benchmark. It is, of course, an easy job to do so on an ex-post basis. The question is, how likely is it that one can accomplish this objective on an ex-ante basis. This is the issue we will explore in our next section.

TRUTH 2

◆

The Past Performance of an Actively Managed Fund Is a Very Poor Predictor of Its Future Performance

When we buy an actively managed fund, we are like gamblers in Vegas. We know it is likely to be a losing proposition, yet somehow we feel we are getting our money's worth.
—Jonathan Clements, *Wall Street Journal*

Investment management is a field fraught with fragility and fallibility, a field in which today's careful, rational fund selections are too often tomorrow's embarrassments.
—John Bogle, *Journal of Portfolio Management*

Yesterday's masters of the universe are today's cosmic dust.
—Alan Abelson and Rhonda Brammer, *Barron's*

Like the investors of every past age, [investors] still search for the money manager with the magic elixir to assure investment success. This search leads to a frenzy of meaningless activity, rarely resulting in sustainable performance.
—Donald Trone, William Allbright, and Philip Taylor,
The Management of Investment Decisions

When presented with both the math of active investing and also the fact that the average actively managed fund has underperformed its benchmark by almost 2 percent per annum on a pretax basis, the usual response is: "So what? I don't care about the performance of the *average* fund. I am not going to buy the 'obvious' losers, the ones with poor track records, the ones that drag the average performance down." The question is: Does screening out the past poor performers produce future winners?

Next to the belief that active management is the winning strategy, the strongest piece of conventional wisdom about investment performance is that the past performance of investment managers is prologue to future performance. The logic is sound enough. For example, when a business seeks to hire a new executive, it will look at candidates who have been successful at similar positions. When a football team looks to add a quarterback, it will try to trade for, or sign as a free agent, someone who has previously performed well in that role. In both cases the rationale is that the person being sought has clearly demonstrated the skills necessary to do the job. While there is no certainty of success, the rationale is sound. Unfortunately for investors, as we have seen, just because something is conventional wisdom doesn't make it correct. In addition, what works in one paradigm might not work in another. Also, unfortunately, it is my experience that "reasoned dialogue has a limited ability to withstand an assault by the mythic power of falsehood, especially when that falsehood is rooted in an age-old social and cultural phenomenon."[1]

As you will see, when it comes to past performance of active managers being prologue, there simply is no substance there. The following are a few selected words of wisdom on using past performance of money managers to predict their future performance.

- Jonathan Clements, *Wall Street Journal* columnist: "I believe the search for top-performing stock funds is an intellectually discredited exercise that will come to be viewed as one of the great financial follies of the late 20th century."[2]
- John Bogle, founder of Vanguard: "No matter where we look, the message of history is clear. Selecting funds that

will significantly exceed market returns, a search in which hope springs eternal and in which past performance has proven of virtually no predictive value, is a loser's game."[3]

- John Rekenthaler, research director for Morningstar, was described as stating that actively managed funds were beginning to show up on his cultural radar as a "marketing scam for suckers."[4] When asked how to pick a winning fund, Rekenthaler responded: "There is surprisingly little that we can say for sure about how to find top-notch stock funds. We should have more answers."[5] And commenting on whether investors should pay attention to mutual fund advertisements, he added: ". . . to be fair, I don't think that you'd want to pay much attention to Morningstar's star ratings either."[6]

Let's examine the evidence on various strategies that are used to pick the future winners based on past success.

A popular approach to selecting mutual funds is to rely on the very popular rating service provided by Morningstar, which rates funds using a star system similar to the one used by film critics. Ads touting four- and five-star ratings are found everywhere. As evidence that investors believe the stars have predictive value, a study covering the period January through August 1995 found that an amazing 97 percent of fund inflows went into four- and five-star funds, while three-star funds experienced outflows.[7]

Diane Del Guerico and Paula A. Tkac of the Federal Reserve Bank of Atlanta investigated how changes in Morningstar's ratings influence mutual fund cash flows. The study, "Star Power: The Effect of Morningstar Ratings on Mutual Fund Flows," covered almost thirty-four hundred domestic equity mutual funds for the period November 1996 to October 1999, and identified over twelve thousand ratings changes.[8] The following is a summary of the key findings.

- The initiation of a five-star rating results in average inflow over the next six months that is 53 percent greater than normal.
- An upgrade from four to five stars increases the rate of inflows over the next six months by 35 percent.
- Even upgrades from two to three stars and from three to four stars generates positive abnormal inflows.
- A downgrade from five to four stars has a negative impact, though to a much lesser degree. Fund inflows fell from their norm by 8 percent. One reason for the smaller impact of a downgrade is that existing investors might be reluctant to sell as capital gains taxes are likely to be incurred as a result of a sale. Another reason is that a five-star fund that is on a recommended list might not be removed from that list unless the fund continues to lag in performance.
- Downgrades from three to two stars and four to three stars also generate abnormal negative flow.
- The influence of ratings changes is observable virtually instantaneously—demonstrating that investors are paying close attention to the ratings and placing a high value on their predictive ability.

The authors also note that funds are "more likely to advertise if they have a five-star rating to tout," and advertising impacts fund flows. The paper cited a study that found that funds that advertise in popular magazines such as *Barron's* or *money* receive significantly greater inflows than a control sample of funds with similar performance.[9] Funds, of course, are only likely to advertise four- or five-star ratings.

For investors the essential question is whether or not chasing ratings is the winning strategy. Let's examine the evidence.

Morningstar gives the coveted five-star rating to the funds it believes are among the top 10 percent of all funds, and a one-star rating to the bottom 10 percent. The *Hulbert Financial Digest* tracked the performance of the five-star funds for the period 1993–2000. For that eight-year period, the total return (pretax) on Morningstar's top-rated U.S. funds averaged +106 percent. This compared to a total return of +222 percent for the total stock market, as measured by the Wilshire 5000 Equity Index. *Hulbert* also found that the top-rated funds, while achieving less than 50 percent of the market's return, carried a relative risk (measured by standard deviation) that was 26 percent greater than that of the market. If the performance had been measured on an after-tax basis, the tax inefficiency of actively managed funds relative to a passive index fund would have made the comparison significantly worse.[10] In another study, *Hulbert* found that a portfolio that was always fully invested in the fifty-five funds that Morningstar rates highest in a twice-a-month newsletter, buying when they climb into this elite group and selling when they drop out, from January 1991 through March 2002 trailed the market by 5.9 percent per annum, after paying sales charges, redemption fees, and other transaction costs.[11]

An FRC (Financial Research Corporation) study covering the period January 1, 1995–September 30, 1998, revealed that two- and three-star funds outperformed their four- and five-star counterparts for the entire period. The study's conclusion: "The linkage between past performance and future realizations is tenuous if not nonexistent."[12]

A study, by Christopher R. Blake, associate professor of finance at Fordham University's Graduate School of Business, and Matthew Morey, assistant professor of finance at Fordham, found that for the five-year period ending December 31, 1997, the average five-star fund underperformed the market by almost 4 percent per annum. The study also found that the differences between the performances of the three-, four-, and five-star funds were so small as to have very little statistical significance.[13] Blake and Morey concluded that while a low star rating was actually a good predictor of relatively poor future performance, high star ratings were not good predictors of future top performance. The top-rated funds did not outperform the next highest or even median-rated funds.[14] Morningstar has even stated: "Over the years, Morningstar's star system has been frequently—and sometimes willfully—misunderstood. Many commentators insist on treating the star rating as a predictive measure or a short-term trading signal. The rating, which is clearly labeled as a historical profile, does neither."[15] Despite this strong admission, it is obvious from the heavy expenditures of advertising dollars by mutual funds that they believe investors perceive the star ratings as having predictive value.

Morningstar's ratings are so popular that there have been many studies on their ratings of funds and future performance. One of these, "The Persistence of Morningstar Ratings," sought to determine if there was any useful information contained in the star ratings.[16] If there is persistence in fund ratings, it would be valuable information. Unfortunately, the authors concluded—after studying variable annuities, equity funds, and bond funds—that there is little evidence of persistence of performance. The study found:

- For four- and five-star equity funds, year-to-year persistence is the equivalent of a coin flip. Less than half of all mutual funds rated four or five star at year-end 1997 still held that high rating at year-end 1998. Basically, there is a reversion to a three-star mean.

- Persistence for variable annuities is worse than a flip of the coin. Year-to-year persistence is only about 40 percent.

- Persistence is the worst for taxable bond funds at just over 20 percent.

- For equity funds with just three-year ratings, the year-to-year persistence of ratings was less than 25 percent. Keep this in mind when you think you have discovered a new guru.

The following is perhaps the most amazing example on using Morningstar's rating system to select future winners. For the period 1995–2001, funds rated one star outperformed funds rated five star by 45 percent.[17]

Even Smith Barney, which heavily advertises its funds that have received five-star ratings on the basis of past performance, had this to say: "One of the most common investor mistakes is choosing an investment management firm or mutual fund based on recent top performance." This was the conclusion they drew from their own study covering seventy-two equity managers with at least ten-year track records. The managers studied covered the full spectrum of investment styles: large cap to small cap, value to growth, and domestic to international. In fact, the study found: "The investment returns of top quintile managers tended to plunge precipitously while the returns of bottom quintile managers tended to rise dramatically."[18]

Here is another powerful example of the fallacy of relying on past performance of active fund managers. Relying on the Micropal database, DFA studied the performance of the top thirty funds for successive five-year periods beginning in 1970 and then compared their performance against that of the S&P 500 Index through 1998. Here is what they found:[19]

- The top thirty funds from 1970 through 1974 went on to underperform the index by 0.99 percent per annum.

- The top thirty funds from 1975 through 1979 went on to underperform by 1.89 percent per annum.

- The top thirty funds from 1980 through 1984 went on to underperform by 2.75 percent per annum.

- The top thirty funds from 1985 through 1989 then went on to underperform by 1.57 percent per annum.

- The top thirty funds from 1990 through 1994 then went on to underperform by 10.9 percent per annum.

In not one case did the top performers from one five-year period continue to outperform.

As further evidence, in his book, *A Random Walk Down Wall Street,* Burton G. Malkiel reported that he did extensive testing through the early 1990s on whether an investor, by choosing the "hot" funds, could outperform the market. The results showed the ineffectiveness of a strategy that chose the top ten, twenty, thirty, or more funds based on the performance of the previous twelve months and then one year later switched to the new top performers. From 1980 through the end of the analysis period, this strategy produced results that were not only below the average mutual fund but also below that of the S&P 500 Index. Similar results were found when Malkiel tried ranking funds by their past two-, five-, and ten-year track records.

As *Fortune* magazine put it: "Despite the solemn import that fund companies attribute to past performance, there's no evidence that the 4 percent who beat the index owe their record to anything other than random statistical variation. The whole industry is built up around a certain degree of black magic." *Fortune* concluded: "Despite volumes of research attesting to the meaninglessness of past returns, most investors (and personal finance magazines) seek tomorrow's winners among yesterday's. Forget it. The truth is, much as you wish you could know which funds will be hot, you can't—and neither can the legions of advisers and publications that claim they can."[20] Despite being the very same magazine that glorifies the latest hot fund manager, they added in another issue: "We have learned that past investment records make lousy crystal balls."[21]

Let's examine another powerful bit of evidence against the wisdom of using the past performance of active managers as a predictor of future performance. A logical proposition is that if anyone could beat the market, it would be the pension funds of the largest U.S. companies. They have access to the best and brightest portfolio managers, all of them clamoring to manage the billions of dollars in these plans. Presumably, these pension funds rely on the excellent track records of the "experts" they eventually choose to manage their portfolios. Surely they never hired a manager with a poor track record.

FutureMetrics Inc. (formerly Piscataqua Research), in a study covering the period 1987–96, found that only 10 (just 7 percent) out of 145 major pension funds outperformed a portfolio consisting of a simple 60/40 percent mix of the S&P 500 Index and the Lehman Bond Index, respectively. The study was updated to include the period through 2000 and also increased the number of participating pension funds to 179—just 19 of the plans (11 percent) outperformed the benchmark.[22] A 60 percent equity/40 percent fixed-income allocation was used, since that is estimated to be the average allocation of all pension plans. The FutureMetrics study provides evidence against not only the strategy of choosing managers based on past performance, but also the use of active managers in general.

Relying on past performance as a predictor can also be viewed as the phenomenon of relying on the "hot hand." Andrew Met-rick, a finance professor at the Wharton School of the University of Pennsylvania, conducted an extensive study on the hot hands issue. Metrick analyzed every buy or sell recommendation on a U.S. stock by 153 investment newsletter editors for the period 1980–96. Metrick then constructed a portfolio consisting of the recommendations of the 10 percent of advisers with the best per-formance during the previous calendar year. He reformed the portfolio at the start of each year based on the new rankings. While the hot hands portfolio returned 15.7 percent per annum, the S&P 500 returned 16.2 percent and the market, as represented by the CRSP 1–10 (Center for Research in Security Prices), returned 15.7 percent per annum.[23]

Let's take a look at another issue. While we know that it is likely that some of today's managers will outperform in the future, what are the odds that we can successfully predict who they will be? A 1999 study looked at all 307 large-cap funds with at least a ten-year history. This methodology creates what is known as "survivorship bias" in favor of active management. Funds that perform poorly close because of redemptions by investors, or they are merged out of existence by their sponsor. Thus their performance data disappears. (A skeptic like me would say that the mantra of active fund management is: If at first you don't succeed, destroy any evidence that you tried.) The returns of the funds were then compared to that of the benchmark S&P 500 Index. Over the twenty-year period, the passive strategy out-performed over 93 percent of all *surviving* funds. For the fifteen-year period, it outperformed over 99 percent of all surviving funds. And for ten-, seven-, five-, and three-year periods, the pas-sive strategy outperformed at least 95 percent of all *surviving* active funds. Finally, for the sixty-one rolling five-year periods, the passive strategy outperformed at least half the active funds fifty-eight (95 percent) times.[24] And all this is on a pretax basis. Based on historical data, it is safe to assume that the results would have been even worse if the returns had been after-tax returns. With the odds so great against success, it is no wonder active management is called the loser's game.

It Actually Is Easy to Find the Future Top-Performing Funds

Mutual fund industry insiders paid FRC to complete a study published in December 2001, "Predicting Mutual Fund Performance II: After the Bear."[25] In an attempt to find predictors of future fund performance, FRC studied five broad mutual fund categories (domestic equities, international-global equities, corporate bonds, government bonds, and tax-free securities) and ten "predictors" (past performance, Morningstar ratings, expenses, turnover, manager tenure, net sales, asset size, and four risk/volatility measures: alpha, beta, standard deviation, and the Sharpe Ratio). FRC's definition of *predictability* was very conservative: A top-ranking fund must stay in the top half of its peer group in future periods. The study, published in December 2001, used quarterly returns for the prior fifteen years, comparing average returns for one-year, three-year, and five-year periods. FRC's conclusion: Most statistics have no predictive value. Among the study's findings were:

- Morningstar ratings "are not very effective as a guide in finding funds with above average future performance potential." The study warned investors: "Don't let the stars get in your eyes!"

- Past performance can't predict future results.

- Turnover and manager tenure are equally useless as predictors.

- Asset size has "very little relationship to future performance."

- Increasing net sales is actually a contrarian indicator. These
  funds actually underperform in future years, "suggesting that
  investors tended to heavily purchase funds right before their
  relative returns were about to become mediocre or worse."

The study did, however, find one reliable predictor—expenses.
Funds with lower expenses delivered "above-average future performance across nearly all time periods." FRC concluded that a
favorable expense ratio is an "exceptional predictor" for bonds
and a "good predictor" for stock funds. This finding is perfectly
consistent with the EMH. Since index and other passive investment vehicles such as ETFs generally have the lowest costs, it is
easy to conclude that the strategy that is most likely to produce
the best returns is passive investing.

Successful Active Management Contains the Seeds of Its Own Destruction

Why have successful funds not been able to deliver encore performances? One explanation is that the past success was very
likely a random outcome, not a skill-based one. However, even if
you attribute skill as the reason for the success, there are also
some very practical reasons why even the most successful active
funds seem to lose their luster over time—successful fund man-

agement contains the seeds of its own destruction. In fact, the more successful a fund is, the more likely it is that its outperformance will be "gone with the wind."

Fund managers know that the more a fund diversifies, the more it looks and performs like its benchmark index (a fund whose holdings are very similar to those of its benchmark is known as a *closet index* fund). Therefore, in order to have the greatest chance to outperform, a fund must concentrate its assets in a few stocks (which is why "focus" funds were created). Unfortunately, while a strategy of owning just a few of a manager's best ideas is the most likely way to generate world-class returns, it is also the most likely way to end up at the bottom of the rankings list.

Let's look at how the mutual fund world works. A new fund is created. The fund starts out with a very small amount of assets under management. Aware of the risks of being a closet indexer (we will cover this issue shortly), the fund concentrates its assets in a very few stocks. The fund also knows that the market for large-cap stocks is highly efficient in terms of information, and thus concentrates its research efforts in the less efficient (at least in terms of information) asset class of small-cap stocks. The fund, of course, must comply with the SEC's (Securities and Exchange Commission) rules on diversification and thus cannot have more than 5 percent of its assets in any one stock. The fund happens to be in the right place at the right time or has one of the very rare truly gifted managers—the "next Peter Lynch"—and earns spectacular returns for a few years. The fund is given the coveted five stars from Morningstar and starts to advertise its great performance. Assets come rushing in. The better the performance, the more funds pour in. The fund is now faced with a dilemma. It must buy very large positions in just a very few small-cap stocks, increase its diversification, or style drift to large-cap stocks. All courses contain the seeds of the fund's likely future inability to persist with its track record of outperformance. Let's see why.

If the fund starts to diversify and buys the stocks of many more smaller companies, it runs into the math of closet indexing. A closet index fund looks like an actively managed fund, but the stocks it owns so closely resemble the holdings of an index fund that investors are unknowingly paying very large fees for minimal differentiation. For example, if we assume that a fund is even as much as 50 percent differentiated from its benchmark index, the hurdle created by the operating-expense ratio is twice the published figure. If the fund is only 20 percent differentiated, the hurdle becomes approximately four times the operating expense ratio. A relatively good indicator of the amount of differentiation is the actively managed fund's correlation with its benchmark index (i.e., the S&P 500 Index for large-cap stocks or the S&P 600 Index for small-cap stocks). The higher the correlation—measured by a fund's r, or the correlation coefficient—the less the differentiation is likely to be. The r-squared ($r \times r$), or the coefficient of determination, is commonly used to measure the degree of differentiation compared to a benchmark. Remember that the larger the fund, the more diversified it will likely become. The more it diversifies, the greater becomes its r-squared and the greater the hurdle the manager must overcome in order to outperform. Add this hurdle to the other expenses actively managed funds and their investors must overcome (bid/offer spreads, commissions, market impact costs, drag of cash, and, for taxable accounts, taxes), and the hurdle becomes virtually insurmountable.

The following is evidence of the difficulty of overcoming a high r-squared. A study found that for the three years ending August 31, 1999, the five largest funds with r-squareds over ninety-five returned between 21 and 26.9 percent per annum.

After taxes an investor would have received between 18 and 24.6 percent per annum. Vanguard's S&P 500 Index Fund beat them all. It returned 28.5 percent per annum pretax and 27.5 percent per annum after tax. Of the eighty largest funds with r-squareds over ninety-five, only three managed to beat the Vanguard Index Fund and just barely did so. (For the record, these were the Vanguard Growth and Income Fund, the Goldman Sachs Capital Growth Fund, and the Pioneer Fund.) And none did so after taxes.[26] That is about $400 billion of underperforming assets and probably over $20 billion per annum that investors left on the table because of their belief in active management.

The second alternative to dealing with the cash inflow is to concentrate assets in the same few stocks. Here the fund runs into the problem of market impact costs. As we discussed in the previous chapter, Barra, a research organization, found that a fairly typical small- or mid-cap stock fund with $500 million in assets and an annual turnover rate of between 80 and 100 percent could lose 3 to 5 percent per annum to market impact costs.[27] Because of their lack of liquidity, the smaller the market cap, the greater the market impact cost. And the larger the fund, the greater the market impact costs become.

It is also worth commenting on the performance of "focus" funds. *Money,* with assistance from Chicago consulting firm Performance Analytics, reviewed the performance of twenty-two private account managers whose performance placed them in the top 20 percent of their peer group. Each firm provided its *single* best idea. For the period beginning in May 1996 and ending in mid-June 1998, the average return of the twenty-two best picks was 53.5 percent, or a negative value added of 13.2 percent when compared to the return of 66.7 percent for the Wilshire 5000.[28] As an amusing note, in early 2002, Morgan Stanley announced that its Competitive Edge "Best Ideas" Fund portfolio was to be merged into another fund (presumably in order to have its poor performance disappear).[29] One can only wonder how their less-than-best ideas turned out.

The third alternative is to style drift to large-cap stocks. This is the alternative that many funds follow. The problem here is that the larger the market cap, the more efficient the market is in terms of information. This makes it extremely difficult to outperform. As was noted in truth 1, a good example of the likelihood of failure is that for the decade of the 1980s only two large-cap growth funds that even survived the entire decade managed to outperform the Vanguard S&P 500 Index Fund after taxes.[30]

No matter which way the manager turns, the likelihood of continued outperformance diminishes. The alternative is to stay small in terms of assets. This can be accomplished by closing the fund to new investors. The problem here is that not many funds are willing to forego the profits from increased assets under management.

"The Perils of Success," a study focused on the issue of persistence of performance of active small-cap managers, found evidence that success does indeed sow the seeds that ultimately result in performance mediocrity.[31] In other words, by the time you learn of a manager's success, it is too late to exploit that information. The authors cited the following reasons as explanations for the future mediocrity:

- Trading costs in the form of market impact costs increase.
- Profits from the flipping of IPOs (initial public offerings) are no longer as great. Flipping is most prevalent in small-cap funds of fund families such as Fidelity. Fund families typically will allocate a very large portion of their total allocation to one small fund, where it can have a large impact on

returns. Two mutual fund companies were recently heavily fined by the SEC for failure to appropriately disclose the impact of IPOs on the returns of their funds.

- Active funds tend to lose their sell discipline as they have to now consider the greater impact of trading costs.

- Fund managers tend to invest less aggressively. With greater assets under management, they have more at stake to lose in the form of fees. They become less willing to risk underperformance (become closet indexers with active management fees), dooming them to mediocre performance.

- The funds have to diversify more in order to limit market impact costs.

- The funds tend to be driven to purchase stocks with larger market caps in order to reduce market impact costs. There is another problem for investors here—style drift. Style drift causes investors to lose control over the risks and expected returns of the portfolio.

The authors concluded that there was a statistically significant relationship between performance and the growth of assets under management. Unfortunately for believers in active management for small-cap stocks, the relationship is negative.

Investors should also note that there are often biases in the active small-cap-fund performance data being reported by the financial press and media. It is important that investors are aware of these biases or they might draw the wrong conclusion. The biases in the data favoring active small-cap managers include:

- Survivorship bias: Poorly performing funds sent to the mutual fund graveyard or merged out of existence.

- IPO bias.

- Incubator bias: Incubator funds are newly created funds, seeded by mutual fund families with their own capital. The funds are not available to the public. Here is one way the game may be played. A fund family creates several small-cap funds, possibly even under the same manager. Each fund might own a different group of small-cap stocks. The fund family incubates the funds, safe from public scrutiny. After a few years they bring public only the fund with the best performance. Magically, the performance of the other funds disappears.

- Front running bias: A large fund family with a small-cap fund has the small-cap fund buy shares of stocks with a low market cap and limited liquidity. The other funds in the same family then pile in, buying more shares. The limited supply of stock allows the large fund family to drive up prices with relatively small purchases by each fund. The returns of the new fund look great.

Encore Performances

John Bogle, the founder and former chairman of the Vanguard Group, studied the encore performances of top-performing active funds. His findings support our theory that successful performance contains the seeds of its own destruction.[32] Bogle compared the performance of the top twenty funds of the period 1972–82 with their performance for the period 1982–92. He found that the top twenty funds did perform slightly better in the second period than the average active fund, finishing in the 54th percentile. However, the margin of outperformance fell from 8.3 percent to just 1.2 percent. More importantly, they *underperformed* the S&P 500 Index by 1.8 percent—and that is even before considering any loads or the impact of taxes. One further point: The dispersion of returns in the succeeding period was huge—rankings ranged from 2 to 245 (out of 309). Investors might have gotten lucky, or they might have paid a big price. There was no way to know before the fact.

Bogle found a similar story when he examined returns for the periods 1982–92 and 1992–September 30, 2001. The top twenty performers from the first period finished the succeeding period with an average ranking at the 58th percentile. However, the average outperformance fell from 4.9 percent to just 0.9 percent. More importantly, they *underperformed* the S&P 500 Index by 1.5 percent. Again, this is before considering any loads or the impact of taxes. Also, once again, there was a wide dispersion of returns—rankings ranged from 14 to 823 (out of 841). Investors were taking lots of unnecessary risks. Simply accepting market returns would likely have delivered superior performance.

Here is another problem for the active management faithful. Since it takes time before a manager demonstrates top performance, most of the outperformance will likely occur when the fund's assets are very small. Thus very few shareholders actually earn the great returns. Most fund assets come piling in only *after* great returns are earned. When the fund's performance reverts to the mean (which is what the evidence suggests is highly likely to occur), despite the fact that the fund may still show high annualized returns, most of the fund's invested dollars are likely to earn below-market returns. This is consistent with several studies on investment behavior and returns—by chasing yesterday's returns, investors earn rates of return well below those of the very funds in which they invest. They tend to buy high (*after* great performance), and sell low (*after* poor performance). Not exactly a prescription for successful investing.

Peter Lynch I

Before drawing any conclusions on the persistence of performance of fund managers, it is worth considering the case of Peter Lynch, generally considered the greatest fund manager of them all. Lynch joined Fidelity in 1966. However, it was not until 1977 that he was given responsibility for the Magellan Fund. The fund was not even available to the public until mid-1981. Prior to that it operated as the Johnson family's (founders of Fidelity) private investment vehicle. From mid-1981 through mid-1990 Lynch outperformed the S&P 500 Index by 6 percent per annum (22.5 percent to 16.5 percent). Lynch started with about $100 million under management, but ended up running $16 billion. The original small-cap fund not only had become a large-cap fund, but it also eventually owned seventeen hundred stocks. While Lynch did outperform over the latter part of his reign, the size of the outperformance deteriorated, just as we would expect. Over the last four years Lynch managed the fund, Magellan managed to beat the index by just 2 percent per annum.[33] Still a great performance, but not the stuff of which legends are made, nor one that might not just as easily be explained by random good luck. Some might even guess that Lynch retired before the game was up and market forces caught up with him. He may have recognized because of, not only the market's efficiency, but also the increased hurdles of closet indexing, market impact costs, and the other burdens of active management, that the odds of his continuing success were not very good. Why not go out on top?

The subject of Peter Lynch and his performance is an excellent transition to the next issue. One explanation for investors buying actively managed funds is what might be called "the lottery effect"—investors are hoping to hit the investment equivalent of the lottery by finding the next Peter Lynch.

Peter Lynch II

The financial press media are forever seeking to acclaim some mutual fund manager as the financial equivalent of the Michael Jordan of investment managers—the "next Peter Lynch." They, along with individual investors, perform intensive searches of databases for fund managers with track records of outperformance. The latest to be acclaimed as the next Peter Lynch is Bill Miller, the manager of the Legg Mason Value Trust. He has managed to do what no other current manager has done—beat the S&P 500 Index twelve years in a row. Surely that cannot be luck. Surely you can rely on that performance as a predictor of future greatness. Before you come to that conclusion, you should consider the following bit of historical evidence.

The last mutual fund to beat the S&P 500 for even eleven years in a row was the Lindner Large-Cap Fund, outperforming from 1974 through 1984.[34] How were investors rewarded if they waited eleven years to be sure they had found a true genius and then invested in the fund? Over the next eighteen years, the S&P 500 Index returned 12.6 percent. Believers in past performance as a predictor were rewarded by their faith in the Lindner Large-Cap

Fund with returns of just 4.1 percent, an underperformance of over 8 percent per annum for eighteen years. After outperforming for eleven years in a row, the Lindner Large-Cap Fund managed to beat the S&P 500 in just four of the next eighteen years, and none of the last nine—quite a price to pay for belief in a discredited theory.

Not yet convinced? Consider the case of David Baker, and the 44 Wall Street Fund. Baker even outperformed the legendary Magellan Fund over the entire decade of the 1970s and was the top-performing diversified U.S. stock fund of the decade. Unfortunately, 44 Wall Street ranked as the single worst-performing fund of the 1980s, losing 73 percent.[35] During the same period, the S&P 500 grew at 17.5 percent per annum. Each dollar invested in Baker's fund fell in value to just twenty-seven cents. On the other hand, each dollar invested in the S&P 500 Index would have grown to just over five dollars. The fund did so poorly that in 1993 it was merged into the 44 Wall Street Equity Fund, which was then merged into the Matterhorn Growth Fund Income in 1996.

Belief in the hot hand and past performance as a predictor of the future performance of fund managers, even with ten years of evidence, can be quite expensive. To paraphrase a famous quotation: Those who do not know their financial history are doomed to repeat it.

Investors should note that Bill Miller's stellar performance was not even unexpected. With thousands of money managers playing the game, the odds are that several, not just one, would have turned in a Millerlike performance. Yet both the press and the public are quick to assume the performance was a result of skill rather than the more likely assumption that it was a random outcome. In other words, there will be future Peter Lynch's and future Bill Miller's, but we have no way of identifying them

ahead of time. And we can only buy their future performance, not their past performance. Investors would be well served to read *Fooled by Randomness,* an excellent book by Nassim Nicholas Taleb.

Another important topic we need to cover before you draw any conclusions regarding the informational value of Miller's superior performance is that you should really compare his performance to that of value benchmarks. The reason is that Miller is a value manager, or at least that is what the name of his fund implies. The following data breaks down the ten-year period (1992–2001) into two five-year periods. It then compares Miller's performance to that of the performance of two passively managed funds, the DFA Large and Small Value Funds. The data is simulated for the DFA Small Value Fund for the first two months of the period, and it is simulated for the first fifteen months for the DFA Large Value Fund. The simulations include estimated trading costs. For the first five years (1992–96), Miller's fund did not outperform either of the two DFA value funds, returning 19.2 percent compared to 19.3 percent for the DFA Large Value Fund and 21.2 percent for the DFA Small Value Fund. Based on this data, I don't see why any investor would have chosen Miller's fund as the value fund of choice. For the latter five-year period (1997–2001), Miller did outperform both DFA funds, returning 16.5 percent per annum. This compares to the returns of 11 percent and 12.5 percent per annum, respectively, for the two DFA funds. However, all of the outperformance occurred in the first three years. In 2000, Miller's fund lost 7.1 percent and in 2001 lost another 9.3 percent. Contrast those losses with gains for the two DFA value funds in both years. The DFA Large Value Fund returned 10.2 percent and 3.9 percent, outperforming Miller's fund by about 17 percent in 2000 and 13 percent in 2001. The DFA Small Value Fund returned 9.0 percent and 22.8 percent, outperform-

ing Miller's fund by about 16 percent in 2000 and 32 percent in 2001.

Miller's underperformance relative to the DFA value funds continued in 2002. While Miller's fund lost 18.9 percent (once again outperforming the S&P 500 Index by over 3 percent), it underperformed both the DFA Large Value Fund by 4 percent (it lost 14.9 percent) and the DFA Small Value Fund by 9.6 percent (it lost just 9.3 percent). Miller's performance no longer looks quite so impressive. For the period 1991–2002, Miller's fund returned 14.2 percent. It outperformed the DFA Large Value Fund that returned 12.2 percent. However, it underperformed the DFA Small Value Fund that returned 14.3 percent. This performance is certainly not the stuff of which legends are made. In addition, here is another problem. Given the dramatic underperformance of the last three years, what do investors in Miller's fund do now? Do they abandon ship or wait for a turnaround? If they decide to wait, for how long do they do so? Or imagine an investor who, at the start of 2000, having examined Miller's superior performance and trusting that past performance is a predictor of future performance, decides to invest in the Legg Mason Value Trust. This investor never benefited by the superior performance and now has had three years of terrible returns. What does he do now? If he waits, for how long does he do so? If he decides enough is enough, how does he decide in which active fund he should now invest, having discovered that past performance is not a good predictor of future performance? I hope that this section has convinced you that the correct answer is to realize that the strategy of relying on the past performance of equity fund managers is a flawed strategy based on a false premise. Let us now turn our attention to fixed-income mutual funds.

The Determinants of Future Performance of Fixed-Income Mutual Funds

Is the past performance of actively managed bond funds a good predictor of their future performance? Is management tenure a good predictor of future performance? How do expenses and turnover impact returns? The answers to these questions provide valuable insights into identifying the winning fixed-income investment strategy.

Christopher R. Blake, Edwin J. Elton, and Martin Gruber studied the performance of nonmunicipal bond funds for the ten-year period 1979–88. The study was free of survivorship bias and covered forty-six funds.[36] The study concluded that there was no correlation of returns in the first five years with the returns of the succeeding five years. When the authors broke the entire period into three-year periods, they found similar results. The authors followed up their initial study with another covering the period 1986–91 and 123 nonhigh-yield funds.[37] They concluded that actively managed funds do not, on average, provide value added in terms of returns. They found that the major cause of underperformance was expenses.

A study by James Philpot, Douglas Hearth, James N. Rimbey, and Craig T. Schuman examined the performance of twenty-seven bond funds that survived the period 1982–1993.[38] They found that there was no relationship between the Sharpe Ratio (a measure of return relative to the risk taken) during the first five years and the second five years. They also found that there was a strong negative correlation between returns and fund expenses, turnover, and loads. The study acknowledged a survivorship bias in that there were thirty-four bond funds at the start of the period. A full 20 percent of the bond funds that existed at the start of the

47

period disappeared, presumably because of poor performance. Even with this bias, the study concluded that a bond fund's past performance doesn't predict its future performance and that bond fund managers generally are ineffective at increasing risk-adjusted returns.

John Bogle of Vanguard studied the performance of bond funds and concluded that "although past absolute returns of bond funds are a flawed predictor of future returns, there is a fairly easy way to predict future relative returns." After he separated the bond funds into their major categories of quality and maturity, he analyzed returns in terms of their expense ratios. Bogle placed funds into four categories: those with expenses of less than 0.5 percent, those with expenses between 0.5 and 1 percent, those with expenses between 1.0 and 1.5 percent, and those with expenses of over 1.5 percent. Bogle found that "in every case, and in every category, the superior funds could have been system-ically identified based solely on their lower expense ratios. At the extremes, in each group, the lowest-cost funds outpaced the highest-cost funds by between 1 percent and 2.2 percent annu-ally."[39] The ability to predict interest rates played no part in the performance of the bond funds.

William Reichenstein's study, "Bond Fund Returns and Expenses: A Study of Bond Market Efficiency," found similar results to those found by Bogle. His study covered the five-year period 1994–98.[40] He sorted bond funds by investment quality (low, medium, high) and by maturity structure (short-term, inter-mediate, and long-term). His conclusion: Fund expenses are dead weight to investors. He found that there was virtually a perfect inverse relationship between expenses and returns—increases in expenses lead to a direct proportional one-for-one reduction in returns.

Another study looked at bond mutual fund returns from a different perspective. Richard Fortin, Stuart Michelson, and James Jordan-Wagner compared the returns of bond funds based on length of the tenure of the fund's management.[41] The working hypothesis was that a fund run by managers with greater experience might provide higher returns. There would seem to be almost a self-fulfilling prophecy at work here as fund managers who have managed to survive for a long time must be good at what they do. Unfortunately, the study found that there was no difference in the returns of funds where the manager's tenure was greater than ten years and those whose tenure was less than five. It seems expenses are far more important than experience.

The study, "Explaining the Future Performance of Domestic Bond Mutual Funds," covered the period 1992–99 and evaluated the effectiveness of various fund attributes in explaining subsequent returns.[42] The authors came to the following conclusions:

- There was no correlation between fund management tenure and returns.
- There was no support for the notion that higher future returns will recoup loads.
- There was a positive correlation between assets under management and returns. This relationship was not statistically significant at the 95 percent confidence level but was at the 90 percent level. There is logic to this positive relationship, as larger funds should achieve some economies of scale.
- Higher risk funds (funds with higher standard deviations) did provide slightly greater returns. However, the effect was very marginal.
- The coefficient for expenses was -0.71. In other words, every dollar of increased expenses reduced returns by seventy-one cents.

- There was some tendency for past winners to repeat. The coefficient for the three-year trailing Sharpe Ratio was 0.42. It was statistically significant at the 95 percent confidence level.

It is clear that active management has had a negative impact on returns. How big is the impact? A study covering as many as 361 bond funds showed that the average actively managed bond fund underperforms its index by eighty-five basis points a year. Furthermore, depending on the benchmark, between 65 and 80 percent of the funds generated excess returns (returns from their active trading) that were negative.[43] Another study covering the ten-year period ending 1998 found that the average actively managed taxable bond fund underperformed the average bond index fund by 0.7 percent per annum.[44] Finally, a 1994 study found that only 128 (16 percent) out of 800 fixed-income funds beat their relevant benchmark over the ten-year period covered.[45]

In the face of this body of evidence, we can draw some conclusions as to the winning investment strategy. First, because bonds within each investment grade are relatively homogenous investments (have relatively similar risk characteristics), there is little opportunity for fund managers to distinguish themselves. Since different bonds of the same investment grade are good substitutes for one another, costs only reduce returns. This is particularly true of short-term fixed-income investments, where little or no value can be added by guessing right on the future direction of interest rates. Thus the winning strategy is to simply choose the lowest cost fund of the maturity and credit risk you seek. That fund is highly likely to be a passively managed one.

Exploiting Anomalies

Before concluding this section, there is one last point we need to cover. Let's suppose that a manager has been able to deliver superior performance because he/she has discovered an anomaly in how the market prices securities. The problem is that because the markets are highly efficient (EMH), the anomaly is not likely to persist, and thus the outperformance is not likely to persist. By the time you discover the manager's skill, it is probably too late. Economics professors Dwight Lee and James Verbrugge of the University of Georgia explain the power of the efficient markets theory in the following manner.

The efficient markets theory is practically alone among theories in that it becomes more powerful when people discover serious inconsistencies between it and the real world. If a clear efficient market anomaly is discovered, the behavior (or lack of behavior) that gives rise to it will tend to be eliminated by competition among investors for higher returns. (For example) If stock prices are found to follow predictable seasonable patterns this knowledge will elicit responses that have the effect of eliminating the very patterns that they were designed to exploit. The implication is striking. The more the empirical flaws that are discovered in the efficient markets theory the more robust the theory becomes. (In effect) those who do the most to ensure that the efficient markets hypothesis remains fundamental to our understanding of financial economics are not its intellectual defenders, but those mounting the most serious empirical assault against it.[46]

While there will likely always be some active fund managers who outperform, the average equity active fund manager underperforms his or her benchmark by close to 2 percent per annum (even before taxes are considered) and the average bond fund manager by close to 1 percent. And the evidence demonstrates that past performance cannot be used to predict future performance. However, perhaps there are other strategies that can be used to identify ahead of time the future winners. That is the subject covered in truth 7.

TRUTH 3

◆

If Skilled Professionals Don't Succeed, It Is Unlikely That Individual Investors Will

The body of credible impartial evidence indicates that active stock portfolio managers do not add value.
> —Richard M. Ennis, director, investment policy research, and Michael D. Sebastian, director, analytical development at Ennis Knupp + Associates, Inc., *Pensions & Investments*

I have personally tried to invest money, my client's and my own money, in every single anomaly and predictive result that academics have dreamed up. And I have yet to make a nickel on any of these supposed market inefficiencies. An inefficiency ought to be an exploitable opportunity. If there's nothing investors can exploit in a systematic way, time in and time out, then it's very hard to say that information is not being properly incorporated into stock prices. Real money investment strategies don't produce the results that academic papers say they should.
> —Richard Roll, financial economist and principal of the portfolio management firm, Roll & Ross Asset Management, *Wall Street Journal*

There is no evidence of any large institutions having anything like consistent ability to get in when the market is low and get out when the market is high. Attempts to switch between stocks and bonds, or between stocks and cash, in anticipation of market moves have been unsuccessful much more often than they have been successful.
> —Charles Ellis, *Winning the Loser's Game*

*There is no reliable way to predict the future performance of
a money manager or mutual fund. By the time a hot mutual
fund, money manager, or even asset class graces the top ten
list of the financial press, the overwhelming odds are that
within a short period of time the performance will decline.*
—Donald Trone, William Allbright, and Philip Taylor,
The Management of Investment Decisions

I f a group of professional basketball players were given a test
of their basketball skills, and the vast majority of them failed
the test, what are the odds that an individual would be able to succeed at that task? I think everyone would agree that the odds
would be very low. And if individuals were offered a chance to
bet on their ability to succeed, the vast majority would not be
willing to take that bet, even if the odds offered were very high. It
would be rational for individuals to conclude that if the very best
can't succeed, the odds of their doing so are "slim to none." However, faced with this same situation in the world of investing, individuals take the very same bet, even with no odds given them. In
fact, the odds are vastly against them succeeding, as you will see.

It appears to be a very common human trait for individual
investors to be overconfident of their skills when it comes to identifying active managers who will outperform the market in the
future. Even if they are aware of the evidence on the dismal performance of active managers overall, a frequent response is: "The
data only represents the average fund. By instituting simple
screens, you can easily eliminate many losers." And even if they
happen to be aware of the equally dismal track record on using
past performance as a predictor, they press on. Typical suggestions
include the screening out of, not only those funds with poor performance, but also those with high expenses, high turnover, tax
inefficiency, or to screen for managers with long tenure. By *care-*

fully selecting funds, rather than looking at all funds, investors believe they can identify funds that will outperform. This approach has a logical appeal, and it will likely even improve the results compared to all actively managed funds; however, it is not likely that it will result in market-beating performance. After reading this section, my hope is that you will agree that it is not logical to think that you can identify the future winners, even with the most logical of approaches. The logic is based on observing the track record of highly respected professional firms, with highly skilled talent and tremendous resources at their disposal, certainly more resources than the individual investor is likely to have. As with our basketball example, if the very best can't succeed, it is not logical to believe that you will be able to do so.

One of the most respected names in the investment business is Frank Russell (creator of the Russell Indices). Russell's firm performs research and due diligence on money managers in its role as a pension plan consultant and chooses the very best to manage funds it sponsors. It would seem logical that if anyone could beat the market by identifying the future great money managers, the Russell organization could. On its Web site (www.russell.com) it touts an extensive process, with sixty analysts studying some seventeen hundred investment managers. These analysts hold over two thousand meetings a year, during which they grill managers on their investment approach. They use both qualitative and quantitative analysis to narrow those seventeen hundred to the best four hundred and seventy, and then subject those to further scrutiny. The list is then narrowed down to the very best, before ultimately selecting the very few "superstars" who will have the honor of comanaging one of Russell's funds. Within investment styles (growth and value, small cap and large cap, domestic and international), Russell funds use a manager-of-managers approach—selecting and monitoring "some of the best money managers in the world." Russell notes that in making the ultimate selection of managers it places the most weight on the investment process used by the manager. The second most important criterion is the strength of the management team. The third, but least important factor, since it is an unreliable predictor, is past performance.

So let's take a ride on Mr. Peabody's (of Rocky and Bullwinkle fame) way-back machine and see just how well the Russell approach has performed. To test the process, we can compare the returns of the actively managed Russell manager-of-manager funds with appropriate passive benchmarks. For an appropriate benchmark for each asset class for which Russell has funds, we can use the passively managed asset class funds of DFA (and simulated returns if the funds were not live for the entire period). We will look at both pre- and after-tax performance. A 35 percent tax rate will be used to calculate after-tax returns. Depending on the availability of live data, we will examine either the five- or ten-year period (whichever is longer) ending in 2002. Let's begin by examining the pretax returns for the large-cap asset class.

1993–2002	Percent
Russell Equity I	8.3
Russell Equity Q	9.9
DFA Large Cap (an S&P 500 Index fund)	9.1

The average return of the two Russell funds was 9.1 percent, exactly the same as for a benchmark index fund. However, once taxes are considered, the story is quite different. The Russell funds each lost about 3 percent per annum to taxes. The index fund lost just 0.8 percent per annum. Thus, on an after-tax basis, the Russell funds underperformed by 2.2 percent per annum on an after-tax basis.

Let's now look at the performance of the large-cap value-oriented Russell Equity III Fund. We will look at the five-year period ending in 2002.

1998–2002	Percent
Russell Equity III	−3.5
DFA Large Cap Value	2.7

As you can see, the Russell fund clearly underperformed by over 6 percent on a pretax basis. On an after-tax basis, the underperformance exceeded 5 percent per annum. The Russell fund lost about 1.5 percent per annum to taxes while the DFA fund lost about 2.3 percent per annum. It is also worth noting that DFA has introduced a *tax-managed* large-cap value fund that should significantly reduce the drag from the negative impact of taxes on returns. In its first three years, this fund lost an average of only 0.51 percent to taxes.*

Let's now examine the performance in the asset class of small-cap stocks.

1993–2002	Percent
Russell Equity II	9.1
DFA Small Cap	9.0
DFA Micro Cap	11.6

On a pretax basis, the Russell fund basically matched the return of the DFA Small Cap Fund. However, on an after-tax basis, it underperformed as it lost 2.9 percent per annum to taxes.

---

*While tax-management strategies should produce greater tax efficiency, the newness of the funds in all likelihood overstates their long-term tax efficiency. A simulated study by Kenneth R. French, depending on the assumptions made about growth of assets under management and investment horizon, indicated improved long-term, after-tax returns of approximately 1 to 2 percent per annum.

The DFA fund was more tax-efficient, losing just 2.4 percent per annum to taxes. The DFA Micro Cap Fund outperformed the Russell fund by 2.5 percent per annum on a pretax basis. Its greater tax efficiency allowed it to outperform the Russell fund by 3.0 percent per annum on an after-tax basis. It is also worth noting that DFA has introduced a *tax-managed* small-cap fund that should significantly reduce the drag from the negative impact of taxes on returns. In its first three years this fund lost an average of only 0.13 percent to taxes (see footnote on previous page).

Let's now examine the five-year performance of the Russell Real Estate Fund as compared to that of the DFA Real Estate Fund.

1998–2002	**Percent**
Russell Real Estate	4.0
DFA Real Estate	4.7

Once again we see no evidence of outperformance. In this case the Russell fund was as equally tax-efficient as the DFA fund. They both lost 2.3 percent per annum to taxes. However, since most investors should hold real estate assets in tax-deferred accounts, after-tax returns are less of an issue. At any rate, on an after-tax basis, the DFA fund outperformed.

Moving on to the asset class of international stocks, we can compare the performance of the Russell International Fund with that of the DFA Large Cap International Fund that basically conforms to the EAFE Index.

1993–2002	**Percent**
Russell International	4.0
DFA Large-Cap International	4.0

While the Russell International Fund matched the return of the DFA fund on a pretax basis, it was less tax-efficient. The Russell fund lost 1.7 percent to taxes. The DFA fund lost just 0.8 percent to taxes. Thus the DFA fund outperformed the Russell fund on an after-tax basis by 3.2 percent vs. 2.3 percent, respectively.

We will conclude our analysis by comparing the performance of the Russell Emerging Markets Fund with that of the DFA Emerging Markets Fund.

1998–2002	Percent
Russell Emerging Markets	−7.8
DFA Emerging Markets	−1.4

In what is supposedly the most inefficient asset class in the world (where active managers claim to be able to add the most value), we actually find the worst performance, with Russell underperforming its benchmark by over 6 percent per annum pretax. It should be noted that, with the low level of absolute returns, neither fund was impacted much by taxes (the tax impact for the Russell fund was 0.2 percent per annum and for the DFA fund it was 0.4 percent per annum).

To summarize, it is very hard to see any evidence of the ability of Frank Russell to add value, especially on an after-tax basis.

There is another piece of strong evidence against the likelihood and wisdom of trying to find the *future* great investment managers. As mentioned in truth 2, it would seem logical to believe that if anyone could beat the market, it would be the pension funds of the largest U.S. companies. They have access to the best and brightest portfolio managers, all of them clamoring to manage the billions of dollars in these plans. Presumably, these pension funds rely on the excellent track records of the "experts" they eventually choose to manage their portfolios. It seems unlikely they would ever choose fund managers with poor past performance. In addition, the pension plans often hire professional advisors such as Frank Russell, SEI, and Goldman Sachs to help them perform due diligence in interviewing, screening, and ultimately selecting the very best of the best. As individuals, we don't have access to many of these great managers since we would not meet their investment minimums. We also don't have the luxury of being able to personally interview the firms and perform a thorough due diligence. And we don't have professionals helping us to avoid mistakes in the process.

As we saw in truth 2, FutureMetrics Inc. found that only a very small percentage of the pension plans covered by their study managed to outperform their passive benchmark.[1] Another study of pension fund managers found very similar results. T. Daniel Coggin and Charles A. Trzcinka studied the performance of 292 pension plans with twelve quarters of data up to the second quarter of 1993.[2] Here is a summary of their findings:

- It is very difficult to find investment managers who consistently add value relative to appropriate benchmarks.
- There was no correlation found between relative performance in one period and future periods.
- There was no evidence that the number of managers beating their benchmarks was greater than pure chance.

The authors concluded: "Those who rely solely on historical style alpha (performance) to predict future style alphas are likely to be disappointed."

Also insightful on the likelihood of finding managers who will beat their benchmark is the experience of the chief investment officer of SURS (the State Universities Retirement System of Illinois), John R. Krimmel. His comments on the firings of the two active fund managers the system had employed were as follows:

- It's a tough area in which to operate.
- Academic research bears that out. Our experience shows that as well.
- Over the long haul we've just about broken even (that is, equaled the index return) but with slightly higher volatility.[3]

Also consider the following cases. In 1995, Intel fired all of its active managers.[4] In 1999, Philip Morris ended the use of active managers on nearly $8 billion of pension assets due to poor and inconsistent performance,[5] and in 2002, ExxonMobil moved the remainder of its $14 billion in retirement assets that were still actively managed into indexing.[6] It is a safe assumption that none of these firms ever hired an active manager who did not have a track record of outperformance. It is probably an equally safe assumption that these firms performed a thorough due diligence on the managers before hiring them. They probably also received outside expert advice before making the final choice. And finally, it is also a very safe assumption that they ultimately fired the active managers because they did not receive the expected or the desired result. These three firms, among many others, recognized that, unfortunately, they were playing the wrong game—the loser's game of trying to outperform the market through active stock selection and market timing.

If you are not yet convinced that trying to find the future great fund managers is a loser's game, perhaps the following amusing tale will convince you. At the very least you should have a good laugh. In 1995, Minneapolis money manager Robert Markman bet Vanguard Group founder John Bogle twenty-five dollars that he could beat the stock market over the long term with a portfolio of professionally managed mutual funds. How did the bet turn out? Between 1995 and 2000, Markman's funds trailed the Vanguard S&P 500 Index Fund by an average of 6 percentage points a year. But the story doesn't end here. In the spring of 2000, just after the NASDAQ bubble burst, Markman bet another five dollars that he could beat the index with an even more aggressive portfolio of funds. Two years later, *U.S. News* reported that Markman was losing again, but this time by an even wider margin. Markman's response: "I've really become disillusioned with the ability of active managers." One can only wonder how investors in Markman's funds feel.[7]

Returning to our starting point: Is it logical for you to believe that you can predict which actively managed funds will outperform, or are you overconfident of your skills? Before you attempt to find the great fund managers who will outperform in the future, ask yourself: What am I going to do differently in terms of identifying the future winning fund managers than do the pension plans and their advisors? Surely these organizations have thought of eliminating from consideration the poorly performing funds and the high-cost funds? And if you are not going to do something different, what logic is there in playing a game at which others with superior resources have consistently failed? Or is it that you believe that you can interpret the data more correctly than have others with far more resources?

By seriously considering these questions, you can avoid the mistake of trying to find the future great fund managers. Yes, it is possible that you will succeed. However, both the evidence and the logic suggest that the odds against success make this a game you are better off not playing. Think about it: Of the 355 equity funds that existed in 1970, only 169 were left standing as of June

2001. Of the survivors, just nine managed to outperform the S&P 500 Index.[8] Daniel Kahneman, professor of psychology and public affairs at Princeton University, put it this way:

> What's really quite remarkable in the investment world is that people are playing a game which, in some sense, cannot be played. There are so many people out there in the market; the idea that any single individual without extra information or extra market power can beat the market is extraordinarily unlikely. Yet the market is full of people who think they can do it and full of other people who believe them. This is one of the great mysteries of finance: Why do people believe they can do the impossible? And why do other people believe them?[9]

TRUTH 4

◆

The Interests of Wall Street and the Financial Media Are Not Aligned with Those of Investors

Economists, when faced with a conflict between theory and evidence, discard the theory. Stockbrokers discard the evidence.
—Andrew Smithers and Stephen Wright, *Valuing Wall Street*

Investor to stockbroker: When we set up my investment plan, I thought the objective was funding MY retirement!
—Anonymous

The most common of all follies is to believe passionately in the palpably not true.
—H. L. Mencken

The stockbroker services his clients in the same way that Bonnie and Clyde serviced banks.
—William Bernstein

How many stockbrokers does it take to change a light bulb? Two. One to take out the burned out bulb and drop it, the other to try and sell it before it crashes.
—Anonymous

It is often the case that important discoveries provoke a confederacy of resistance from those who embrace the established doctrine.
—Mark P. Kritzman, *Puzzles of Finance*

Trading often and heavy is not something that makes you a lot of money. Now, that's contrary to my own interests, but it is the truth.
—Joe Ricketts, Ameritrade founder, Fortune.com

D espite the superior returns generated by passively managed funds, financial publications are dominated by forecasts from so-called gurus and the latest hot fund managers. I believe there is a simple explanation for the *mis*information: It's just not in the interests of either the vast majority of investment firms or the financial media to inform investors of the failure of active managers. It is extremely unfortunate that our education system has left the vast majority of Americans without the knowledge to understand either the conflicts of interest that exist or the ability to recognize investment propaganda when they see or hear it. Most Americans, having taken a biology course in high school, know more about amoebas than they do about investing. Despite its obvious importance to every individual, our education system almost totally ignores the field of finance and investments. Unless you earn an M.B.A. in finance you probably never were taught how financial economists believe the markets work and how you can best make them work for you.

Just as nature abhors a vacuum, Wall Street and the financial media rush in to fill the void. Investors, lacking the protection of knowledge, are susceptible to all the investment graffiti, hype, and sales pressure that the investment establishment is capable of putting out. The problem with this hype is that, in general, the only people who are enriched by it are part of the investment establishment itself.

In this section we will examine the nature of the conflict of interest between most investment firms and financial media, and the investing public. We begin with the misalignment of interests between most investment firms and investors.

Investment Firms

It is fairly common knowledge that it may be in the interest of life insurance salespeople to sell whole or variable life insurance instead of much less expensive term insurance. The reason is that while in some cases term insurance may be the better choice for the individual, insurance agents often earn far higher commissions from selling other products. In the same manner, it is clearly in the interests of Wall Street to charge you 1.5 percent for an underperforming and tax-inefficient actively managed fund rather than 0.25 percent to 0.5 percent for a passively managed fund with superior performance and greater tax efficiency. It is also in their interests to sell you funds with loads or commissions rather than index funds carrying no such expenses. It is important to note that there are exceptions. The two main ones are Vanguard and DFA, both providers of index/passively managed funds that are low cost, tax efficient, and carry no commissions of any kind (though DFA does require you to use an approved fee-only financial advisor to access their funds). Let's examine both the nature of the conflict between most investment firms and individual investors, and also the danger this conflict presents.

Unless you are a do-it-yourself investor, you are working with an investment advisor of some kind. That person is typically either a stockbroker or a registered financial advisor. It is my strong advice that you should only work with advisors who are fee only, not commission based.

A fee-only relationship is the best way you can seek to ensure that the advisor's interests are aligned with yours. The only thing they are selling is their advice. No one else is providing them with any compensation. Most fee-only advisors work on a fee that is based on a percentage of assets under management, in which case there is an alignment of interests. The more your portfolio is worth, the greater their compensation. Their only incentive is to help you grow the value of your portfolio. If you work with an advisor who is paid on a commission basis, there is no guarantee that the person selling you a product is not suggesting that particular product because he/she gets a large commission upon sale, even though there might be a better alternative for you. Remember, commission-based advisors are not just selling advice but also products.

The worst example of this conflict of interest is that investors in profit-sharing plans and other tax-deferred accounts have been sold expensive variable annuities. It should be noted that, by law, under the "old" 403(b) plans, an individual could only hold variable annuities. When the new 403(b)(7) was added, that changed. Considering that the only valuable benefit of a variable annuity is the tax deferral, there is virtually no reason anyone should be paying the expensive charges of a variable annuity when the account structure already provides the benefit of the tax deferral. Of course the salesperson will have received a commission of as much as 8 percent. It is also worth noting that no-load, no surrender charge, and low-expense variable annuities are available. Therefore, there is no reason to buy a high-expense load annuity with heavy surrender charges.

Commission-based advisors most likely will also push for expensive and tax-inefficient actively managed funds over index funds. The likely reason is not that they believe that the actively managed funds will provide better performance but that they will be paid a load and/or receive a trailing fee as long as you hold the fund. Of course, it is possible that they might actually believe, despite all evidence to the contrary, that somehow they can identify the few active managers who will beat their benchmarks in the future. But you could not be certain of their motives unless they were fee-only advisors whose interests were aligned with yours. Consider the following memo sent in response to requests from a brokerage firm's sales force for the firm to offer index funds. The sales force was simply responding to similar requests from clients who had heard about the superior performance of these passively managed funds.

> Index funds are passively managed mutual funds. They simply buy and hold all the stocks of a particular market index such as the S&P 500. Because their portfolio turnover is low and they don't require large research staffs, most have low operating expenses. The returns of an index fund are a function of two factors: 1) the performance of the index, and 2) the fees to operate and DISTRIBUTE the mutual fund. For a fund to be successful in the brokerage community it must adequately compensate brokers either through an up-front commission or an ongoing service fee or both. As a result, a broker-sold index fund would underperform not only the index but also a no-load index mutual fund. These are reasons why most index funds are offered by no-load fund groups. (emphasis mine)

The reason that brokers do not sell index funds is not because these funds do not perform well; they don't sell them because investors can buy them cheaper elsewhere. In addition, there is just not enough revenue available to compensate the broker, whose first priority is generating fees, not obtaining the best possible results for clients. Mutual fund sponsors avoid indexing because, while the record demonstrates that it is the winning strategy for investors, it is not very profitable for fund sponsors. They see indexing as the losing *business* strategy. This is clearly a conflict of interest, as the following tale will demonstrate.

CIBC (the Canadian Imperial Bank of Commerce) is one of

Canada's largest banks. In the mid-1990s, it made the decision to focus on growing their wealth-management business. The problem was that the family of CIBC mutual funds had delivered poor results, leaving them with a marketing dilemma. (It's tough to market poor performance.) The bank decided that the solution to their problem was to tout index funds as the winning strategy for investors. The bank created a family of index funds and placed Ted Cadsby in charge. His mission was to spread the gospel of the benefits of passive investing. He became a very public spokesman for the bank. Cadsby even wrote a book, *The Power of Indexing,* in which he railed against the evils of active management—high costs and poor and inconsistent performance.[1]

Cadsby was highly successful in his mission—assets under management doubled to $24 billion in just four years. CIBC had the second-fastest growing fund family among Canadian banks. And suddenly, Cadsby virtually disappeared from public view. According to the story in the *Financial Post,* sources told the paper that Cadsby had been told to "quiet down." Why? Because the winning strategy for investors was the losing strategy for the bank! The bank had recently purchased Merrill Lynch Canada's retail brokerage arm (including $4.5 billion in actively managed mutual fund assets), as well as TAL Global Asset Management Inc., which managed over $50 billion in assets, including $4 billion in retail mutual funds (under the Talvest name). These funds charged the kind of outrageously high fees against which Cadsby had been railing. The typical Talvest fund charged about 2.5 percent per annum. Some of its global funds charged over 3 percent per annum. Merrill's fund fees were similar.[2] And index funds, or their equivalent ETFs, can be purchased with operating-expense ratios of well below 1 percent. And then you have the issue of the poor and inconsistent performance you get for the privilege of owning those high-cost actively managed funds. As Rex Sinquefield, the cochairman of DFA, is fond of saying: "Poor performance doesn't come cheap, you have to pay dearly for it." While passive/index investing is clearly the winning strategy for investors, it did not generate the kind of profits (from the pockets of investors) that active management did. By allegedly "muzzling" Cadsby, CIBC appears to have made the decision that the interests of the bank's shareholders were more important than the interests of the bank's clients.

The same conflict of interest exists when it comes to the trading of individual stocks. Commission-driven compensation requires investors to trade in order to generate profits, both from commissions and market-making activities. (They can earn the bid-offer spread if they make a market in the particular stock being traded.) Thus there is an incentive to have the investor actively trade an account, when doing nothing might be in the investor's best interests. The activity, known as "churning," has been the cause of the filing of many investor lawsuits.

There is one other issue related to dealing with brokerage firms as advisors that has nothing to do with the form of compensation. A conflict of interest may arise when an investor wants to purchase bonds. A brokerage firm might be holding an inventory of bonds that it wants to dispose of. The firm will typically provide incentives for its brokers to dump these bonds on unsuspecting clients by offering them larger commissions. An investor then might end up being sold a bond that might not be the most appropriate one for him/her based on the desired maturity and credit risk. In addition, although commissions will generally appear on a purchase statement, the firm may mark up its bond inventory so that the investor ends up paying an above-market price without the client's knowledge of this occurring. Investors are particularly vulnerable to this with municipal bonds, as prices for municipal bonds are not generally posted as they are for stocks.

Therefore, while you might see a commission charge, there might also have been a markup of 1 percent, or even more. The investor will never see this cost, except, of course, through lower returns. This can be avoided by requiring that the advisor shop several wholesale market makers for the best price.

Evidence of Conflicting Interests

Citing from the NASD's (National Association of Securities Dealers) dispute-resolution Web site, www.nasdadr.com, Dan Solin, a securities attorney, told me that the types of controversies that cause complaints to be filed against brokers fit into the following categories: breach of fiduciary duty, negligence, misrepresentation, failure to supervise, unsuitability, unauthorized trading, omission of facts, churning, margin calls, and on-line trading. Dan added that, in general, many brokers sell whatever the client will buy. It is his experience that some brokers make little or no effort to diversify or to contain transaction costs. To the contrary, these costs are often the prime motivation behind the sale. He told me of a case in which he represented a client against two major firms where the turnover was around 150 percent per month. It was estimated that the portfolio would have had to earn 30 percent a year to break even!

Dan explained to me that in his experience most clients have no idea how often their accounts are being turned over, how much they have lost in their accounts, or how risky their portfolios are. The concept of diversification means to most of them that they should not be invested solely in tech stocks—and this has been only a recent revelation. To his surprise, unauthorized trading is far more frequent than one would imagine. The broker believes that if the stock goes up, the client will not complain. If it goes down, he will offer to waive the commissions or to give the client a shot at an IPO. Dan added: "The number of outright crooks in the securities business is alarming. These include 'pump-and-dump' operations, boiler rooms, and firms infiltrated by organized crime. Many firms are financially irresponsible or unscrupulous or both. The number of investors willing to deal with such firms (without any prudent investigation) is mind-boggling. These are the firms that go out of business and do not pay awards." Dan provided me with the following data, again from www.nasdadr.com, as well as from his insights on arbitration awards:

- In 2000, there were 5,558 new matters filed with the NASD and approximately 600 new matters filed with the NYSE. Given the number of investors, and the ethics of brokers, it is apparent to Dan that most investors (and their advisors) do not know they may have claims against their brokers.

- Recently there has been an increase in the number of claims filed with the NASD. Total filings for 2001 were projected to be over sixty-seven hundred. This is still far less than the number of investors who have claims.

- Investors prevail at the NASD approximately 54 percent of the time. This number drops to 45 percent for cases before the NYSE.

- When investors are not represented by attorneys, the odds of prevailing drop by 27 percent.

- The NYSE awarded $161 million to investors in 1998. In Dan's opinion, if investors knew their rights, this number would be over $1 billion.

- Surprisingly, 49 percent of these awards were not paid because many of the guilty brokers left the industry.

- Most of the relatively few attorneys who specialize in these matters will not take a case unless the losses are at least one hundred thousand dollars. These cases are typically done on a contingency-fee basis, with the lawyer's fee ranging from 33.3 percent to 40 percent. The client pays expenses, which typically run from five thousand to fifteen thousand dollars, mostly for outside experts. Investors with smaller claims can bring them without counsel if they cannot find counsel to assist them.

Dan summed up the conflict-of-interest problem this way in his excellent book *Does Your Broker Owe You Money?*

For the broker to truly look after your interests while at the same time earning the best living possible is like trying to ride a horse in both directions at the same time. The bottom line in all of this is that your broker is not your friend, and your broker is not necessarily looking out for your best interest. The first conflict, of course, is that many brokers are still compensated through sales commissions. The more they sell, the more they earn. The more they recommend that you invest in products that pay a high commission, the more they earn. But their earnings are your costs. And costs are one of your portfolio's worst enemies.

In his book Dan relates the highly revealing tale of Robert Magnan, a former broker barred from the industry for life. In an April 2001 interview with Scott Cohn of CNBC, Magnan stated that he had received "a lot of training on how to sell over the phone, how to build relationships, and how to gather assets and how to convince clients to send you a lot of money and how to keep it with you. But I never received any training on how to make a client money."

If you are not yet convinced that working with a commission-based advisor can be dangerous to your financial health, perhaps the following quote will convince you.

> My branch managers only want producers who will pick the gold from their grandmother's teeth. Now that we have the gun to your head and we are into your pockets, do as you are told, sell what we want you to sell when we want you to sell it, or we'll fire you and hire someone else. Then we will sue you for what we lent you and make damn well sure that you never see your book of business again.

The source is an unnamed former vice president of sales of a major broker-dealer. The source is unnamed because arbitration cases prevent disclosure. Dan Solin told me that he has represented an ex-broker who worked for two major firms, and the ex-broker testified to almost precisely this speech being given to him. Dan added that he has reviewed tens of thousands of pages of internal broker-dealer documents and that in his view this statement accurately reflects the prevailing views of management in the brokerage industry.

Highly revealing about the question of whether Wall Street firms have your interests at heart is the following quotation: "It has been a problem since the dawn of the retail brokerage business. Brokers have a strong incentive to get customers to trade when it might be in [the] clients' interests to do nothing."[3] This inherent conflict of interest is why the following definition of a stockbroker is often appropriate: Someone whose objective it is to transfer assets from your account to their account. It is also why investors should be aware that if they get their investment advice from a stockbroker, they might end up dealing with another kind of broker, the pawn kind. To paraphrase advice from Prof. 'Enry 'Iggins in *My Fair Lady:* You should rather a new edition of the Spanish Inquisition than to ever let a broker in your life.

Once again the best way to avoid any conflict of interests is to work with an advisor on a fee-only basis. That assures alignment of interests and unbiased advice. No matter how good an advisor's intentions are, it is too easy to be swayed from those good intentions by commission-based compensation.

Before leaving the world of investment banks, we need to cover another area of conflict of interest, the conflict between the interests of investors and the relationship of an investment firm with its investment-banking clients. The following tales are evidence of these conflicts and the dangers they present.

CSFB (Credit Suisse First Boston) banking analyst Mike Mayo had become a guru for his December 1994 forecast that bank stocks were bottoming out and would stage a rally. He made a gutsy call and turned out to be right. Over the next few years the S&P Bank Index rose 254 percent. Thinking (mistakenly) that he could change the ratings game on Wall Street—Mayo actually thought he could be honest and tell people to SELL—in the spring of 1999 he stated: "In no uncertain terms sell bank stocks." He turned out to be right. Banks began to issue earnings warnings, and from their peak on July 7 to the end of 1999 the benchmark index fell 21 percent. This was the worst performance relative to the S&P 500 Index in fifty-four years. It continued to tumble through February 2000. How did Mr. Mayo fare? After many irate calls from their investment-banking clients (including at least one who threatened to cease all underwriting and trading business with CSFB), Mr. Mayo was fired. Why? Was it for making a great forecast? In fact, his forecast actually had just earned him the *Wall Street Journal*'s number-two ranking in its annual stock-picking poll! He also came out second in *Institutional Investor*'s 2000 ranking. I think the answer is obvious. Wall Street's interests are simply not aligned with those of investors. Their interests are to drive investment-banking profits, and in order to do that they must keep their investment-banking clients happy. This is why you see virtually no negative recommendations from them. As *Fortune* magazine put it: "If, in fact, stocks are headed for a disastrous slide, you won't hear it from the researchers paid to predict it." *Fortune*'s article pointed out that more than 70 percent of the twenty-seven thousand First Call/Thomson Financial analyst recommendations are either buys or strong buys. How likely is it that 70 percent of the stocks will outperform the market? Amazingly, only 1 percent are sell recommendations. How likely is it that only 1 percent of stocks will underperform the market?[4]

The following tale is another one that reveals the danger to an analyst's personal financial wealth of making a negative forecast. In the summer of 1998, Ashok Kumar, an analyst at Piper Jaffray, downgraded the stock of Gateway from a *strong buy* to a simple *buy*. Now keep in mind, Kumar did not issue a sell or even a hold recommendation. He simply warned investors that "the long-term growth rate implicit in the current level of the stock may be unrealistic." During the next Gateway conference call, Kumar found that he couldn't ask any questions. After the call, a couple of portfolio managers who did business with Piper Jaffray called Kumar's boss and told him that "if this guy doesn't stop pissing on the stock, we'll yank our business." When Kumar gave similar warnings on Dell's stock, he was kicked off the company's conference call with analysts. The danger of candid, unbiased commentary is very clear to analysts.[5] Therefore, the danger of following analysts' advice should be equally clear to investors. The following are further examples of why this is so.

Richard Lilly was an analyst at JW Charles Securities in 1992. Convinced he had uncovered fraud in a company he had previously been recommending, he was about to issue a sell recommendation. The company learned what Lilly was planning and threatened both Lilly and the firm. Lilly refused to comply and sent letters to the media and investors outlining his concerns. He was fired. Shortly thereafter, the company collapsed.[6]

The results of a study done by Roni Michaely of Cornell and Tel-Aviv Universities and Kent Womack of Dartmouth are quite revealing on the issue of analyst bias. Their study, "Conflict of Interest and the Credibility of Underwriter Analyst Recommendations," compared recommendations made by underwriters and nonunderwriters of 391 companies that conducted IPOs in 1990 and 1991. They tracked stock performance for up to two years after the IPO date. They found significant evidence of bias and possible conflict of interest between an analyst's responsibility to his investing clients and his incentive to market stocks underwritten by his firm. The study also concluded that contrary to conventional wisdom the market doesn't come close to recognizing the full extent of this bias. They found that the stocks of companies that were recommended only by analysts from the underwriting firms were terrible performers. After two years, the average IPO recommended only by nonunderwriters outperformed the group recommended by their own underwriters by more than 55 percent. They considered that a logical explanation for this underperformance is that the analysts know that they are misleading the public but do so anyway because they have been directed to or because it is good for their compensation.[7]

Another study, "The Relation Between Analysts' Long-Term Earnings Forecasts and Stock Price Performance Following Equity Offerings," turned up similar results. The study found that, in general, sell-side analysts' long-term growth forecasts are systematically overly optimistic around equity offerings and that analysts employed by the lead managers of the offerings make the most optimistic growth forecasts. The study concluded that there was a positive relationship between the fees paid to the affiliated analysts' employers and the level of the affiliated analysts' growth forecasts.[8]

One of my favorite examples of the potential for bias in analysts' forecasts as well as the lack of value of such forecasts goes as follows. On May 31, 2000, Goldman Sachs analyst Anthony Noto ranked thirty-two e-commerce companies he covered into three groups in terms of likely survival: winners, a middle tier, and losers.[9] Of the eight winners, 88 percent (all except Amazon.com) were Goldman Sachs investment-banking clients. Only one of the nine middle-tier companies, and none of the fifteen losers, were Goldman clients. Let's roll the videotape.

An investor who had purchased, on June 1, 2000, the stocks of the companies Noto had forecast to be the winners by December 26 of that same year would have experienced an average loss of 73 percent. One would have been slightly better off actually purchasing the stocks of the companies he forecast as the losers as the loss would have been only 72 percent. It is also worth noting that during the same time frame, the S&P 500 Index fell from 1,449 to 1,315. Including dividends, the loss to an investor would have been slightly less than 9 percent.

One last example on the dangers of conflicting interests. Marvin Roffman was an analyst at Janney Montgomery Scott in 1990. He was at the firm for sixteen years and had been in the business for thirty. He followed the gaming industry and put out a report that called an investment in Trump's Taj Mahal in Atlantic City too risky. Donald Trump demanded he be fired, and he was, within days. Trump's Taj Mahal filed for bankruptcy shortly thereafter.[10]

The conflicts between the vested interests of most investment firms and investors are both many and dangerous. At the very least, forewarned is forearmed.

The Financial Media

Unfortunately for investors, because of the alignment of their interests, the investment firms have as allies most of the media. Investors need to understand that it is not in the interests of financial publications that tout "The Best Ten Funds" to inform investors of what is in their best interests. The following two quotations are good examples. The first is from the August 1995 edition of *MONEY* magazine. "Bogle wins: Index funds should be the core of most portfolios today." The headline for the cover story read: "The New Way to Make Money in Funds." The second is from the February 1996 edition of *Worth* magazine. "The index fund is a truly awesome invention. A cheap S&P 500 or a Wilshire 5000 Index fund ought to constitute at least half of your portfolio." The irony in these two statements is that neither magazine will give passive management a whole-hearted endorsement. If passively managed funds (i.e., index funds) are so good, why shouldn't they be the only ones an investor should use? These magazines withhold such whole-hearted endorsement because their interests are not aligned with those of their audience.

Investors need to understand the following about the advice provided by financial publications. They are in business to provide profits to their shareholders. In order to maximize their profits, they use attention-getting headlines such as *sell stocks now!* Their goal is to turn the boring world of investing into an exciting industry. They need you to *tune in*. Much of what they present is simply investment propaganda, a speculative feeding frenzy pretending to know what cannot be known. They sell noise, not disciplined investment strategies designed to provide investors with the greatest likelihood of achieving their financial objectives. If they told you to simply buy and hold index funds, there would be little reason for you to subscribe to their publications (or tune in to their shows). Their objectives of selling magazines and generating advertising revenue presents them with a conflict of interest that they choose to, at best, ignore. Their interests are simply not aligned with those of their readers (and viewers). They are not about creating wealth. Instead, they are about creating sensationalism, the noise to stir you into action you would be better served not taking. They know that, not only is passive management boring, but if they told you to buy and hold a globally diversified portfolio of passive asset class or index funds, what would be left to say? They can't keep repeating the same story every week. In addition, their publications carry a large amount of advertising from actively managed mutual funds. The publishers do not want to risk losing valuable advertising revenue. The broadcast media (i.e., CNBC, CNNfn, and MSNBC) have the same dilemma.

Perhaps the most telling comments on this conflict of interest come from financial reporter Patrick Regnier of *MONEY* magazine. Regnier began his career as a fund analyst at highly regarded Morningstar. While there he interviewed hundreds of professional money managers. In his efforts to gain insights and be the best at what he was paid to do, he read an even greater number of fund prospectuses and shareholder reports. Yet Regnier now admits that he will never understand why one fund manager will succeed and another fail. Here are some of the insights he presented in the August 2000 issue of *MONEY,* along with my own commentary in italics.

- Every financial publication I know—*MONEY, Fortune, SmartMoney, Forbes,* and countless others—has dismally underestimated some managers while overhyping others. *In other words, they are selling hype and hope, not valuable insights.*

- A list of the glossy magazines' favorites of five years ago now reads like a memorial to the fallen might-as-well-be-dead. *In other words, yesterday's masters of the universe are today's cosmic dust.*

- Most fund managers are very smart. Unfortunately being smart is not enough. *In other words, the competition is very tough.*

- A manager's skill matters less than the trend he is riding or failing to ride. *In other words, markets make great managers.*

Regnier concluded: "The market is unpredictable, leaving all at its mercy." Regnier also concluded that based on his experience, a rational investor should choose index funds.

Investors can benefit from listening carefully to the following anonymous confession of a financial reporter for *Fortune.*[11] "I was assured that in personal-finance journalism it doesn't matter if the advice turns out to be right, as long as it's logical. You're supposed to produce the most stories that 'end in investment decisions,' so publications substitute formula for wisdom. The formula for recommending funds: Filter according to returns, then add something trendy—high tech, no tech, whatever." She went on to confess that she knew that recent returns don't predict the future and then added: "Nothing predicts future results. The best you can do is to hold on to low-cost, diversified funds and be oblivious to short-term static." She admitted that while financial publications preach long-term, buy-and-hold investing, their recommendations are explicit endorsements of what she called "hot-fund promiscuity." She also admitted that the fund reporters she knew, while writing hot-fund stories, secretly favored low-cost index funds for their own investments.

Why do financial publications preach disciplined long-term indexing and write investment propaganda? The reason is simple. As the anonymous *Fortune* writer stated: "Unfortunately, rational, pro-index-fund stories don't sell magazines, cause hits on Websites, or boost Nielsen ratings."[12]

Merton Miller, a Nobel laureate, in an interview with *Barron's,* was asked what advice he would give the average investor. His response: "Don't quote me on this, but I'd say don't read *Barron's.*" He continued, ". . . because it will only tease you about investment opportunities that you'd best avoid."[13]

It is important to note that just as there are exceptions in the investment banking community, there are exceptions in the media. Although I cannot list them all, there are a few that command my great respect for two reasons. First, they have the interests of investors at heart. Second, while it is easy to write a regular column about the latest noise of the market or the latest outperforming manager who gets declared a guru, it is much more difficult to write basically the same message every week, that passive investing and the discipline to adhere to a well thought-out investment plan is the winner's game, and keep it interesting. Luckily for investors there are a few who manage to do so. Among them are Scott Burns, Jonathan Clements, Humberto Cruz, Beverly Goodman, Jane Bryant Quinn, and Jason Zweig. Zweig, who writes for *MONEY,* related the following tale to me. He told me that it reflects his view of the state of personal-finance journalism in this country better than anything he has ever heard—and I agree. On his deathbed Zweig's father, himself a journalist, told him: "You can make money in this world by lying, or by telling the truth. In the short run, you can make a little money by lying to people who want to hear the truth, or a lot of money by lying to people who want to be lied to. But you can't ever make any money by telling the truth to people who want to be lied to. In the long run, you make the most money by telling the truth to people who want to hear the truth."

While not defending the media, this observation by Zweig's father contained an important truth: A large group of investors want to be lied to. They want to believe that there is an easy way to beat the market. They want to believe that they will find the next Microsoft—somehow they will win the stock market's equivalent of the lottery. So the media delivers what they want to hear.

Jean Baptiste Colbert, finance minister to Louis XIV, described the act of generating revenue in this colorful way: "The art of taxation consists in so plucking the goose as to obtain the largest possible amount of feathers with the least possible amount of hissing." The same can be said of active managers—they want to keep plucking those large management fees from the pockets of individual investors with the least possible amount of hissing. In order to continue doing so, they must keep alive the myth that active management works. And the media are their coconspirators. Frank Knight, a professor of economics at the University of Chicago from 1928 until his death in 1972 at the age of eighty-seven, said it best when, as described by Peter Bernstein in his book *Against the Gods,* Knight "claimed that economic theory was not at all obscure or complicated, but that most people had a vested interest in refusing to recognize what was insultingly obvious." And as Charles Ellis, author of *Winning the Loser's Game,* points out, "Investment advice doesn't have to be complicated to be good. [For example,] there is no better advice on how to live longer than to quit smoking and buckle up when driving."

I believe that the financial press has an obligation to inform investors of the poor performance of active managers. They should also make far greater efforts to present the public with the results of the ongoing academic research on financial markets. For example, I am sure that most investors do not know that in 1990 the Nobel Prize in economics was awarded to three economists for their contributions to MPT (modern portfolio theory). Building on their work, financial economists have demonstrated that efforts to beat the market are not only nonproductive, they are counterproductive because of the expenses and taxes that are generated. The only winners in the game of active management are the Wall Street firms that generate commissions, the publications that offer "expert" advice, and Uncle Sam, who collects more taxes.

If the media did a better job of presenting the public with the facts about investing, investors would get much better investment returns—mainly because Wall Street and Uncle Sam would be taking a smaller cut out of their investment pie. On the other hand, if they had been doing their job well, there would have been no need for me to write this book.

TRUTH 5

◆

Risk and Reward Are Related: Great Companies Provide Low Expected Returns

The most important principle of finance is the positive relationship between risk and expected return—riskier assets must provide an ex-ante risk premium as compensation for investors accepting incremental risk. As the following example will illustrate, this principle is easily understood when it is related to fixed-income investing.

Consider the following hypothetical situation. You just inherited one hundred thousand dollars. With a thirteen-year-old child, you are anticipating having to begin paying college tuition in five years. Given the relatively short horizon, you conclude that investing in equities is too risky. You thus decide to invest the inheritance in a fixed-income asset. You call an investment firm and they tell you they have three investments of five-year maturity for you to choose from: a U.S. Treasury note yielding 5 percent, an IBM bond yielding 5 percent, and a JCPenney bond yielding the same 5 percent. Which one would you choose? You should choose the U.S. Treasury because, while the Treasury note has the same rate of return as the others, you would have none of the credit risk the other instruments carry. Thus this hypothetical world could never exist. No investor would ever choose the other alternatives. Thus neither IBM nor JCPenney would ever be able to raise capital at those rates.

Let us now alter our hypothetical world to a more real world example. Now the Treasury note is yielding the same 5 percent, but the IBM bond is yielding 6 percent, and the JCPenney bond is yielding 13 percent. Which instrument would you now choose? This time the answer is much more complex. In fact, there is no correct answer. The answer depends on your tolerance for risk. If you are a very conservative investor, you would choose the Treasury note. If you are willing to accept some degree of risk, but not too much, you might buy the IBM bond and earn an expected 1 percent risk premium over the riskless Treasury note. And if you were willing to accept a lot of risk, you might consider buying the JCPenney bond and earn an expected risk premium of 8 percent. Another perfectly logical choice might be to diversify the risk and buy some combination of all three instruments. At this point it is important to make the following points:

- The greater yields on the two corporate bonds are not guaranteed. The higher returns are compensation for the risk the companies might default. Even great companies default. If you doubt that, just consider the bankruptcies of Polaroid and Enron.
- The greater the perceived risk of default, the greater the risk premium investors demand.
- The higher interest rates paid by IBM and JCPenney are the flip side of the higher returns investors *expect* to earn when they invest in the company's debt.

I would like to make one more point. Even if you were a highly risk-tolerant investor, it would not be prudent to invest your entire sum in a JCPenney bond. That would be taking what is known as "uncompensated risk." It is single company risk that can easily be diversified away. Instead of buying a one-hundred-thousand-dollar JCPenney bond, you might buy a five-thousand-dollar bond from twenty different corporate issuers with the same credit rating as JCPenney. Another alternative would be to buy a mutual fund that invests in a broad range of corporations with a similar credit rating to JCPenney. In either case, you would be addressing the issue of too many eggs in one basket.

When shown this fixed-income example, every investor understands very clearly the nature of the positive relationship between risk and reward. If you seek safety, you must be willing to accept low returns. On the other hand, if your goal is a high return, you must accept greater risk. However, when we switch to equity investing, individuals seem to forget this basic principle. Let's examine this strange phenomenon.

One of the most persistent, and incorrect, beliefs among equity investors is that "growth" stocks have provided, and are expected to provide, higher returns than "value" stocks. Growth stocks are stocks of the glamorous high P/E (price-to-earnings) or low BtM (book-to-market) companies, while value stocks are the stocks of distressed companies, trading at low P/E ratios and high BtMs. If you are watching CNBC or reading a financial publication, almost invariably the stock recommendations go something like this: If you want great returns, you have to buy great companies— companies that have growing markets, are gaining market share, and are generating superior growth in earnings. However, as I hope to convince you, statements of this type are not only incorrect, they are as illogical as believing that the hypothetical fixed-income world we looked at, with U.S. Treasury notes yielding the same as IBM and JCPenney bonds, could exist. Let's see why this is true.

The problem of believing that growth companies provide greater ex-ante returns than value companies arises from the confusion between *earnings* generated by growth (or value) companies and *returns* earned by their shareholders. Let me explain. It is true that growth companies *outearn* value companies. For example, for the thirty-eight-year period ending in 2001, the ROA (return on assets) for growth stocks was 9.1 percent per year. This was over twice as great as the 4.2 percent ROA for value stocks. Over the thirty-nine-year period ending in 2002, however, the annualized compound return to investors in value stocks was 15.5 percent per annum—53 percent greater than the 10.1 percent return to growth-stock investors.

The simple explanation for this seeming anomaly is that investors discount the future expected earnings of value stocks at a much higher rate than they discount the future earnings of growth stocks. This more than offsets the faster earnings growth rates of growth companies. The high discount rate results in low current valuations for value stocks and higher expected future returns relative to growth stocks. Why do investors use a higher discount rate for value stocks when calculating the current value? The following example should provide a clear answer.

Let's consider the case of two similar companies, Wal-Mart and JCPenney. Most investors would say that Wal-Mart is a far better run company and a safer investment. If an investor could buy either company at the same market capitalization, say $20 billion, the obvious choice would be Wal-Mart. It not only has far higher current earnings but also is expected to produce much faster growth of future earnings. Investors recognizing this opportunity would buy shares of Wal-Mart, driving its price up, and sell shares of JCPenney, driving its price down. What is happening is that investors are lowering the risk premium they demand on Wal-Mart and raising it on JCPenney. Now let us say that Wal-Mart's price rises relative to JCPenney—say $100 billion for Wal-Mart and $10 billion for JCPenney—until the two have the same *expected* (not guaranteed) future rate of return— say 10 percent. Given that Wal-Mart is perceived to be the better company, and therefore a less risky investment, investors would still choose Wal-Mart. The reason is that although we now have equal expected returns, there is less perceived risk in owning Wal-Mart. So our process of investors buying Wal-Mart and selling JCPenney continues. It does so until the expected return of owning JCPenney is sufficiently greater than the expected return of owning Wal-Mart to entice investors to accept the risk of owning JCPenney instead of owning Wal-Mart—say a price of $200 billion for Wal-Mart and $5 billion for JCPenney. In the same way that the size of the yield differential between the U.S. Treasury note and the IBM and JCPenney bonds was correlated with the perception of their respective credit risk, the size of the price differential (and thus the difference in future expected returns) between Wal-Mart and JCPenney is directly related to the difference in perceived investment risk. Given that Wal-Mart is perceived to be a much safer investment than JCPenney, the price differential (risk premium) may have to be very large to entice investors to accept the risk of owning JCPenney.

Would these price changes make Wal-Mart "overvalued" or "highly valued" relative to JCPenney? The answer is "highly valued." If investors thought Wal-Mart was overvalued relative to JCPenney, they would sell Wal-Mart and buy JCPenney until equilibrium was reached. Instead, the high relative valuation of Wal-Mart reflects low perceived risk. Wal-Mart's future earnings are being discounted at a very low rate, reflecting the low perceived risk. This low discount rate translates into low future expected returns. Risk and reward are directly related, at least in terms of expected future returns—"expected" since we cannot know the future with certainty. JCPenney's future earnings are discounted at a very high rate. It therefore has a low relative valuation, reflecting the greater perceived risk. However, it also has high expected future returns.

Value Stocks

Value stocks are the stocks of distressed companies. A study by
Nai-fu Chen and Feng Zhang found that there are three very common characteristics of value stocks that all have simple intuitive
risk interpretations: high volatility of dividends; high ratio of
debt to equity; and high volatility of earnings. The three factors
all capture the returns information (produced high correlations)
contained in portfolios as ranked by BtM value. When these three
factors are present, returns are greater. Since all three factors have
simple intuitive risk interpretations (are associated with firms in
distress), it isn't surprising that the risk factors are highly correlated and are also highly correlated with BtM rankings. The
authors concluded that value stocks are cheap because they tend
to be firms in distress, with high leverage (high ratio of debt to
equity), and face substantial earnings risk; thus they provide
higher returns due to the greater risks facing value investors.[1]

Another conclusion is that the risks of value stocks are most
likely to show up at the worst of times for investors—in times of
economic distress. A perfect example of this is the period from
1929 through 1932. During this period, while the S&P 500 Index
fell 22.7 percent per annum, risky large-value stocks fell 33.9
percent per annum. The even riskier small-value stocks fell 38.7
percent, underperforming the S&P 500 Index by almost 16 percent per annum for four years. Since investors are on average
highly risk averse, the value premium has been quite large.

Another study, "The Value Premium," by Lu Zhang, provides
further support to this risk story. He concluded that the value
premium could be explained by the asymmetric risk of value
stocks. Value stocks are more risky than growth stocks in bad
economic times, but less risky than growth stocks in good eco-

nomic times. However, the size of the difference in risk is much lower in good times than in bad times. In other words, value stocks are much riskier in bad times and only moderately less risky in good times.[2] Zhang explains that the asymmetric risk of value companies exists because value stocks are typically companies with unproductive capital. Asymmetric risk is important because:

- Investment is irreversible—once production capacity is put in place, it is very hard to reduce. Value companies carry more nonproductive capacity than do growth companies.

- In periods of low economic activity, companies with nonproductive capacity (value companies) suffer greater negative volatility in earnings because the burden of nonproductive capacity increases and they find it more difficult to adjust capacity than do growth companies.

- In periods of high economic activity, the previously nonproductive assets of value companies become productive while growth companies find it harder to increase capacity.

- In good times, capital stock is easily expanded, while in bad times adjusting the level of capital is an extremely difficult task and is especially so for value companies.

Zhang also observes that:

- Recessions happen with far less frequency than good economic times.

- The longevity of recessions is far shorter than that of good times.

When these facts are combined with a high aversion to risk by investors (especially when that risk can be expected to show up when their employment prospects are more likely to be in jeopardy), the result is a large and persistent value premium. Zhang and colleagues Joao Gomes and Leonid Kogan reached the same conclusion in another study, "Equilibrium Cross-Section of Returns."[3]

The Value Effect and Economic-cycle Risk

A study by Gerald R. Jensen and Jeffrey M. Mercer examined the relationship between economic-cycle risk and the size, as well as the value, effect. The authors used monetary policy as the variable determining economic-cycle risk.[4] They used three different measures of monetary policy:

- Changes in the discount rate. An increase would be viewed as a contraction of monetary policy and a decrease as an expansion.

- Changes in the Fed Funds Rate. An increase would be viewed as a contraction of monetary policy and a decrease as an expansion.

- Interpretation of the minutes of the Federal Reserve Board meetings.

Using data from COMPUSTAT, covering the period 1965–97, and adding monetary policy as a fourth variable to the Fama-French three-factor model (exposure to the risk factors of equities, size [small cap vs. large cap], and value [value vs. growth], determine the vast majority of the risk and return of an equity portfolio), they found that all three measures resulted in the same conclusions in regard to the size effect:

- When size is isolated, there is a significant small-firm premium only in periods of expansionary monetary policy.
- In restrictive periods, the small effect is not statistically significant.

They came to similar conclusions regarding the value effect:

- There is a significant value premium in expansionary periods.
- The premium is smaller in restrictive periods, but it is still statistically significant.

The authors concluded that monetary policy has a significant impact on the size and value effects. Good economic times generally occur when the Fed is either expansionist in its policy or simply "leaning against the wind," and bad times occur when the Fed is being restrictive in its policy. The authors also noted that since small and value firms are typically highly leveraged, they are more negatively impacted in their ability to access capital during periods of restrictive monetary policy. Thus small and value firms are more susceptible to distress in times of restrictive monetary policy (weak economy).

This study supports the hypothesis that the value effect is a premium related to the risk of distress. While it provides support for the Fama-French three-factor model, it also adds another important "dimension" by explaining the variation in the size of the risk premium based on changes in monetary policy. Unfortunately, there is no evidence of a persistent ability to forecast changes in either economic conditions or monetary policy in a manner that leads to abnormal trading profits.

Hopefully, you now understand why value stocks have provided, and are likely to continue to provide, greater returns than growth stocks despite having much lower growth rates of earnings. It is a simple risk story. Relating this information back to our fixed-income example:

- The greater expected returns on value stocks are not guaranteed. The higher returns are compensation for risk.

- The greater the perceived risk, the greater the risk premium investors demand and the higher the expected return.

- The flip side of the much lower price investors pay for the shares of value companies is the high cost of capital value firms must pay to raise equity. The flip side of the high cost of capital is a high expected return to the providers of that capital.

- If your objective is to invest in companies with less risk, then invest in growth companies. However, you should anticipate lower returns in exchange for accepting less risk.

- Even if investors are highly tolerant of risk, they should not invest all their eggs in one value stock. This would be taking "uncompensated risk" that can easily be diversified away by owning a mutual fund that buys the stocks of many different value companies.

We now need to turn to a related problem that investors have regarding growth stocks. They wonder: How can growth stocks, with their very high prices, be considered safe investments? For example, as we entered the new millennium, the P/E ratio of the large-cap growth-dominated S&P 500 was approximately 30, and the P/E of the even more growth-oriented NASDAQ-100 was almost 150. Value stocks, on the other hand, had a P/E ratio of only about 12. Investors who wonder how stocks that have such a high valuation can be considered safe are confusing *business* (operating) risk with *price* risk. JCPenney has more *business* risk than Wal-Mart. Therefore, the price of JCPenney's stock falls until investors are compensated for the *business* risk. The distinction is in the risk of the *companies,* not the risk of their *stock prices.*

On the other hand, *stock* risk, or *price* risk, increases with increases in price. This concept can be clarified by an analogy related to the fixed-income markets. Long-term bonds have greater price risk than short-term bonds—the longer the maturity, the greater the risk. For example, if interest rates rise 1 percent, a one-year note will fall in value by 1 percent, a ten-year note by about 7 percent, and a thirty-year bond by about 13 percent. Here is the analogy to growth and value stocks. Growth stocks are like long-term fixed-income instruments. Because of their high P/E and low BtM ratios, much of their value is derived from expected earnings far into the future. For value stocks, on the other hand, because of their low P/E and high BtM ratios, most of their current value is derived from liquidation value and expected earnings in the near future. As we saw, when interest rates go up, long-term (long-duration) fixed-income assets fall in value more than short-term fixed-income assets. The same is true of equities. Growth stocks are longer duration assets than value stocks. Thus, when the rate at which you discount future earnings rises (because either the risk-free rate or the risk premium rose), the longer duration growth stocks will fall in price more than the shorter duration value stocks. So growth stocks have more price risk than value stocks in the same manner that long-term Treasury bonds have more price risk than short-term Treasury notes.

There is another reason that growth stocks might be considered to have more price risk. The less the perceived likelihood of a company failing to reach its projected earnings, the lower will be the risk premium and the higher the stock price. Taken to an extreme, a stock with very little perceived risk might be said to be "priced for perfection." Simply put, there is little room for any upside surprise. If everything goes as expected, you get low returns (because of the low-risk premium). On the other hand, if almost anything goes wrong, the risk premium might rise sharply, and because of the long duration the stock could fall dramatically. This is the type of price risk that existed in the NASDAQ-100 stocks that were trading at astronomical P/E ratios prior to our entering the new millennium. Conversely, with value stocks being so distressed, there is far less likelihood of disappointment (when the risk premium would rise further) and lots of opportunity for upside surprise (the risk premium would fall and the price would rise dramatically).

In addition, if all the risk already perceived occurs, investors in value stocks will still earn high returns as that risk was already reflected in the price when the stock was purchased. Some value stocks are so distressed, due to such high perception of risk, that almost nothing else can go wrong that has not been anticipated already. Thus the stock might have a high upside potential should the risk premium fall. This was exactly what happened to emerging-market stocks during the so-called Asian Contagion. Emerging-market stocks were priced almost as if they were more likely to submerge rather than emerge. The DFA Emerging Markets Fund fell almost 20 percent in 1997 and another 10 percent in 1998. Eventually the perception of risk was lowered as investors recognized that the emerging markets were not going to submerge. With the fall in the risk premium, the DFA Emerging Markets Fund rebounded over 70 percent in 1999.

Let's look at another example of why growth stocks with their high P/E ratios have a high degree of *price* risk. Keep in mind that a high P/E ratio reflects both the market's expectation for rapid growth in earnings and investor perception of low *business* risk.

Anyone who follows the market closely has observed that frequently when a growth stock misses its forecasted earnings by even just a few cents its stock falls dramatically—seemingly far out of proportion to the small shortfall in earnings. The explanation is simple. Let's assume we have a high-flying technology stock with projected earnings of one dollar per share and selling at one hundred dollars per share and that earnings come in at only ninety cents. The shortfall in earnings might cause the price to drop to ninety dollars, given the one hundred P/E ratio. However, the shortfall in earnings will also likely affect the risk premium, causing it to rise. Let's assume that the rise in the perception of *business* risk causes the risk premium to rise so that the P/E ratio now falls to a still sky-high eighty. Instead of falling just 20 percent as the P/E ratio fell (from one hundred to eighty), the price falls further due to the combination of the fall in the P/E ratio and the shortfall in earnings. The stock will actually fall to seventy-two dollars, or a drop of 28 percent. It is the rise in the risk premium (perception of business risk) that causes the sharp fall, not the 10 percent shortfall in earnings.

Hopefully we have resolved the seeming conundrum of the riskiness of value and growth stocks, as well as their expected returns. To summarize, it is the perception of a high degree of *business* risk, and thus a high-risk premium applied to valuations, that causes the price of value companies to be distressed. The same high-risk premium creates high expected future returns. It is the perception of low *business* risk, and thus a low-risk premium applied to valuations, that causes the price of growth stocks to be elevated. It is high prices that create much higher *price* risk in the longer duration *growth* stocks than the shorter duration value stocks.

There is a simple principle to remember that can help you avoid making poor investment decisions. Risk and expected return should be positively related. While we do not have a perfect model to explain the risk of value stocks, the value premium has been large and persistent for a very logical reason—value stocks are not only risky, their risk is highly correlated with economic-cycle risk, tending to manifest itself during recessions that are also deflationary periods. Remember that if prices are high, they reflect low perceived risk, and thus you should expect low future returns; and vice versa. This does not make a highly priced stock a poor investment. It simply makes it a stock that is perceived to have low risk and thus low future returns. Thinking otherwise would be like assuming government bonds are poor investments when the alternative is junk bonds.

TRUTH 6

◆

The Price You Pay Matters

The last half of the twentieth century was a golden era for U.S. equity investors. From 1950 through 1999, the S&P 500 Index produced annualized returns of 13.6 percent per annum, or a real rate of 9.2 percent per annum. Even more impressive are the returns of the last quarter of that century. From 1975 through 1999, the S&P 500 Index produced an annualized return of 17.2 percent and a real rate of return of 11.8 percent. That is the good news. The bad news is that for today's investors the result of those great returns is that future expected returns are now much lower, even after considering the bear markets of 2000 and 2001. The reason is that the price you pay for future earnings determines the rate of return you can expect to earn.

Unfortunately, most investors don't understand the math of investing. They mistakenly simply extrapolate past returns into the future. Bull markets lead investors to expect higher future returns, and bear markets lead them to expect lower future returns. However, you need to understand that the price you pay for an asset has a great impact on future returns. This bit of wisdom seemed to have eluded Henry Blodgett, Merrill Lynch's Internet analyst, when he made the following statement in a report on ICG (Internet Capital Group): "Valuation is often not a helpful tool in determining when to sell hypergrowth stocks."[1] He made this statement on January 10, 2000, shortly before the Internet bubble collapsed. Blodgett resigned before the end of the following year.

Forecasting future returns by simply extrapolating past returns is illogical as is demonstrated by the following example. From 1926 through 1974 (the bottom of the second worst bear market in postwar history), the S&P 500 returned 8.5 percent per annum. An investor simply extrapolating into the future would project returns of 8.5 percent per annum. By 1999, the returns since 1926 had increased to 11.3 percent per annum. An investor simply extrapolating returns would project returns of 11.3 percent. But prices being paid for the same assets were much higher now. P/E ratios had risen to more than double their historical averages, and dividend yields had fallen to a small fraction of their historical levels. How can one logically expect higher returns when paying much higher prices for the same assets? After the bear markets of 2000 and 2001, the long-term return had fallen below 11 percent. Once again, if you simply extrapolated returns, does it seem logical that with prices substantially lower, future returns are also expected to be lower?

The high prices that existed as we entered 2000 reflected a low perception of risk and low future returns, not high future returns. Making the mistake of simply extrapolating past returns can lead to very poor decisions about saving and investing. Let's explore the nature of risk and reward and how the price you pay impacts returns.

As we have discussed, the relationship between risk and reward is positively correlated—in order to attract investors to take more risk, they must *expect* higher returns. (The key word is *expect*. If the higher *expected* returns were guaranteed, there would be no risk.) The greater the perceived risk, the higher the *expected* return must be. Higher *expected* returns are reflected in lower valuations. Conversely, the lower the perceived risk, the lower the *expected* return must be, as investors willingly pay more to achieve a lower level of risk. Let's examine the mathematical process by which the market determines equity prices.

The first step is to forecast earnings. The second step is to calculate the present value of those earnings by discounting them at the *risk-free rate* (the rate on a riskless short-term instrument such as a three-month Treasury bill) plus a *risk premium* (the size of which is commensurate with the amount of perceived risk). The lower the denominator (the riskless rate and/or the risk premium), the higher the present value, and vice versa. Let's explore the impact shifting risk premiums have on prices and how this impacts future expected returns.

If the risk premium of an asset class falls (as investors perceive less risk), two things occur: First, investors in that asset class benefit from a one-time increase in the price of the asset as future earnings are now discounted at a lower rate; this is similar to the impact of falling interest rates on bond prices. The second impact is on future expected returns. Since risk premiums are a reflection of future expected returns, the falling risk premium reflects lower future returns. The reverse would be true if the risk premium of an asset class increased due to an increase in perceived risk. The first impact would be a drop in equity prices as future expected earnings are now discounted at a higher rate, reflecting the now higher risk premium. The second impact would be that investors would now receive greater expected future returns, reflecting the greater risk premium. This process is exactly the opposite of what investors perceive when they extrapolate the recent outperformance of an asset class into the future. Bull markets should lead investors to expect lower, not higher, future returns. Bear markets should lead investors to expect higher, not lower, future returns.

Let's examine some of the historical data to see what observations we can make about the size of risk premiums and future expected returns, or at least the changes in them. To do so we will examine the valuation characteristic called the P/E.

The average historical P/E ratio for the market has been around fifteen. For the period 1926 through the second quarter of 1999, an investor buying stocks when the market traded at P/E ratios of between fourteen and sixteen earned a median return of 11.8 percent over the subsequent ten years.[2] This is remarkably close to the long-term return of the market. The S&P 500 returned 11.0 percent per annum for the seventy-four-year period 1926–2000. It is also important to note that the inverse of the P/E ratio (called the E/P ratio or earnings yield) has been about 7 percent. The real return to stocks since 1926 has been about the same. This is not a coincidence. The E/P ratio has been a reasonably good predictor of returns over the long term (though not very useful in the short term).

Let's now look at the returns investors received when they bought stocks when the perception of risk was low, for instance, during good economic times and a bull market and when the perception of risk was high, during a recession or financial crisis and a bear market. Investors purchasing stocks when the P/E ratio was greater than twenty-two (when investors are highly optimistic and there is great enthusiasm for buying stocks) earned a median return of just 5 percent per annum over the next ten years.[3] High P/E ratios generally reflect a strong economy and a bull market. During such times investors perceive relatively low levels of risk, which translates into high prices and low-risk premiums. Those low-risk premiums, however, also translate into low future expected returns—exactly the opposite of what most investors expect.

Let's now look at the returns investors received when they purchased stocks when the perception of risk was high. Investors who purchased stocks when P/E ratios were below ten earned a median return of 16.9 percent per annum over the next ten years.[4] Low P/E ratios generally reflect a weak economy and a bear market. During such times investors perceive relatively high levels of risk, which translates into low prices and high-risk premiums.

Those high-risk premiums, however, also translate into high future expected returns. Investors buying stocks when the P/E ratios were below ten (when perceived risk was high and seemingly no one wanted to own stocks) outperformed investors who bought stocks when P/E ratios were above twenty-two (when perceived risk was low and seemingly everyone was jumping on the equity bandwagon) by almost 12 percent per annum.

A study, "P/E Ratios and Stock Market Returns," examined the historical relationship between P/E ratios and subsequent returns from a variety of perspectives.[5] It thus provided some valuable insights. The authors examined the returns of the S&P 500 Index, twenty-year bonds, and one-month Treasury bills for the period from 1949 to 1997. The P/E ratios used were those published by S&P's Statistical Service. They split the data into three P/E categories: high P/E (greater than fifteen), medium P/E (between ten and fifteen), and low P/E (less than ten). The following is a summary of their conclusions:

- Buying when the P/E is low outperformed buying when the P/E is high, regardless of the investment horizon. At the one-year horizon, buying when the P/E is low outperformed when the P/E was high by 23.8 percent to 11.31 percent. At the ten-year horizon, the figures are 16.3 percent and 6.9 percent, respectively.

- As the P/E ratio increased, there was a corresponding lowering of future returns. This was true of all holding periods.

- As the horizon lengthened, the standard deviation of returns was reduced. Buying when P/Es were low produced a standard deviation of 16.1 percent at one year but just 1.6 percent at ten years. Buying when P/Es were high produced standard deviations of 14.6 percent and 3.5 percent, respec-

103

tively. The significance of the lower standard deviations is that the dispersion of returns was reduced. This gives you more confidence in the predictability (reliability) of the returns.

- When the investment horizon is ten years, buying when P/Es were low makes the lowest returns much higher (12.7 percent higher), but the highest returns only somewhat higher (just over 4.1 percent). This is very important given that investors are, on average, risk averse—they care more about doing well in poor times than in good times.

- The statistical significance of the P/E ratio increases as the investment horizon lengthens. While one would hope that investors have more than a one-year horizon, even at the one-year horizon the data is close to being statistically significant at the 5 percent level of error (the outcome might be a matter of luck). A t-stat of 2 is generally considered to be a measure of statistical significance. At one year the t-stat was 1.86, and at ten years it was 8.43 (statistically significant at the 1 percent level). The r-squared (measure of correlation) also increased from 0.07 to 0.65. This means that the P/E ratio explained only 7 percent of returns at the one-year horizon (has almost no explanatory power), but almost two-thirds of returns at the ten-year horizon (has high explanatory power). Thus as the period lengthens, the explanatory power of the P/E ratio increases.

- The model does not work perfectly. There are periods when P/E ratios are high but future returns are high. This is likely to be true during recession, as earnings may only be temporarily depressed (stock prices reflect expected earnings over the long term). During the 1991 recession, the P/E ratio was high, but subsequent returns were still high as not only did earnings improve but the equity risk premium collapsed and interest rates fell.

The authors point out that we should not be surprised by the fact that we see high P/E ratios produce low future returns. Expected returns to stocks should be low when the risk-free rate is low (because future earnings are discounted at a low rate). Thus the low future returns might be due to low interest rates. The data supports this hypothesis. They found that even when high P/E ratios produced low future returns, stocks still outperformed riskless instruments. However, there still is an inverse relationship between P/E ratios and the equity risk premium. For ten-year holding periods, the risk premium was only 1.3 percent when buying when the P/E was high, but there was a 10.3 percent risk premium when the P/E was low.

There is one problem with using P/E ratios as indicators of future returns that we must consider. As we discussed, a high P/E ratio can be a result of temporarily depressed earnings due to a weak economy. Since stocks are valued based on long-term earnings, not just one year's earnings, we might get misleading information by looking at a P/E ratio that considers only the previous year's earnings. This problem can be addressed by using a ten-year moving average of inlation-adjusted earnings—smoothing out the peaks and troughs. Clifford S. Asness, managing partner at AQR Capital Management, LLC, used this technique to examine the historical relationship between the "normalized" P/E ratio and future returns. His study, covering the period 1926–2001, placed every ten-year period into one of six buckets based on the starting P/E of the S&P 500 Index. He then looked at the decade-long returns in each bucket. He found that buying when the P/E was in the lowest of six buckets (P/E of 5.2–10.1) provided returns over the next ten years of 15 percent per annum. Even the worst period provided a 45 percent cumulative real return. Buying when the P/E was in the highest bucket (P/E of 19.0–31.7) provided returns that were negative after inflation. The worst period produced a loss of 36 percent of purchasing power.[6]

A study, "P/E and Price-to-Book Ratios as Predictors of Stock Returns in Emerging Equity Markets," examined the evidence on the predictive value of these indicators in nineteen emerging-markets countries for the period 1986–1999.[7] The authors used the IFC's (International Finance Corporation, an arm of the World Bank) database. The study ranked the E/P ratio in all markets in descending order and divided them into quintiles, from the highest to the lowest E/P ratio. They then examined returns over the next three-, six-, and twelve-month periods. The following summarizes their findings:

- For all three horizons, average returns decrease as the E/P ratio declines.

- The average return for all horizons was negative following periods when the E/P ratio was in the lowest quintile.

- The relationship strengthens as the horizon lengthens.

- The return in the first quintile (highest E/P) was over 40 percent for the succeeding twelve-month period.

- Virtually the same observations were made when BtM was used as the indicator. None of the above should be surprising. First, it is consistent with data in the U.S. markets. Second, the price you pay matters. If you buy when prices are high (low E/P) that reflects a low perception of risk. Hence future returns are likely to be low. And of course, the reverse is also true. When the E/P ratio is high, that reflects a high perception of risk and thus high expected returns.

In summary, the study on emerging markets provides out-of-sample support to the evidence in U.S. markets. This is important because markets don't know where investors live—if a theory works it should work in all markets. Thus we have further evidence to support the view that value indicators such as P/E and BtM ratios provide valuable insights into future returns. The reason really is simple: The price you pay matters. The lesson for investors is: When the world looks darkest and prices are most distressed is just when future returns have been the greatest for those with the discipline to avoid the noise of the market and stay the course. When the world looks brightest (and it appears to be the safest time to invest) and investors are typically chasing great returns is when future returns have turned out to be the poorest.

Collapsing Risk Premiums—the Impact on Future Returns

From 1995 to 1999, we experienced a collapse in the risk premium for the large-cap stocks that dominate the S&P 500 and NASDAQ-100 indices. At year-end 1994, the P/E ratio for the S&P 500 was just under sixteen, not much higher than its historical average. However, by the end of the first quarter of 2000, it had risen to just under thirty, well above the twenty-two P/E ratio that historically has produced 5 percent returns over the succeeding ten years. The NASDAQ was trading at a P/E ratio of well over one hundred. Also worth noting is that the P/E ratios for the other domestic asset classes had remained virtually unchanged. For large-value stocks (as represented by the DFA U.S. Large Cap Value Fund), the P/E ratio rose from 10.3 to just 11.3. For small-cap stocks (as represented by the DFA Micro Cap Fund), the P/E ratio actually fell from 14.1 to 13.7. And for small-cap value stocks (as represented by the DFA Small Cap Value Fund), the P/E remained virtually unchanged, falling from 11.7 to 11.6.

What conclusions, if any, should you draw from the above information? First, investors in 2000 who chased yesterday's returns by purchasing mostly or even exclusively the then-popular large-cap growth stocks were *highly likely* to be disappointed since those high prices reflected low perceptions of risk and thus low future *expected* returns. Second, while the prices of the large-cap growth stocks had risen to levels that have historically resulted in low future returns, the prices of other asset classes had not changed in relative valuation since 1994 and were basically trading at around historically average levels. Thus, between 1995 and 1999, the valuation of large-cap growth stocks relative to the valuations of other asset classes increased significantly. This lowered the future expected return of large-cap growth stocks relative to other asset classes. Of course, in the short term, anything could have happened. For example, the already low-risk premiums for large-cap growth and technology stocks could have fallen even further. This is how bubbles occur. Remember that although the market is very rational in the long term, it can be quite irrational in the short term—it can also stay irrational for a relatively long time.

I hope the above has set the stage for you to understand a very important issue: There is only one way to achieve spectacularly high returns like those achieved by U.S. investors in the latter half of the last century—you must start out with the price of assets at very distressed levels and end up with them at very elevated levels. This is exactly what happened. Let's go to the videotape to see how the world looked in 1950.

As we entered the second half of the last century, what kind of investment climate did investors perceive? The United States had just experienced two world wars and a great depression. The Korean conflict was brewing, and communism was a great threat. Europe and Japan were in ruins. Not exactly a world safe for democracy, let alone equity investing. Those investors courageous enough to invest in equities would have been "rewarded" over the previous twenty-one years, from 1929 through 1949, with an annualized rate of return of just 3.8 percent, or a real rate of just 2.2 percent per annum. Disappointing rates of return for today's investors. Clearly the world was a very risky place, and prices reflected that risk.

The world turned out to be far less risky a place moving forward than it was perceived to be at the time. Capitalism and democracy won out. Russia collapsed. The SEC dramatically improved the regulatory environment, making investing safer. And the economy grew with only one major interruption, the oil-induced recession of 1973 and 1974. The change in perception of risk led investors to require a much lower risk premium to entice them to invest in equities. This reduction in the size of the risk premium provided a very large one-time capital gain to investors. The offset is that the lower perception of risk translated into much higher prices and, of course, much lower expected returns going forward. It cannot be any other way. The following analogy should help clarify this issue.

A bond investor purchases for one hundred dollars a bond of a risky company paying twelve dollars in interest (yield is 12 percent). The next day the company is acquired by another company with a much better credit rating (lower risk). The rate on the new company's bonds is just 6 percent. The market price of our investor's bond will rise, reflecting the lower risk of the acquiring company. This provides a one-time capital gain. However, the ongoing return is now 6 percent, not 12 percent. This is analogous to what happened to U.S. stock prices. The world was perceived to be very risky. Prices were very low (expected returns were very high). The world turned out to be less risky than perceived at the time, and investors began to lower the premium they demanded to accept the risk of equity investing. Prices rose, providing the dramatic returns investors experienced. However, those spectacular returns are not repeatable, unless the perception of risk were to once again fall by similar amounts, something that is virtually impossible as we shall see. The high prices we now have reflect a low perception of risk and thus low expected returns. Of course, the world could turn out to be far more risky than currently perceived. The result would be the reverse of the experience of the last fifty years—we would experience a collapse of prices, and then expected returns would once again be higher.

Let's again turn to the math of investing. Estimating stock returns over the long term is really not that difficult. (Over the short term it is impossible; market timing is a loser's game.) We saw the historical evidence on using P/E ratios to provide some guidance. However, the reason that it is relatively easy to forecast stock returns over the long term is that earnings ultimately determine stock prices, and corporate earnings tend to be a relatively stable percent of GNP (gross national product). If corporate earnings grew faster than GNP in the long term, they would "crowd out" other components of the GNP, like welfare, defense, government, wages, etc.

If we assume that the GNP will grow at a rate of about 3 percent per annum (about the very long-term historical average), we can estimate equity returns by simply adding to that rate the dividend yield provided by stocks. As we entered 2003, that rate was about 2 percent. Add a 3 percent estimate of long-term growth in GNP and we get an expected real rate of return to stocks of about 5 percent (2 + 3). If we add to that rate the expected rate of inflation (observed by subtracting the yield on TIPS [Treasury

Inflation-Protected Securities] from the bond yield), we get a nominal rate of return of about 7 percent. Note that the real estimated return of 5 percent is not much more than 50 percent of the real rate earned from 1950 through 1999, and not much more than 40 percent of the real rate earned from 1975 through 1999. Investors simply extrapolating returns are highly likely to be disappointed. Investors depending upon those high rates in order to retire are highly likely to find themselves working a lot longer or living a much lower-than-desired lifestyle.

Those forecasting higher returns must be assuming either a further drop in the risk premium (highly unlikely as we shall shortly see) or faster earnings growth. Can the economy grow faster than 3 percent, generating faster earnings growth? Sure, anything is possible. But the historical evidence suggests that 3 percent is a very good estimate. Even if it were to grow much faster, say 4 percent, it would only add 1 percent to returns. And it would not be prudent for investors making retirement plans to count on faster than historical growth occurring. (They might end up broke.) Another caveat is that it is actually logical to expect earnings to grow at a somewhat slower rate than GNP growth as some of the growth in future earnings will come from companies that do not yet exist. The historical evidence supports this view. Earnings have grown at a rate somewhat below that of the GNP.

There is another important caveat to our forecast of an expected real return of 5 percent. It is dependent on an important assumption. That assumption is that the risk premium demanded by investors remains unchanged. Given that we currently have a virtually riskless instrument, called TIPS, yielding in excess of 2 percent, it seems unlikely that the equity risk premium could fall. After all, why would any rational person take the risk of equities without a compensating risk premium, which appears to be less than 3 percent? It seems that with this low a premium, current equity prices reflect a world with little perception of risk (despite the events of September 11, 2001). On the other hand, it seems quite possible that investors could once again demand a higher risk premium. (The world could turn out to be more risky.) If this were to occur, we would see a one-time drop in equity prices and then once again higher expected returns, reflecting that now greater perception of risk. Returning to our bond example, it would be as if a highly rated company paying 6 percent on its bonds were to be acquired by a poorly rated company that had to pay 12 percent on its bonds. A one-hundred-dollar bond paying six dollars in interest would immediately drop in price to fifty dollars (a one-time capital loss), but the expected future return would now be 12 percent. Bear markets restore equity premiums; bull markets deteriorate them.

It is extremely important for investors to have a working knowledge of financial history (or rely on an advisor who does). The reason is that, to paraphrase a common expression, there is nothing new, only the financial history you don't know. Knowledge of financial history enables an investor to avoid the clarion call of, "This time it's different." Today's low forecasted returns to equities are not unusual. In fact, they are very similar to those that prevailed in 1968 when the Nifty Fifty and technology bubbles broke. The then very high prices implied very low future returns. And that is exactly what occurred. For the period 1968–84 large-growth stocks returned 5.8 percent per annum, 1.1 percent below the rate of inflation and 3.1 percent below the rate of return on riskless, government-insured, bank CDs. The risk premium was restored to equity markets when the S&P 500 Index fell 14.7 percent in 1973 and a further 26.5 percent in 1974. (It took until 1985 before the damage done to large-growth stocks would turn into a realized equity premium over one-month CDs.) The severity of the 1973–74 bear market set the stage for the spectacular returns of the last quarter of the century. The lower prices that resulted from the bear market meant higher future *expected* returns.

It is important to understand that the above analysis is done at the broad market level. The small-cap premium and the value premium are still alive and well. Those investors gaining exposure to those asset classes have higher expected returns than indicated above. In addition, those asset classes never experienced quite the bubble that did the large-cap asset class, thus their risk premiums never eroded to quite the same levels. One should *expect* that going forward the small and value premiums would be at least as large as they have been historically.

To summarize:

- Spectacular returns require that prices start at very distressed levels, a time when most people are afraid to invest in equities. Only bold and disciplined investors benefit.
- Very high prices must reflect both a very low perception of risk and low expected returns.
- There is a rational limit to how low equity premiums can fall (the benchmark riskless real rate on TIPS). This does not mean, however, that prices cannot rise above that level temporarily. In other words, greed and irrationality sometimes take over markets.
- Current prices reflect very low expected future returns. Prudent investors build these low expected returns into their plans in order to have the greatest chance of achieving their financial goals (or they adjust their goals accordingly).
- Investors should be prepared to adjust their investment/ spending decisions on an ongoing basis as capital market returns impact their portfolios. A bull market leading to high returns can lower the need to take risks. Investors benefiting

from that bull market should consider lowering their equity allocation accordingly (especially since expected future returns are now lower). Investors now expecting lower future returns may need to either increase their savings or lower their financial goals accordingly. Ignoring market valuations is not prudent investing.

- Bear markets restore risk premiums.

- Young investors should root for a bear market so that future returns will be higher. Older investors should be very conservative in their equity allocations given the likelihood of low expected returns. If your need to take risk is low, taking it when risk premiums are low is certainly not prudent investing.

- And finally, as Wes Wellington of DFA states: "Just because I want to maximize my current spending but have a high degree of certainty that I won't exhaust my resources doesn't mean the markets owe me such an outcome."

TRUTH 7

◆

The Most Likely Way to Achieve Above Average Returns Is to Stop Trying to Beat the Market

As I traipse around the country speaking to investing groups, or just stay in my cage writing my articles, I'm often accused of "disempowering" people because I refuse to give any credence to anyone's hope of beating the market. The knowledge that I don't need to know anything is an incredibly profound form of knowledge. Personally, I think it's the ultimate form of empowerment. You can't tune out the massive industry of investment prediction unless you want to: otherwise, you'll never have the fortitude to stop listening. But if you can plug your ears to every attempt (by anyone) to predict what the markets will do, you will outperform nearly every other investor alive over the long run. Only the mantra of "I don't know, and I don't care" will get you there.

—Jason Zweig

It's a staple of personal finance advice: Buy and hold, because trading the stock market is a sucker's bet.

—Business Week

Imagine the following scenario: The NBA is holding a free-throw shooting contest open to all players. Each participating player will shoot one hundred free throws. Players will receive one hundred dollars for each free throw they make. Players are also given the choice of either participating in the contest or accepting the average score of all players who do participate. You are one of the league's better free-throw shooters. The best free-throw shooter in the league shoots about 90 percent, the average player shoots just 65 percent, while you shoot 80 percent. Should you compete or accept the average score of all players who do participate? You quickly calculate that while the average of a 65 percent success rate will return sixty-five hundred dollars, your average score would earn you eight thousand dollars. So you decide to participate. Is this the correct answer? While the obvious answer would seem to be that you should play, game theory provides a different answer.

The fact that you are an above-average shooter is not really relevant to the problem. Here is why. Knowing that he is the worst free-throw shooter in the league, Shaquille O'Neal would clearly be better off not participating. He decides to accept the average score. All the other weak shooters quickly come to the same conclusion. Thus the average score of the remaining players starts to rise. Anticipating this occurrence, the weakest of the remaining players logically drop out as well. This process would repeat itself until you are the weakest player left, at which point you should decide to accept the average score. This process would continue until only one player would remain, the best shooter in the league. This is the thought process that is logical. Only the best should compete. All others should accept the average score, which should now earn you nine thousand dollars.

What does this problem and game theory have to do with deciding on whether active or passive investing is the winning strategy? Before explaining the importance of this example to investment strategy, we need to explore one other issue, the difference between market and average returns. Wall Street wants and needs you to be confused about this important issue.

As we learned in the first section, the mathematics of investing tells us that, in aggregate, active investors earn lower net returns than passive investors. While both earn the same market return before expenses, the greater expenses of active managers leads to lower returns after expenses. Wall Street tries to obfuscate this issue. Listen to Edward C. Johnson III, chairman of Fidelity Advisors: "I can't believe that the great mass of investors are going to be satisfied with just receiving *average* returns. The name of the game is to be the best."[1] (emphasis mine) This is what a typical stockbroker's pitch might be when confronted with an investor who asks about investing in index funds as a good strategy: "If you index [passively invest], you will get average rates of return. You don't want to be average, do you? Don't you think you can do better than that?" Both stockbrokers and Edward Johnson are appealing to what seems to be the very human need to be "better than average." Now listen carefully to Jonathan Clements: "It's the big lie that, repeated often enough, is eventually accepted as truth. You can beat the market, trounce the averages, outpace the index, beat the street. An entire industry strokes this fantasy."[2]

The mistake Wall Street wants you to make is to fail to understand that by simply earning *market* returns, you will earn *greater* after-tax returns than the *average* investor. The reason is that the average actively managed fund underperforms its benchmark by almost 2 percent per annum on a pretax basis, and by far more on an after-tax basis. In other words, if you earn *market* returns, you will outperform the *average* investor, and that includes professional investors. The most likely way to achieve above-average returns is not to play Wall Street's game of active investing.

Hopefully, the analogy between our hypothetical free-throw shooting contest and the choice between active and passive investing is now clear. In our example, unless you were the best free-throw shooter in the world, you were better off accepting "market" returns. The analogy to investing is that unless either you believe you can succeed in doing what professionals have long failed at, identifying ahead of time the very few active managers who will beat their benchmark, or when you look in the mirror you see Warren Buffett, you should decide to accept market returns.

The following hypothetical situation should also lead you to the winning strategy. Called "outfoxing the box," it was created by my good friend Bill Schultheis, author of *The Coffeehouse Investor.* Once again, it is a game that you can choose to either play or not. In this game you are an investor facing the following choice. You are shown nine boxes, each representing a rate of return you are guaranteed to earn. The returns each box represents are presented in this table.

%	%	%
12	8	7
6	**10**	14
5	0	12

You are told that you have the following choice: You can either accept the return of 10 percent, or you will be asked to leave the room, the boxes will be shuffled around, and you will then get to choose a box, not knowing, of course, what return the box holds. You quickly calculate that the average return of all nine boxes is just above 8 percent. This is just like the world of investing, where the average active fund underperforms its benchmark by close to 2 percent per annum. And just like in the real world, while you might be lucky and earn as much as 14 percent, you also might be unlucky and earn 0 percent. Any rational, risk-neutral, or risk-averse investor should logically decide to outfox the box and accept the "market" return of 10 percent. In my years as an investment advisor, whenever I present this game to an investor, I have never once had an investor believe that it would be better to play. While they might be willing to spend a dollar on a lottery ticket, when it comes to their life's savings, they become more prudent in their choice. Like our free-throw shooter, the winning strategy is not to play.

Before concluding this section, let's address one more issue: What if everyone indexed? This is a question I am asked with great frequency. First, we are a long way from that happening, even at the current pace of change. It is estimated that today institutions have in the neighborhood of 40 percent of their assets committed to passive strategies. By comparison, it is estimated that individuals still have about 90 percent of their financial assets in actively managed funds or individual stocks. Second, there will always be some trading activity due to the exercise of stock options, estates being distributed, mergers and acquisitions, divorces, etc. Also, remember that even if individuals stopped trading stocks, companies would still be active in buying other companies. With that in mind, let's deal with the real issue of the likelihood of active managers either gaining or losing an advantage as the trend toward passive management marches on.

Let's first address the issue of information efficiency. With less active management activity, there will be fewer professionals researching and recommending securities. Active management proponents would correctly argue that it would therefore be easier to gain a competitive information advantage. However, this is the same argument they currently make about those really "inefficient" asset classes such as emerging markets. Unfortunately for active managers, their underperformance against their proper benchmarks has been just as great, if not more so, in "inefficient" asset classes as it has been in the large-cap arena. One of the reasons, and perhaps the main reason, is that in these inefficient asset

119

classes the costs of trading, both in terms of bid-offer spreads and market impact costs, are much greater than they are in the large-cap asset class. Less efficient markets are typically characterized by lower trading volumes. The lower trading activity results in less liquidity and therefore greater trading costs. As more investors move to passive strategies, it is logical to conclude that trading activity would decline. Yet while we have seen a shift to passive management by both individuals and institutions, trading volumes have continued to set new records. The only conclusion to draw is that the remaining active participants are becoming more active—increasing their turnover. However, if as investors shifted to passive management, trading activity fell, liquidity would decline and trading costs would rise. The increase in trading costs would raise the already substantial hurdle that active managers have to overcome in order to outperform. Based on the evidence we have from the "inefficient" emerging markets, it seems highly likely that any information advantage gained by a lessening of competition would be more than offset by an increase in trading costs. Remember, for active management to be the winning strategy, it is a necessary, but not sufficient, condition that the markets are inefficient. The other condition is that the costs of implementing an active strategy must be small enough that market inefficiencies can be exploited, after expenses.

There is another interesting conclusion that can be drawn about the trend toward passive investing. Remember that for active managers to win, they must exploit the mistakes of others. It seems likely that those abandoning active management in favor of passive strategies are investors who have had poor experience with active investing. The reason this seems logical is that it doesn't seem likely that an individual would abandon a winning strategy. The only other logical explanation I can come up with is that an individual simply recognized that he/she was lucky. That conclusion would be inconsistent with behavioral studies that all show individuals tend to take credit for their success as skill based and attribute failures to bad luck. Thus it seems logical to conclude that the remaining players are likely to be the ones with the most skill. Therefore we can conclude that as the "less skilled" investors abandon active strategies, the remaining competition, on average, is likely to get tougher and tougher. Returning to our free-throw shooting contest, in this world only the Warren Buffetts of the world should be attempting to win. And I only know one Warren Buffett who sees himself in the mirror.

While it is highly unlikely that everyone will abandon active strategies (hope springs eternal), I see nothing in the trend to passive investing that gives reason for optimism among the believers in active management. In fact, just the opposite appears to be true. Game theory leads us to the logical conclusion that the winning strategy is not to play the game of active management but to simply accept market returns.

TRUTH 8

◆

Buying Individual Stocks and Sector Funds Is Speculating, Not Investing

*R*isk is a word that contains four letters. However, it is not a four-letter word, at least not in the colloquial sense. When it comes to investing, we need to distinguish between two very different types of risk, good risk and bad risk. Good risk is the type that you are *compensated* for taking. The compensation is in the form of greater expected returns. Bad risk is the type for which there is no such compensation; thus it is called *uncompensated* risk. Let's begin by taking a look at examples of compensated risk

We will begin our tour of the world of compensated risk with short-term U.S. Treasury bills, which are riskless instruments—they entail neither credit nor principal risk. Because they are riskless instruments, they provide the lowest rate of return. Investors seeking higher returns must be willing to accept greater risk. They can do so by purchasing long-term U.S. government instruments (assuming the yield curve is positively sloped—which it is the vast majority of the time—longer maturities will carry higher interest rates). For example, from 1926 through 2001, one-month Treasury bills returned 3.8 percent while U.S. government bonds with an average maturity of twenty years returned 5.3 percent. Investors were *compensated* with a risk premium of 1.5 percent per annum for taking the price risk of longer maturities. The standard deviation (a measure of risk) for one-month bills is only about 3.2 percent per annum. For longer term bonds it jumps to

9.4 percent per annum. Investors can also seek higher returns by accepting credit risk. By investing in corporate bonds with the same twenty-year maturity, investors would have earned 5.7 percent and were *compensated* with a risk premium of 0.4 percent. The more credit risk an investor is willing to accept, the greater the expected return. Obviously junk bonds will provide significantly higher *expected* returns than investment-grade corporate bonds.

With equity investing there are also forms of compensated risk. Equities are more risky than fixed-income investments. Therefore, they must *compensate* investors by providing greater *expected* returns to attract investors. For example, for the period from 1926 through 2001 the annual equity premium over one-month Treasury bills was 8.4 percent. Just as equities are more risky than fixed-income instruments, the stocks of small-cap and value companies are riskier than their large-cap and growth counterparts. Therefore, they too must carry risk premiums—individuals investing in these asset classes did so only because they expected to be compensated with greater returns. The annual risk premium for small-cap and value stocks from 1964 through 2001 was 3.5 and 5.1 percent.

We have seen how risk and reward are related in that investors taking greater risk receive compensation in the form of an *ex-ante, expected* risk premium. Remember, if the greater expected returns were guaranteed, there would be no risk and no risk premium. Thus the compensation investors receive must always be considered an *ex-ante* risk premium. Now let's turn to the "four-letter" type of risk, the *uncompensated* kind.

Diversification of Equity Portfolios

As we have seen, equity investors face several types of risk. First, there is the idiosyncratic risk of investing in stocks. Second, various asset classes carry different levels of risks. Large-cap stocks are less risky than small-cap stocks, and glamour (growth) stocks are less risky than distressed (value) stocks. These first two risks cannot be diversified away. Thus investors must be compensated for taking them. The third type of equity risk is that of the individual company. The risks of individual stock ownership can easily be diversified away by owning passive asset class or index funds that basically own all the stocks in an entire asset class/index. Exchange-traded funds also can be used to accomplish this objective. Each of these vehicles eliminates the single-company risk in a low-cost and tax-efficient manner. Note that asset class risk can also be addressed by the building of a globally diversified portfolio, allocating funds across the various asset classes of domestic and international, large and small, value and growth, and even real estate and emerging markets. Individual investors can build portfolios that reflect their own unique ability, willingness, and need to take risk, tilting the portfolio to either higher or lower risk asset classes as best suits their personal investment plan. Since the risks of single-stock ownership can be diversified, the market does not compensate investors for taking that type of risk. This is why investing in individual companies is speculating, not investing. Investing means taking compensated risk. Speculating is taking uncompensated risk, like buying a lottery ticket.

The benefits of diversification are obvious and well-known. Diversification reduces the risk of underperformance. It also reduces the volatility and dispersion of returns without reducing expected returns, thus a diversified portfolio is considered to be more *efficient* than a concentrated portfolio.

Given the benefits of diversification, the question is: Do investors actually hold diversified portfolios? A study by William Goetzmann and Alok Kumar, "Equity Portfolio Diversification," sought the answer to this question.[1] The authors examined over forty thousand equity investment accounts at a large discount brokerage firm during the six-year period 1991–96. They found that the vast majority of investors held portfolios that were clearly undiversified, with holdings typically concentrated in just a few stocks—the average investor holds a portfolio consisting of just four stocks. Amazingly, they found that less than 5 percent of investors held at least ten stocks. They also found that even investors holding large numbers of stocks benefited very little from diversification, as their holdings were highly correlated (in the same asset class). They found that "the average correlation among the stocks in portfolios containing a large number of stocks is not lower than the average correlation among stocks in portfolios with fewer stocks." Finally, they found no evidence that investors with undiversified portfolios compensated for this by investing in mutual funds.

The authors found that the lack of diversification caused portfolio variance (a measure of risk) to be three to four times that of well-diversified portfolios. They also found that only a small fraction of investor portfolios exhibited a better risk-return trade-off than the market. Given the evidence on individual investor stock-picking skills, it seems investors are getting the worst of all worlds—lower returns and greater risk.

Why Do Investors Fail to Diversify?

Given the obvious benefits of diversification, why don't investors hold highly diversified portfolios? This failure has its roots in two distinctly different sources: lack of knowledge and human behavioral traits.

Because most investors have not studied financial economics, read financial economic journals, or read books on modern portfolio theory, they do not have an understanding of how many stocks are really needed to build a truly diversified portfolio. Similarly, they don't have an understanding of the nature of how markets and stocks behave in terms of risks and rewards (the issue of compensated versus uncompensated risk). The result of the lack of knowledge is that most investors hold portfolios with assets concentrated in relatively few holdings. Let's now examine the other source of the failure to diversify, human behavior. We will begin by examining the all-too-human characteristic of overconfidence.

Individuals Are Overconfident of Their Investment Skills

Prof. Richard Thaler of the University of Chicago and Robert J. Shiller, an economics professor at Yale, note that "individual investors and money managers persist in their belief that they are endowed with more and better information than others, and that they can profit by picking stocks."[2] This insight helps explain why individual investors don't diversify: They believe that they can pick stocks that will outperform the market. They also believe that they can time the market (so that they're fully invested when it is rising and out of it when it is falling) and identify the few active managers who will beat their respective benchmarks.

The following are examples of investor overconfidence:

- A June 1998 survey by the *Wall Street Journal* found that the average investor expected the market to return 13.4 percent for the next twelve months. Of course, on average, each investor expected to individually earn almost 2 percent more than the market. The survey was repeated three months later with similar results. Investors, on average, expected the market to return 10.5 percent for the next twelve months, yet they expected their own portfolios to return almost 13 percent.[3]
- A February 1998 survey by Montgomery Asset Management found that 74 percent of investors interviewed expected their funds to consistently outperform the market.[4]

Even when individuals think that it is hard to beat the market, they are confident that *they* will be successful. Let's take a look at some further evidence on investor overconfidence. Brad Barber and Terrance Odean of the Graduate School of Management, University of California, Davis, have done a series of studies on investor behavior and performance. The following is a summary of their main findings:

- Individual investors: Individual investors underperform appropriate benchmarks.[5] Obviously, on average, they were overconfident of their skills.
- Men vs. women: Though the stock selections of women do not outperform those of men, women produce higher net

returns due to lower turnover (lower trading costs). Also, married men outperform single men.[6] The obvious explanation is that single men do not have the benefit of their spouse's sage counsel to temper their own overconfidence. Behavioral economist Meir Statman, a professor of finance at Santa Clara University, attributed both the greater trading activity and the purchasing of riskier stocks by men to overconfidence. "More so than women, men simply think that they are better at investing than they actually are. Men also get a thrill from trading, and thrill seeking is likely to be biologically based."[7] Women, on the other hand, often feel intimidated by the market and, therefore, tend to stay put.[8]

- Frequent traders vs. less active investors: Individuals who traded the most (presumably due to misplaced confidence) produced the lowest net returns.[9] The findings of the study by Goetzmann and Kumar were consistent with this theory of overconfidence. They found a positive correlation between turnover rates and lack of diversification: The higher the turnover (reflecting greater confidence), the lower the degree of diversification.[10]

- Individuals who switched from telephone trading with a discount broker to e-trading: Presumably, these individuals switched to Internet trading because of their past success. Unfortunately, they performed worse after the switch. Once again, overconfidence led to increased trading, and the greater costs associated with increased turnover led to lower returns.[11]

How expensive is overconfidence? DALBAR, an independent financial services research firm, found that for the seventeen-year period ending in 2000, the S&P 500 returned 16.3 percent per annum. However, the average individual investor buying and selling individual stocks and no-load mutual funds (average holding period for the funds was less than three years) earned an average return of just 5.3 percent. Clearly, overconfidence can be very expensive.[12]

Examining the results of the Mensa Investment Club provides an amusing bit of evidence on overconfidence. It would seem logical that if anyone had a right to be confident of being able to translate their intellectual skills into superior investment results it would be members of Mensa. However, their results make the Beardstown Ladies look like Warren Buffett. The June 2001 issue of *SmartMoney* reported that over the past fifteen years the Mensa Investment Club returned just 2.5 percent, underperforming the S&P 500 Index by almost 13 percent per annum. Warren Smith, an investor for thirty-five years, reported that his original investment of $5,300 had turned into $9,300. A similar investment in the S&P 500 Index would have produced almost $300,000. One investor described their strategy as buy low, sell lower. The Mensa members were overconfident that their superior intellectual skills could be translated into superior investment returns.

As author and personal finance journalist James Smalhout puts it, "Psychologists have long documented the tendency of Homo sapiens to overrate his own abilities and prospects for success. This is particularly true of the subspecies that invests in stocks and, accordingly, tends to overtrade."[13]

There are other behavioral explanations for the failure to diversify.

Other Behavioral Explanations for the Failure to Diversify

Another explanation of why individual investors fail to diversify is that they have the false perception that by limiting the number of stocks they hold, they can manage their risks better. While this belief has been confirmed by a study by Werner DeBondt, it is an illusion; it is just another form of overconfidence.[14]

Investors may also gain a false sense of control over the outcomes by being involved in the process. They fail to understand that it is the portfolio's asset allocation that determines risk, not who is controlling the switch.

Another mistake that we will discuss in greater detail later is that investors confuse the familiar with the safe. They believe that because they are familiar with a company, it must be a safer investment than one with which they are unfamiliar. This leads them to concentrate their holdings in a few companies. It also leads them to hold stocks that have high correlation, as they tend to concentrate holdings in the same small group of familiar large-cap growth stocks (e.g., Coca-Cola, IBM, Microsoft, etc.).[15]

Another interesting finding of the Goetzmann and Kumar study was that there was a positive correlation between age and diversification (i.e., as we age, we tend to increase our diversification).[16] Perhaps investors were learning from their experiences. Perhaps it is the benefit of increasing wisdom with age. Or it might simply be a growing aversion to risk as we age.

The bottom line is that an illusion of control and overconfidence in their stock-picking skills leads investors to ignore the benefits of diversification.

There is one other possible explanation for the failure of investors to diversify that we need to consider. Because investors confuse information with knowledge they don't recognize the simple investment truth that, as legendary investor Bernard Baruch stated, "something that everyone knows isn't worth knowing." The failure to understand this leads to a false sense of confidence. Which, as we have seen, in turn leads to a lack of diversification.

Investors Confuse Information with Knowledge

Information is a fact, data, or an opinion held by someone. Knowledge, on the other hand, is information that is of value. In other words, for information to be of value, you must be able to exploit it. Confusing information and knowledge is a major investment mistake. Let's take a look at what I call the "information paradox."

As we discussed in the introduction, at the core of the EMH (efficient markets hypothesis) is that *new* information is disseminated to the public so rapidly and completely that prices instantly adjust to new data. If this is the case, an investor can consistently beat the market only with either the best of luck or with inside information (on which it is illegal to trade). The logical conclusion seems *illogical* to most investors: If information is valuable, it has no value because either the market already knows it and has incorporated it into prices or it is illegal on which to trade. Thus we have the information paradox. Keep in mind that the only other way you can exploit information is to interpret that information differently (and correctly) from the way in which the market collectively interprets it.

The following example illustrates the logic of the information paradox. You are watching CNBC. David Faber is interviewing a fund manager about his single best stock pick. While the conversation is hypothetical, it will probably sound familiar (though perhaps exaggerated).

David Faber: Tell us why Cisco is your best pick.

Fund manager: Our analyst who covers Cisco is a genius. She graduated first in her M.B.A. class at Wharton. She then graduated first in her class at MIT, receiving a Ph.D. in electrical engineering. She worked for several years at Cisco in product development and several more in marketing and sales. She then joined our firm and has been our technology analyst. She has personally visited all Cisco plants and research facilities; she has also visited with all competitors. She even visited with all of Cisco's major customers to check on how they perceive Cisco products and service and on the status of new orders. And she met with Cisco's suppliers to check on the quality of their work. The stock is currently selling at twenty. Given the great new pipeline of one hundred great new products and the growth in sales that will result, the stock is worth fifty if it's worth a penny.

David Faber: Thank you for your insights.

What is critical for investors to understand is that even if we assume everything the fund manager said was absolutely true, there is a very logical reason for you to ignore all such prognostications—there is something very wrong with the picture. The reason is that although the fund manager probably does have a very smart analyst covering Cisco, there are literally dozens of other very smart analysts covering Cisco. They all probably have M.B.A.s from top schools and lots of experience.

They are all highly paid and motivated. They all work diligently to gather the facts. They all have the same information. If the other analysts and fund managers thought Cisco was worth fifty, obviously the stock would already be trading there and not at twenty. Do you think all those smart people would let a stock that is obviously worth fifty sit there at twenty without rushing to buy it at this obviously undervalued level? The reason Cisco is trading at twenty is that the market collectively thinks that it is only worth twenty, not fifty. The fund manager simply believes that the rest of the world has got it wrong. Their analyst is *right* and the rest of the world is *wrong*. Only their analyst really knows this stuff, and the rest of the smart analysts are simply misinterpreting the information.

It is also important to keep the following in mind. Beating the market is a zero-sum game—for one fund manager to outperform, another must underperform. Is it really logical to believe that an analyst at, for example, Merrill Lynch is superior and knows more than the analyst at Goldman Sachs or Janus? Actually, it doesn't even matter. What really matters is that the evidence is clear that it is highly unlikely that any one individual will be able to consistently identify securities the rest of the market has somehow mispriced.

The next time you watch CNBC and listen to an analyst or fund manager explain all the good reasons why to buy a specific stock, sector, or equities in general keep the information paradox in mind. Even though you might be impressed with the intellectual capacity of the person and the information presented, as well as the logic of the recommendation, keep these four points in mind before you leap into action:

1. Capturing *incremental* insight is very difficult, if not impossible, to achieve. The reason is that security analysts are

competing with so many other smart and highly motivated people researching the same stocks. It is this tough competition that makes it so difficult to gain a competitive advantage. Imagine an art auction where you are the only expert among a group of amateurs. In that circumstance, it might be possible to find a bargain. On the other hand, if you are one of a group of mostly experts, it is far less likely that you will find bargain prices. The same is true of stocks. Competition among all the professional active managers ensures that the market price is highly likely to be the correct price.

2. Think about where you just heard the new insightful information—*on national television.* In the unlikely scenario that this information was a secret, it no longer is. The same analogy could be made for recommendations from any of the high-profile publications such as *Barron's, Business Week, Fortune, Forbes, MONEY, or SmartMoney.*

3. As Rex Sinquefield, the cochairman of DFA points out: "Just because there are some investors smarter than others, that advantage will not show up. The market is too vast and too informationally efficient."[17]

4. If the person is a fund manager, it is possible that he/she is touting the stock because the person already owns it. He/she may need you to buy the stock so that the person can sell it to you at a higher price.

The information paradox also applies to the recommendations of such gurus as Harry Dent. If you read his books, you would say Dent makes a lot of sense. However, before you leap to invest in individual stocks or mutual funds based on Dent's (or any guru's) insightful analysis, you might want to consider: Is Dent the only person who knows that the demand for health care will rise as the population ages? Aren't all investors aware of this? Don't the big institutional investors and mutual funds that manage the vast majority of financial assets know all the things Dent predicts are likely to occur? Doesn't the market already incorporate this knowledge into current prices? The alternative is to believe the market is simply asleep—a highly unlikely scenario. If the market is aware of this information, it has already been incorporated into prices. Therefore, the knowledge cannot be exploited.

Confusing information with knowledge can lead investors to stray from the strategy of prudent diversification by creating an undeserved confidence. The best way to avoid this mistake is to simply tune out all such forecasts, unless you enjoy them for their entertainment value.

Why Broad Diversification Is More Important Than Ever

The evidence on lack of diversification is particularly distressing given that changes in the equity markets have made diversification more important than ever. In December 1968, a study by J. L. Evans and S. H. Archer concluded that an investor needed to construct a portfolio containing as few as fifteen randomly selected stocks before the benefits of diversification (as measured by standard deviation) were basically exhausted.[18] A similar study from the same era found that 90 percent of the diversification benefit came from just sixteen stocks and 95 percent of the benefit could be captured by just thirty stocks.[19]

Almost three decades later (1996), a study by two University of Nevada, Las Vegas, professors, Gerald Newbould and Percy

Poon, came to a far different conclusion. They found that "investors needed to hold more than one hundred small-cap or large-cap stocks to remain within five percent of average risk, which they define as the average volatility of the forty thousand simulated portfolios created for the study."[20]

Consider now an investor who wants to achieve broad global asset class diversification. He/she would need to hold over one hundred small-cap and one hundred large-cap stocks. And then the person would probably have to add a similar number of small- and large-value stocks, real estate stocks, foreign large-cap stocks, emerging-market stocks, etc. There is simply no way to achieve this type of diversification by building your own portfolio of individual stocks.

The results of Newbould and Poon's study are supported by the results of a similar study published in 2000, "The Truth About Diversification by the Numbers."[21] The authors measured the percentage of possible reductions in dispersions of returns achieved by portfolios of various sizes on the average compared to a single-stock portfolio. The study covered the period January 1986–June 1999 and included all stocks within the COMPUSTAT database. The following table summarizes their findings.

Number of stocks	15	30	**60**	Market
Standard Deviation	16.5%	15.4%	15.2%	14.5%
R-squared	.76	.86	**.88**	1
Tracking error	8.1	6.2	**5.3**	
Percent reduction in dispersion of returns	82%	86%	88%	

Note that even with a portfolio of as many as sixty stocks, the correlation of returns was still below 90 percent. Perhaps more important, the tracking error to the market was still over 5 percent per annum. With the historical return to the market (as measured by the S&P 500 Index) being just over 11 percent, I wonder how many investors would be comfortable with a tracking error that is equal to almost 50 percent of the average market return.

What has caused this increased need for diversification? A study, coauthored by Burton Malkiel, John Campbell, Yexiao Xu, and Martin Lettau, argues that a dramatic increase in the volatility of individual stocks, along with a declining correlation of stocks within the S&P 500 Index, has led to a significant increase in the number of securities needed to achieve the same level of portfolio risk. They found that for the two decades prior to 1985, in order to reduce excess standard deviation (a measure of diversifiable portfolio risk) to 10 percent, a portfolio would have had to consist of at least twenty stocks. From 1986 to 1997, that figure increased to fifty. Whereas the study found that there was a large increase in the volatility of individual stocks, the authors found no increase in overall market volatility or even industry volatility. The implication of the combination of increased volatility of individual stocks and unchanged volatility of the S&P 500 is that correlations between stocks have declined. Reduced correlation between stocks implies that the benefits of, and the need for, portfolio diversification have increased over time.[22]

The authors offer three explanations for the increased volatility of individual stocks, the first of which is the increased influence of institutional investors over the past forty years. Institutional investors have exhibited a herd mentality; thus, when hundreds of funds and pension plans rush to buy or sell at roughly the same time, price changes are now more exaggerated. A second explanation is the advent of retail day traders. The third explanation is the tendency for companies to go public at a much earlier stage, when they are likely to be more volatile.[23]

The investment results of the year 2000 perfectly illustrate the risks of targeting narrow market sectors rather than diversifying risk. The *Wall Street Journal*'s year-end mutual fund survey found that while the S&P 500 Index fell less than 10 percent that year, 487 funds lost 30 percent or more.[24]

Perhaps the following is the most dramatic example of the need for and logic of broad diversification as the winning strategy. While the 1990s witnessed one of the greatest bull markets of all time, 22 percent of the 2,397 U.S. stocks in existence throughout the decade had negative returns. Not negative real returns, but negative absolute returns.[25] Even this shocking figure is inaccurately low. The reason is that it includes only stocks that were in existence throughout the decade—thus there is survivorship bias in the data.

Stocks are much riskier than investors believe. The reason is that stock returns are not normally distributed—the dispersion of individual stock returns does not resemble a bell curve where the median return is the same as the mean return. If the dispersion of individual stock returns resembled the bell curve then the returns of half the stocks would be above the mean and half would fall below the mean. Unfortunately for investors in individual stocks, this is not the case. The reason is that while your profits are unlimited, you can only lose 100 percent. Thus a few big winners (e.g., Microsoft) cause the average return to be above the median return. As a result, there are more stocks that have below "average" returns than there are stocks with above "average" returns. This makes the purchase of individual stocks a loser's game.

As we have discussed, the problem that investors have is that each of them thinks that he/she can find the few outperformers while avoiding the many losers. However, the stock market is not

Lake Wobegon. Less than one-half of all stocks provide greater than market returns, and probably about 30 percent or more underperform riskless instruments. And as we just saw, a fairly high percentage actually lose money, even over periods as long as ten years. Thus investors in individual stocks are far more likely to underperform than outperform. The conclusion I draw, and I hope you draw as well, is that the purchase of individual stocks should be viewed as speculating, not investing.

Sector Funds

As we saw, investors purchasing individual stocks are speculating by taking uncompensated risk. They are basically operating under the assumption that the market has mispriced the stock they are purchasing. Purchasing a sector (single industry) fund is making a similar, but not quite as bad, mistake. It is similar in that it entails taking uncompensated risk. In their seminal paper, "The Cross-section of Expected Stock Returns," Professors Eugene F. Fama and Kenneth R. French demonstrated that it was the exposure to the risk factors of size and value that determined over 90 percent of the risk and reward of a portfolio, not stock selection, sector selection, or market timing.[26] It is important for investors to understand the importance of this finding: Stocks with the same market cap and BtM have the same risk and expected return. This is why there should be no expected compensation for owning one large-growth stock instead of another. Another issue of importance is that since the exposure to a sector (e.g., technology or health care) is not the major determinant of risk and reward, then investors in sector funds are taking uncompensated risk, risk that can be diversified away. And at least in one sense, purchasing a sector fund is making an even greater mistake than purchasing an individual stock (though purchasers are at least achieving some diversification of individual company risk). The reason is as follows. As we have discussed, the buyer of an individual stock is assuming the market has mispriced the stock—and there is no evidence that the market makes this mistake, at least in a manner that is exploitable. On the other hand, the buyer of a sector fund is assuming the market has mispriced an entire sector (otherwise why would the buyer take uncompensated risk?). Again, there is no evidence of any such exploitable mispricing.

There is one other issue regarding diversification that needs to be addressed. It has to do with a mistake related to the purchase of mutual funds. I call it diversification by the numbers.

Diversification By the Numbers

Far too many investors believe that they can achieve effective diversification by purchasing a large number of mutual funds. To see why this may not be true, let's look at an example that is fairly typical. It is one of an investor buying several different funds within one or two fund families. In this case we will assume that to diversify an investor buys twenty different funds, the ten largest in terms of assets under management from each of Fidelity and Janus (two of the most popular fund families for actively managed funds). When we examine such a portfolio under the microscope of the Fama-French model, we find that in the case of Fidelity, seven of the ten funds were first decile by size and three were second decile. All ten were first decile by BtM. None had any international exposure. The results are similar with Janus: Seven of the ten are first decile by size and three are second decile. Nine are first decile by BtM, with one in the second decile. While the investor would own twenty different funds, and there would be some international diversification with some of the Janus funds, every single one of the funds is basically a domestic large-cap growth fund. Thus, the investor achieved very little in terms of effective diversification (with the exception, again, of some international exposure).

Fidelity	Janus
Magellan 1/1	Worldwide 1/1
Growth and Income 1/1	Twenty 1/1
Contrafund 2/1	Mercury 1/1
Growth Company 1/1	Growth and Income 2/1
Blue Chip Growth 1/1	Overseas 1/1
Equity Income 2/1	Aspen Worldwide Growth Inst. 1/1
Puritan 2/1	Enterprise 2/1
Spartan U.S. Equity Index 1/1	Olympus 1/1
Fidelity 1/1	Global Technology 2/1
Aggressive Growth 1/1	Balanced 1/1

Source: Morningstar Database as of February 28, 2001; "X/Y" = Size ranking/BtM ranking

Conclusion

I hope that the evidence presented convinces you that the purchase of individual stocks and/or sector funds is speculating, not investing. I also hope that you are convinced that diversification does not work "by the numbers," but is instead determined by the exposure of an equity portfolio to the risk factors of size and value. The implication for individual investors is that broad-based index or passively managed asset class mutual funds (or their equivalent exchange-traded funds) provide the most effective diversification and do so at a very low cost. And the advent of index and passively managed funds that are also tax managed basically eliminates any advantages that an individually tailored private account might offer. Privately managed stock accounts just cannot achieve the same level of diversification that a fund can achieve. And as we saw, the evidence is clear that there now is a greater need for diversification than ever before.

We need to cover one more point about the risks of concentration. It has to do with investors making the mistake of confusing strategy and outcome. Only one example is really needed to convince you that this is a mistake. With the benefit of hindsight we know that a 100 percent concentration in Microsoft would have made an investor a millionaire. However, a 100 percent concentration in Enron, Polaroid, Xerox, and hundreds of other once great companies also made sense, at least for a while. Concentrating assets means accepting uncompensated risk. While it is the surest way to make a large fortune, it is also just as likely to turn a large fortune into a small one (or go broke).

TRUTH 9

◆

Reversion to the Mean of Earnings Growth Rates Is One of the Most Powerful Forces in the Universe

One of the most fundamental principles of economics is that profitability is mean reverting. In a free market, capitalist society when profits are "abnormally" high (far in excess of the cost of capital), more capital gets allocated to that industry, product, or service. The result is that supply and competition increase and profits revert to the mean (approach the cost of capital). This eventually eliminates the "abnormal" profits. When profits are below normal, capital gets allocated away from that industry. Thus supply and competition is reduced, and normal profitability is restored.

Despite the logic, there is a growing body of evidence that suggests that stock market analysts and investors alike ignore this principle. They do so at their peril as this ultimately can lead to poor and even disastrous investment results. To understand why this is so we begin by looking at the historical evidence on the returns of growth vs. value stocks. In general, growth companies are the glamour companies that are projected to have rapid growth in earnings, with a high probability of achieving those projections. Investors thus ascribe a low-risk premium to these stocks. In contrast, value companies are projected to have a low rate of earnings growth. In addition, because they are perceived to be risky companies, investors perceive a greater degree of risk that they will not hit their earnings projections. Investors thus ascribe a high-risk premium to these stocks.

As we have discussed, despite the fact that the glamorous growth companies have provided much higher rates of earnings growth than value companies, value stocks have provided higher returns to investors than growth stocks over the long term. For example, for the period 1927–2002, U.S. large-value stocks outperformed large-growth stocks by 11.7 percent to 9.4 percent and U.S. small-value stocks outperformed small-growth stocks by 14.4 percent to 9.3 percent. The evidence is just as strong in international markets. For the period 1975–2002, international large-value stocks outperformed the EAFE Index (international large-growth stocks) by 16.2 percent to 11.0 percent.

While there is no debate over the issue of past outperformance, there is much debate over the cause of the difference in returns. In one camp are financial economists who argue that the value premium is a risk story—value stocks are riskier than growth stocks. Therefore, investors must be compensated with higher expected returns. Others argue that the explanation lies in a persistent overvaluation of the earnings prospects for growth stocks. Let's examine the evidence on the "overvaluation" story. The data is very compelling. However, as I will explain, investors must be careful before drawing conclusions from the data. The exception to this note of caution is that investors should conclude under either scenario that growth stocks have lower expected returns.

Richard Harris sought to determine a possible cause of any persistent "overvaluation" of securities.[1] His study covered 6,666 five-year earnings forecasts of NYSE, AMEX (American Stock Exchange), and NASDAQ firms in the IBES (Institutional Brokers Estimate System) database for the period beginning in 1982. He then compared the forecasts to actual profits using the S&P and COMPUSTAT databases. Here is what he found:

- The earnings forecasts were extremely biased, with actual profits overestimated by 7 percent per annum. A simple forecast of no change in earnings would have produced more accurate results. An even better forecast would have been to assume that a firm's earnings would grow in line with the overall economy.

- The errors were highly correlated with themselves. Low-profit forecasts had low errors, and high-profit forecasts had high errors. Thus high-growth forecasts had the worst errors. Large companies with high BtM ratios (value stocks) had the fewest errors.

- The forecasting errors were not from having overestimated the growth of the overall economy. Most errors were from individual company forecasts, with a small contribution from overestimating industry profits.

Harris hypothesized that the source of the errors might easily be explained by the following:

- The sell side of investment banking firms might want to hype the stock they follow in order to help with the sale of securities.

- Analysts are afraid to publish negative reports for fear they will lose access to management as a source of information.

- Analysts hype the stock to win favor with company management in the hope that they will win more investment banking business for their respective firms.

All these explanations have appeal, though they do not explain why the errors are worse for growth stocks than for value stocks.

A similar study sought to discover the source of any persistent overvaluation in international markets, and the authors came to the same conclusion as did Harris. The study covered twenty developed country markets for the eleven-year period 1986–96. The authors found that earnings forecasts for growth stocks were consistently too high, thus creating "overvalued" stocks. The actual earnings announcements disappointed growth investors the most, and their stocks (since they had the greatest expectations) were punished. The overestimation of earnings fully explained the value effect.[2]

The question remains as to why analysts err in overestimating earnings growth rates. One explanation that seems plausible is that analysts are overly confident about the growth companies they follow being able to overcome the tendency for reversion to the mean of profits. Analysts might also underestimate the ability of value companies to reinvent themselves by bringing in new management and/or reorganizing. This often restores profitability. Furthermore, value companies are often acquired by growth companies using their less expensive capital (thus forcing a reinventing of the company and a more efficient allocation of capital). Remember, reversion to the mean occurs for both growth and value companies.

In their study, "Forecasting Profitability and Earnings," Professors Eugene F. Fama and Kenneth R. French tested whether or not the theory of profitability reverting to the mean stood up to the historical data.[3] They examined the profits of an average of 2,304 firms per year for the period 1964–95. Their conclusions:

- There is a strong tendency for profits to revert to the mean.
- Reversion to the mean is strongest when profits are highest (greatest incentive for competition to enter) and lowest

(greatest incentive to leave an industry and reallocate assets, thereby reducing competition and restoring profits).

- Abnormally low earnings tend to revert even faster than abnormally high profits.

- Reversion to the mean occurs at a rate of about 40 percent per annum.

- Real-world forecasts tend to underestimate the speed at which reversion to the mean in profitability occurs.

Fama and French offered a possible behavioral-oriented explanation for abnormally low earnings reverting faster than abnormally high earnings. They cite a study published by S. Basu in the December 1997 *Journal of Accounting and Economics.* Basu hypothesized that when reporting bad news, companies become very conservative and try to get all the bad news out of the way at one time (possibly blaming the previous management). On the other hand, they tend to spread good news out over time.

If, in fact, reversion to the mean occurs faster than the market is anticipating, this would help explain why growth stocks underperform value stocks. The market may simply be overestimating the amount of time that growth companies can generate *abnormal* profits. Ultimately, earnings expectations are not met, and this gets reflected in lower equity returns. The reverse is true of value companies. The market appears to overestimate the time it takes for abnormally low profits to revert to the mean. Ultimately, earnings expectations are exceeded, and this is reflected in higher returns.

Several studies summarized in *The New Finance* by Robert A. Haugen come to the same conclusion. A study by A. C. Raynor and I. M. D. Little sought to determine whether the fastest growing companies tended to repeat their past performance in the future.[4] They examined the performance of British companies over the period 1951–61. They ranked firms by their rates of growth in earnings per share and then formed them into groups: fastest growing, fast, slow, and slowest. The rankings were based on their performance for the period 1952–56. While there was a dramatic difference in the preformation period, there was virtually no difference in earnings growth rates among the four classifications in the postformation period. Even intraindustry there was no persistence in earnings growth rates. The authors concluded: "Certainly investors are wrong to think that a few years' above average rise of earnings is evidence at all that good management, which will result in a continued rise, must be present."

Another study by Harvard professors John Lintner and Robert Glauber tried to answer the question: What percentage of the difference in growth rates in one period was explained by the difference in growth rates from the *preceding* period? They examined the performance of U.S. companies for the period 1946–65.[5] The authors concluded: The persistency of earnings growth rates is close to zero. The rankings from one period to the next were virtually independent of one another. At the most they found that only 1.7 percent of the difference in growth rates in one five-year period could be explained by the difference in growth rates of the preceding period. One might conclude that the past is a very poor predictor when it comes to forecasting growth rates. However, there is valuable information contained in the data—it clearly shows that profits tend to revert to the mean.

Another study sheds considerable light on just how quickly profits tend to revert to the mean. The study broke U.S. stocks into four categories, lowest E/P (growth), low E/P, high E/P, and highest E/P (value). The study then examined the rates of growth of earnings of both value and growth companies postformation of the portfolios. The period covered was 1973–90. The study concluded that while growth companies continued to grow faster than value companies, there was a clear and persistent reversion to the mean. Thus, after about five to six years, earnings growth rates had reverted to the mean, virtually eliminating any difference.[6] The problem for investors is that analysts' forecasts and market prices reflect the projection that earnings growth rates for both growth and value companies will not revert to the mean in that short a time span. Thus growth investors are ultimately disappointed and value investors ultimately surprised. This would explain the greater historical returns to value investors.

Investors would be well served to keep the following in mind. From 1960 through 2000, corporate profits grew at a rate of 8 percent, right in line with nominal GNP growth. Obviously, a company growing at a rate of 15 percent has to do about twice as well as the average company. To demonstrate just how difficult a task it is to grow at 15 percent per annum for a long time, only three of the Nifty Fifty growth stocks of 1972 were able to grow at that rate or better over the next twenty-five years. And none grew faster than 18 percent per annum. For the period from 1960 to 1980, just three companies were able to grow at 15 percent or greater (Standard Oil of Ohio, Philip Morris, and Boeing). For the period from 1970 to 1990 just four did so (Boeing, Philip Morris, Merck, and PPG Industries). And from 1980 to 1999, only five companies accomplished that goal (Fannie Mae, United Airlines, Philip Morris, Merck, and Abbott Laboratories). Even the mighty Microsoft is subject to reversion to the mean of its rate of growth. In 1996, revenues were growing 46 percent per annum. By 2000, that figure had fallen to just 16 percent.[7]

The following is another example of just how difficult it is to maintain a very high growth of earnings rate. According to the researchers at Sanford C. Bernstein & Co., over the past half century (ending in 2000) only 10 percent of companies in the S&P 500 have increased their earnings at an average rate of at least 20 percent a year for five years running. Only 3 percent have raised earnings at least 20 percent annually for a decade. And none have sustained 20 percent earnings growth for fifteen years or more. In the long run, it's just not possible for stock prices to rise faster than the earnings of the companies they represent.[8]

A study on the ability of companies to maintain high levels of earnings growth, "The Level and Persistence of Growth Rates," provided both compelling evidence and valuable insights for investors. The authors used a COMPUSTAT database covering all domestic stocks for the period 1951–97.[9] The study covered 359 companies at the start and 6,825 at the end. The authors analyzed long-term growth rates in earnings across broad cross sections of stocks using several different indicators of operating performance—net sales, operating income before depreciation, and operating income before extraordinary items available for common equity. Even with the acknowledged survivorship bias that produces an upward bias in the data (poorly performing companies often don't survive and thus disappear from the database), they found the following:

- While some firms have grown at high rates historically, they are relatively rare instances and about what we would randomly expect. Specifically, only four firms a year achieved annual growth rates above the median for a full ten-year run. This was just 0.2 percent of all firms, and just 0.1 percent more than randomly expected. Only 3.6 percent achieved that goal for just five years. Randomly we would expect 3.1 percent to do so. This was true even in fast-growing industries like technology and pharmaceuticals.

150

- There was no persistence in long-term profit growth rates beyond chance, and there was low predictability even using a wide variety of predictor variables.

- Valuation ratios have little predictive ability in terms of future growth rates. They have little ability to differentiate between firms with high or low future growth rates.

The study thus concluded that analyst forecasts were overly optimistic. IBES earnings forecast for the period 1982–98 averaged 14.5 percent. (IBES, since merged into FirstCall.com, is an analytic system that combines earnings forecasts, company accounts data, real-time brokerage research, and notes.) The after-the-fact reality proved to be just 9 percent. The overestimation problem was worst for the most optimistic forecasts for fast growth. The average five-year forecast for the top quintile firms was for a growth rate of 22.4 percent. However, the realized growth rate proved to be just 9.5 percent, about the average for all firms. The problem is that forecasts of high-growth rates in earnings lead to high P/E ratios. When those high-growth rates are not realized, investors are smacked with a double whammy. Not only do the earnings fail to achieve the targets, but the failure to achieve the anticipated growth rate also leads to a collapse in the P/E ratio and a geometric fall in price. Let's look at just how devastating an impact the double whammy can have.

At year-end 1999, 12 percent of the total stock market's capitalization was made up of firms with P/E ratios in excess of *one hundred*. The authors assumed that over a ten-year period, the P/E would fall to twenty (well above the market's long-term historical P/E ratio of about fourteen). A company would then have to achieve a 30 percent per annum growth in earnings to achieve just a 10 percent rate of return on investment. Earlier we saw just how hard that is to achieve. Here is another stunning example. At year-end 1999, the 90th percentile of companies ranked had forecasted earnings growth rates averaging 40 percent per annum (vs. just under 9 percent for the tenth decile). If the P/E eventually reverted to twenty, and assuming earnings would grow by almost 15 percent, it would take a full thirty-eight years for investors to achieve a 10 percent rate of return. Keep in mind that real earnings for all companies grew at a rate of just 3.5 percent for the full period covered by the study, right in line, as expected, with real GNP growth of 3.4 percent. Add in 3.5 percent inflation and the result is just 7 percent nominal growth in earnings.

The authors concluded that even loosening standards for faster growth to allow for a few bad years within a long run leaves the persistence of growth rates at very low levels and not much more than would be randomly expected. They also concluded that "the chances of being able to identify the next Microsoft are about the same as the odds of winning the lottery."

Sometimes the Math Doesn't Add Up

To illustrate just how dangerous it is to ignore the principle of mean reverting profits, consider the evidence from the following study. It was completed just a few months after the NASDAQ bubble burst. I believe the evidence will convince you that investors put themselves at great risk when they ignore this basic economic principle. The study, by Thompson, Plumb & Associates, presented a compelling case that the March–May 2000 NASDAQ dive was likely to be only the beginning of either a bigger crash or a prolonged period of underperformance for the once red-hot high-tech sector.[10] Their study looked at the seventeen largest technology companies in the S&P 500 Index. A Value Line Investment Survey said those companies—which included the likes of Cisco Systems, Oracle, and Qualcomm—would be able to increase their earnings by an average of nearly 26 percent a year. According to their analysis, such growth would give investors an average annual return of almost 19 percent over the next ten years (using May 25, 2000, stock prices).

Here's why the authors thought that could not happen. Since 1940, earnings for the S&P 500 Index had increased at between 5 and 7 percent a year. If those earnings rose at a 7 percent rate for the next ten years, and the seventeen tech companies grew at the rates Value Line was projecting, by 2009, the tech companies would contribute 74 percent of the earnings for the entire index—hardly a likely scenario. The seventeen companies would also be worth more than the entire S&P 500 if, in 2009, they traded at just thirty times earnings vs. twenty times for the S&P 500. The firm concluded that "we've proved it's impossible for investors to get a 20 percent return because seventeen companies can't be worth more than themselves plus 483 other companies. That means GE, Wal-Mart, Home Depot and Coke would have to have negative values." This study clearly showed that the NASDAQ Index at 5000 was a bubble. Prices could not be justified by any logical economic assumptions.

While these studies all seem to confirm the underestimation of the power of economic theory on profitability reverting to the mean, there does seem to be a puzzle. With all the evidence on analysts' errors, should not market prices already reflect those errors? Is the market simply ignoring the evidence? It is an interesting conundrum. At the very least, while I don't recommend purchasing individual stocks, investors choosing to do so should be very careful to make sure their analysis includes a reversion to the mean of earnings growth. Also, investors should consider this issue when deciding on the appropriate asset allocation of their equity portfolios—how much exposure should there be to the asset class of growth stocks?

Before concluding this section, there is a related issue of which investors should be aware: Just as the profits of individual companies revert to the mean, equity prices in general cannot grow faster than the economy forever.

Equity Prices Can't Grow Faster Than the Economy Forever

From 1988 through 1999, investors in U.S. equities experienced the greatest bull market in history with twelve straight years without a major correction. In fact, there was only a single down year, 1990, when the S&P 500 Index dropped just over 3 percent. Furthermore, 1995–99 was the first five-year period in history when the S&P 500 Index rose over 20 percent each year. The returns for the period had been far in excess of the rate of growth of the economy. The question, then, was: Could equity prices continue to grow faster than the overall economy? The answer should have been a resounding NO! To understand why they couldn't, we need to understand that three factors determine equity prices. These factors are future earnings expectations, the risk-free rate of return, and the equity risk premium. Let's examine how the three factors impact both current returns and the implications for future returns.

Let's begin with the risk-free rate of return. The benchmark for the risk-free rate is short-term U.S. Treasury bills. If these rates rise, the value of future earnings falls. If these rates fall, the value of future earnings rises. However, interest rates cannot fall to zero. Thus there is a limit to the impact falling interest rates can have on stock prices.

Investing in equities entails risk. This results in equities carrying a risk premium as compensation for that risk. Over the seventy-five-year period 1926–2000, equities provided a risk premium of about 7 percent. The risk premium, of course, has not been stable. It has been much higher during times of economic distress (recessions), as investors perceive greater risk in equity investments. The higher equity risk premium drives the value of future expected earnings, and therefore equity prices, lower. However, the higher risk premium results in higher future expected returns. The reverse is true in good times, when investors perceive less risk. The equity risk premium falls, driving the value of future expected earnings and equity prices higher. It should be obvious that while the equity risk premium could rise to infinity, it cannot fall to zero (since equities are riskier than risk-free instruments, nobody should purchase them if there were no expected compensation for doing so).

Understanding the impact of rising and falling risk premiums (and rising and falling interest rates) helps us understand why periods of high returns are generally followed by periods of low returns, and vice versa. This process is called reversion to the mean (long-term average).

Now let's address the third factor, earnings growth. Historically, corporate earnings have grown in line with both the GNP and overall income. While there are short-term fluctuations around averages, the tendency for corporate earnings to grow along with the economy is very logical. Believing that corporate earnings can grow faster than the overall economy leads to the conclusion that corporate profits will eventually consume the entire economic pie—leaving no returns to labor, interest, and other recipients of national income. Obviously, this is a nonsensical conclusion, straining not only credulity but also the evidence. From 1950 to 1980, pretax corporate profits rarely wandered much beyond the range of 8 to 12 percent of GNP. Over the past forty years, pretax corporate profits have rarely wandered much beyond the range of 6 to 10 percent of GNP.

It is important for investors to understand that it is the shifts in interest rates, the equity risk premium, and expectations of corporate profits that account for the volatility of the market. The way these factors impact the market has proven to be virtually unpredictable, particularly in the short term (otherwise we would see active managers outperforming simple benchmarks).

To summarize, equity prices in the long term must reflect the overall growth in the economy. Equity prices can rise faster than the economy for some period of time as interest rates and risk premiums fall and earnings grow faster than the overall economy. However, this process must end at some point. It is very important for investors to understand that if either or both the risk-free rate and the equity premium fall for an extended period of time, there will be two results, not one. First, investors will receive very large capital gains; however, these will be one-time gains. Second, future expected returns will be dramatically lower.

TRUTH 10

◆

The Forecasts of Market Strategists and Analysts Have No Value, Except as Entertainment

It cannot be possible to make reliable predictions about when the market will rise or fall. If it were possible, the market would respond in advance and it could not then rise and fall in the way it does. The fact that market timing must be unpredictable, but that investors nonetheless clamor to know when things will happen, is probably the single main reason why so much nonsense is written about the stock market. It is an old English adage that if you ask a silly question, you will get a silly answer.
　　—Andrew Smithers and Stephen Wright, *Valuing Wall Street*

Basically, we were guessing on interest rates. What we've come to believe is that no one can guess interest rates.
　　—Fred Henning, head of fixed-income investing, Fidelity
　　　　　　　　　　　　　　　　　　Investments, *Los Angeles Times*

Economists, if they are smart, learn to never make forecasts. If they have to make a forecast, they learn to never give a number. And if they have to give a number, they learn to never give a date. In that way they can never be proven wrong. They learn this both from being students of history and also from personal experience.

Forecasting is an extremely difficult thing to get right, especially (as Yogi Berra would say) if you are forecasting the future. The track record of economists is dismal. (Perhaps that is the real reason it is called "the dismal science.") The track record of market strategists is equally dismal. Despite the dismal records, the press and media focus on both economic and market forecasts (though rarely holding the forecasters accountable, for accountability would end the game). The reason for the high degree of focus is that there is probably no arena for predictions where the payoff for being correct is more rewarding than the stock market. In their search for market-beating returns, investors therefore pay great attention to forecasts, allowing the forecasts to influence or even determine their investment strategy. The question for investors is whether or not they should rely on the forecasts of industry professionals. The evidence suggests that the answer is an emphatic, "No!"

Despite all the innovations in information technology and all the academic research, forecasting stock market prices with any consistency or accuracy remains an elusive goal. William Sherden, author of *The Fortune Sellers,* was inspired by the following incident to write his book. In 1985, when preparing testimony as an expert witness, he analyzed the track records of inflation projections by different forecasting methods. He then compared those forecasts to what is called the "naive" forecast—simply projecting today's inflation rate into the future. He was surprised to learn that the simple naive forecast proved to be the most accurate, beating the forecasts of the most prestigious economic forecasting firms equipped with their Ph.D.s from leading universities and thousand-equation computer models.

Sherden reviewed the leading research on forecasting accuracy from 1979 to 1995 and covering forecasts made from 1970 to 1995. He concluded:

- *Economists cannot predict the turning points in the economy.* He found that of the forty-eight predictions made by economists, forty-six missed the turning points.

- *Economists' forecasting skill is about as good as guessing.* Even the economists who directly or indirectly run the economy (the Federal Reserve, the CEA [Council of Economic Advisors], and the CBO [Congressional Budget Office]) had forecasting records that were worse than pure chance.

- *There are no economic forecasters who consistently lead the pack in forecasting accuracy.*

- *There are no economic ideologies that produce superior forecasts.*

- *Increased sophistication provided no improvement in forecasting accuracy.*

- *Consensus forecasts do not improve accuracy.*

- *Forecasts may be affected by psychological bias.* Some economists are perpetually optimistic and others perpetually pessimistic.[1]

Economist and Nobel laureate Paul Samuelson observed: "I don't believe we're converging on ever-improving forecasting accuracy. It's almost as if there is a Heisenberg [uncertainty] Principle."[2] Michael Evans, founder of Chase Econometrics, confessed: "The problem with macro [economic] forecasting is that no one can do it."[3]

Since the underlying basis of most stock market forecasts is an economic forecast, the evidence suggests that stock market strategists who predict bull and bear markets will have no greater success than do the economists. Let's examine some of the evidence against the wisdom of relying on economic and/or market forecasts. We will begin by looking at the forecasts of market strategists, then turn to the record on specific stock-picking recommendations, and conclude with the record of investment newsletters.

The Case Against Market Strategists

- A Goldman Sachs study examined mutual fund cash holdings from 1970 to 1989. In their efforts to time the market, fund managers raise their cash holdings when they believe the market will decline and lower their cash holdings when they become bullish. The study found that mutual fund managers miscalled *all* nine major turning points.[4]

- At year-end 1999, the *Wall Street Journal* polled the market strategists from eleven of the top investment banking firms on their forecast for the S&P 500 Index at year-end 2000.[5] The index had closed 1999 at 1,469.25. The average forecast of the eleven strategists called for the S&P 500 to close at 1,579. This translates into a projected gain of 7.5 percent. It is worth noting that with the benefit of further information one analyst, Goldman Sachs's highly regarded Abby Joseph Cohen, in March actually raised her forecast by 50 points from 1,525 to 1,575. The S&P 500 Index managed to close the year 2000 at 1,320, a loss of just under 10 percent. The index would then have to rise 20 percent from its year-end closing levels to reach the average projected forecast. The superstar forecasters not only dramatically missed their target, but only one single analyst even managed to get the direction correct. When the market is rising, it really makes no difference how bullish a market strategist is. The real value of any forecaster is his/her ability to call the market turns correctly. The year 2000 handed those investors with faith in any such ability a very large tuition bill.

- At year-end 2000, the *Wall Street Journal* polled the market strategists of nine leading investment houses. With the S&P

500 Index closing the year at 1,320, the forecasts ranged from a high of 1,715 (Ed Kerschner of UBS Warburg) to a low of 1,320 (Richard Bernstein of Merrill Lynch). One forecaster, Steve Galbraith of Morgan Stanley, provided a range of 1,375–1,225. Since the index closed the year at 1,148 (down 13 percent) not one of the eight forecasters who provided a single point estimate even got the direction correct. Certainly, getting the direction correct is the most important part of the forecast. Kerschner's forecast of a 30 percent gain proved to be almost *50 percent* above the year-end close. And the press's darling of the late 1990s, Abby Joseph Cohen, had a forecast that proved to be "only" 43 percent too high.[6]

• Each quarter the *Wall Street Journal* reports on the performance of the stock recommendations of major brokerage houses.[7] The firms participating in the survey include many of the major firms: Bear Stearns, Credit Suisse, Goldman Sachs, JPMorgan, Lehman Brothers, Merrill Lynch, Morgan Stanley, Prudential, Salomon Brothers, UBS Warburg. Also included in the contest are large regional firms: A.G. Edwards, Dain Rauscher, Edward Jones, Raymond James, and U.S. Bancorp Piper Jaffray. For the quarter ending September 2001, the S&P 500 lost 14.7 percent. Just six of the fifteen firms' recommendations beat the index. The average performance, including a 1 percent assumed cost of trading, was a negative 16.7 percent, or an average underperformance of 2 percent. The best performer beat the index by 6.1 percent, while the worst performer underperformed by 15.4 percent. The average outperformance was just 2.5 percent, while the average underperformance was 5.1 percent. For the trailing twelve months, the S&P 500 Index lost 26.6

percent. Seven firms outperformed. The average return was a negative 30.7 percent. The average underperformance increased to 4.1 percent. The best performer beat the index by 11.9 percent, while the worst underperformed by 28.3 percent. The average outperformance was by just 6.6 percent, while the average underperformance was 13.3 percent. For the trailing five-year period, the S&P 500 returned 62.7 percent (or an annualized return of 10.2 percent). While data was only available for twelve of the fifteen firms, just two outperformed, and one just barely did so. The average return was 45.8 percent (or an annualized return of just 7.8 percent). The best performance beat the index by 22.4 percent, while the worst underperformed by almost 45 percent. The average outperformance was 12.3 percent, while the average underperformance was by 22.7 percent.

Market strategists are not alone in their misery—stock-picking professionals join them. Let's examine some of the evidence.

The Case Against Stock Pickers

I'd compare stock pickers to astrologers, but I don't want to bad-mouth astrologers. —Prof. Eugene F. Fama, *Fortune*

- Several decades ago, *Institutional Investor* magazine created an all-star team consisting of the "top" analysts in each industry. These analysts are chosen based on a poll of hundreds of institutional investors. Each year the magazine puts its all-star team on the cover of its publication. A while back, *Financial World* set out to measure the performance (hold them accountable) of these all-stars. They stated that it was not an easy task to get the brokerage houses to release the forecasts. We shall see why. After months of digging, the magazine managed to come up with the recommendations of twenty superstars. For the period in question, while the market rose 14.1 percent, following the recommendations of the all-stars would have provided a return of just 9.3 percent. And it is likely that there is survivorship bias in the data— the firms that wouldn't release their analysts' forecasts probably had even worse results. Surely they would have been happy to publish superior returns.[8]

- "The Worth Portfolio" stock selection that appeared in the September 2000 issue of *Worth* magazine likely reflects the collective opinions of some of the most intelligent minds on Wall Street, achieved the following returns:

Stock Name	July 21, 2000 Price* ($)	Feb. 14, 2003 Price* ($)	Total Return (%)
Applied Materials	39.06	12.40	−68
Broadcom Corp.	229.94	13.93	−94
Cisco Systems	68.12	13.68	−80
CMGI	41.75	0.78	−98
eBay	58.75	75.00	+28
Enron	73.00	0.05	−100
Millennium Pharm.	56.38	6.71	−88
News Corp.	52.46	25.85	−51
Nokia	53.38	13.95	−74
Oracle	37.72	11.70	−69
Charles Schwab & Co.	36.83	8.19	−78
Sun Microsystems	52.00	3.30	−94
Sycamore Networks	138.75	3.11	−98
WorldCom	45.13	0.14	−100

* Prices reflect end-of-day closing prices on July 21, 2000, as reported in *Worth,* and most current end-of-day closing prices at the time of writing. Prices have been adjusted for dividends and stock splits.

During this same period, the S&P 500 Index declined 41.2 percent. In absolute terms, this performance certainly does not look good. However, relative to the returns achieved by the above stock picks, they look much better. Outside of a 100 percent allocation to eBay, an investor who followed *Worth* magazine's stock recommendations did not fare well. An investment equally weighted in all fourteen of these stocks would have resulted in a decline of 76 percent.

• David Dreman and Michael Berry examined approximately 500,000 quarterly earnings forecasts from brokerage analysts for the period 1973–91. The average forecasting error was a whopping 44 percent. Also of note was that in recent years the average error got worse—in the last eight years of the study, the average error was 50 percent. When even small errors in forecasts can lead to huge losses, it seems that relying on forecasts of analysts is not a prescription for success.[9] Each year *Fortune* selects its all-star team of security analysts—the very best of the gurus. How did the year 2000's all-stars' stock recommendations made in July of that year perform? While the S&P 500 Index was falling 9 percent, their stock picks were falling 22 percent through the end of May 2001.[10]

- *Business Week* held a stock-picking contest in which they chose four top mutual fund managers to build a portfolio, each consisting of ten stock picks. The contest ran for the period December 8, 2000, through December 14, 2001. The contest winner was Buzz Zaino, manager of the Royce Opportunity Fund. His ten picks only lost 12.5 percent. The other contestants lost 25.5 percent, 27.2 percent, and 39.7 percent, respectively. So much for the skills of active managers as well as *Business Week*'s ability to preselect outperforming fund managers. As an interesting side note, while Zaino's hypothetical stock portfolio lost 12.5 percent, his real small-cap value Royce Opportunity Fund actually performed considerably better, returning 14.3 percent.[11] However, in comparison, the passively managed DFA Small Value Fund rose 22.7 percent (calendar year 2001). Thus the Royce fund significantly underperformed an appropriate benchmark.

- A study, "Can Investors Profit from the Prophets? Security Analyst Recommendations and Stock Returns," examined whether security analysts can correctly forecast which stocks will outperform the returns of their respective asset class, and if so, can investors benefit from their insights by exploiting the information?[12] The study used the Zacks database for the period 1985–96 and covered over 360,000 recommendations from 269 brokerage houses and 4,340 analysts. The study found that analysts did have stock-selection skills. Buying the stocks with the most favorable consensus recommendation earned an annualized return of almost 19 percent per annum, outperforming the market by over 4 percent per annum and the least favorable consensus stocks by 13 percent per annum. After controlling for market risk, size, BtM, and momentum factors, a portfolio of the most highly recommended stocks provided abnormal gross returns of just over 4 percent per annum. The least favorably recommended stocks provided abnormal gross returns of almost a negative 5 percent.

It is important to note that among the very largest companies the study found no reliable differences between the returns of the most highly rated stocks and those with the least favorable recommendations. All the "outperformance" occurred in the smallest stocks. So the news is mixed on the ability of security analysts to identify future under- and outperformers. It appears that they are successful with very small stocks and not successful at all regarding very large stocks. Unfortunately, the evidence is that investors *cannot exploit* the stock-selection skills that appear to be evident in small-cap stocks. The reason is that investors attempting to exploit the analysts' recommendations earn net, not gross, returns. Thus we must account for trading costs such as bid-offer spreads and commissions (mutual fund or other institutional investors would also incur market impact costs). The strategy of daily rebalancing based on changes of recommendations required turnover in excess of 400 percent per annum.

To estimate the cost of turnover, the study used the estimates of institutional trading costs provided by Donald Keim and Ananth Madhavan in their 1998 study, "The Cost of Institutional Equity Trades."[13] The estimated trading costs for a round-trip trade for large- (70 percent of stocks), medium- (20 percent of stocks), and small-cap stocks (10 percent of stocks) are 0.727 percent, 1.94 percent, and 4.12 percent, respectively. The weighted-average estimated trading costs for the portfolio for a round-trip trade was 1.31 percent. Given a 458 percent annual turnover rate, the abnormal return for the most highly recommended stock portfolio not only disappears, it turns negative. Even with the small-cap stocks, which produced the greatest abnormal return of almost 7 percent per annum, the trading costs resulted in negative net returns. With a turnover of 265 percent and estimated round-trip expenses in excess of 4 percent, turnover costs reduce returns almost 11 percent per annum, leading to net returns of about negative 4 percent.

The study found that strategies of reducing turnover still resulted in negative net returns. The authors investigated a large number of trading strategies and did not find any that produced positive net returns. The bottom line is that a strategy of exploiting the stock-selection skills of professional analysts required high-turnover rates. The cost of that high turnover is great enough to suggest that, while market inefficiencies may exist, they are not easily exploitable by investors. This conclusion can be drawn without even taking into account the considerable impact that taxes would have on such a high-turnover strategy in a taxable account. The market is efficient enough that active strategies are likely to produce losing results.

An appropriate conclusion for this section on stock-picker skills is the following quote from Lehman Brothers technology analyst Karl Keirstead. It is one you should keep in mind before you take any analyst's forecast seriously: "My peer group has enough trouble trying to predict the next six months. Trying to predict over the next five-year period is virtually anyone's guess. It is generally a meaningless, throwaway number for most analysts."[14]

Another Excuse Exposed as Myth

An often-heard excuse for the great persistence with which active managers fail to outperform their benchmarks is that the typical fund is "overdiversified." By owning so many stocks, the value of the manager's best ideas are diluted. The solution (or sales pitch) is to create "focus" funds: funds that own just the manager's top ten or twenty best ideas. By owning just the best ideas, concentrated funds should be able to easily trounce both the competition and an appropriate passive benchmark. Based on this premise, there are even funds that hire several submanagers for just their single best idea. Let's examine the evidence.

- In the September 2001 issue of their *FundInvestor* publication, Morningstar sought the answer to the question: Does a fund's largest holdings (which logically should reflect its best ideas) outperform the rest of its holdings? They compared the returns of a fund's top ten holdings with the overall returns of the portfolio. The study covered a five-year period. The result was about what believers in efficient markets would expect: Forty-eight percent of the funds produced higher returns from their top ten picks—about what randomness would suggest. On average, the top ten picks underperformed the return of the entire portfolio by sixteen basis points per annum. The top ten picks must have underperformed the "not best picks" by an even greater amount.

- *MONEY* magazine, with assistance from Chicago consulting firm Performance Analytics, reviewed the performance of twenty-two private account managers whose performance placed them in the top 20 percent of their peer group. Each firm provided their *single* best idea. For the period beginning in May 1996 and ending in mid-June 1998, the average return of the twenty remaining stocks from the twenty-two best picks was 61.6 percent, or a negative value added of 5.1 percent when compared to the return of 66.7 percent for the Wilshire 5000.[15]

- Zacks Investment Research studied the performance of the "best picks" of the analysts they cover. In 1998, while the S&P 500 rose 28 percent and the Russell 2000 (a small-cap benchmark) fell just 8.2 percent, the "best picks" fell 11.5 percent. In 1999, while the S&P 500 rose 21 percent and the Russell 2000 rose 7.6 percent, the "best picks" again fell, this time by 12 percent.[16]

- The October 7, 2001, issue of the *New York Times* examined the performance of some of the leading "best idea" funds. Here is what they found. In November 1999, Paine Webber (now UBS PaineWebber) rolled out its Strategy Fund, run by their global strategist Edward Kerschner. The idea was to own only the top forty to fifty stocks that met Kerschner's criteria for growth. Despite a 4.5 percent upfront load (or a back-end load of as much as 5 percent) and annual expenses of almost 2 percent, the brokerage firm's sales force pulled in over $2 billion—one of the most successful launches in fund history. The fund promptly lost 32 percent in 2000 (the S&P 500 Index fell just 9 percent). For the twelve months ending September 2001, the fund lost 49 percent, underperforming the benchmark Vanguard 500 Index Fund by 22 percent. From inception through September 2001, the fund underperformed the benchmark by almost 22 percent per annum. Apparently trying to bury the embarrassing performance, Paine Webber changed the fund's name to Brinson Strategy. Commenting on the fund's performance, Morningstar's Christopher Davis stated: "If we were trying to give investors a reason to ignore market pundits, we could use Brinson Strategy Fund as our example."

- The "focus" funds of such other leading investment firms as Morgan Stanley (Morgan Stanley Competitive Edge Best Ideas), Goldman Sachs (Goldman Sachs's Research Select), and MFS (MFS Research, the oldest "best ideas" fund) did not fare much better than did Paine Webber's. Morgan's fund lost 37 percent over the twelve months ending September 2001, underperforming its benchmark by 10 percent. From its inception through September 2001, the fund underperformed by almost 15 percent per annum. Goldman's fund lost 41 percent over the prior twelve months, underperforming its benchmark by 14 percent. From inception, the fund underperformed by over 8 percent per annum. The MFS fund lost 39 percent over the prior twelve months, underperforming its benchmark by 12 percent (no other data was available on this fund).[17]

- At the start of the year 2000, *USA Today* polled ten of Wall Street's top strategists for their absolute top picks. By early July, the average year-to-date return was a negative 22 percent. Of the fifty stocks recommended, forty-three were down for the year, eleven had fallen more than 50 percent, and four fell at least 75 percent.[18] Contrast this performance with the returns of such passive investment alternatives as the S&P 500, which had fallen less than 7 percent, and DFA's Micro Cap, Small Value, and Large Value Funds that had risen by 23 percent, 23 percent, and 9 percent, respectively. Obviously, if the strategists really had insights into the market they could have easily outperformed a market benchmark such as the S&P 500 by simply buying small-cap stocks, and small- and large-value stocks, or the index funds that represent those asset classes. As Gus Sauter of Vanguard stated: "Like everybody else in this industry I have an ego large enough to believe I'm going to be one of the *select few* that will outperform."[19] (emphasis mine)

- Researchers at the University of California and Stanford reviewed almost forty thousand stock recommendations from 213 brokerages during the year 2000. They found that the most highly rated stocks had a negative 31 percent return for the year. Amazingly, they also found that the least favorably recommended (the sell recommendations) actually *rose* an annualized 49 percent.[20]

The Case Against Investment Newsletters

- Mark Hulbert, publisher of *Hulbert's Financial Digest,* studied the performance of thirty-two of the portfolios of market-timing newsletters for the ten years ending in 1997.[21] During this period, the S&P 500 Index was up over 18 percent per annum. He found that the timers' annual average returns ranged from 5.84 percent to 16.9 percent, that the average return was 10.09 percent, and that *none of the market timers beat the market.*

- MoniResearch studied the performance of eighty-five market-timing managers with a total of $10 billion under management.[22] They found that the timers' annual average return ranged from 4.4 percent to 16.9 percent, that the average return was 11.04 percent, and that *none of the market timers beat the market.*

- Two researchers, from Duke University and the University of Utah, respectively, collaborated on a study examining the performance of the stock selections of 237 market-timing newsletters over the period June 1980–December 1992. An investor holding an equally weighted portfolio of all the newsletters would have earned an 11.3 percent rate of return. This compared to the rate of return of 15.8 percent earned by an S&P 500 Index fund. If the costs associated with the trading recommendations of these financial tout sheets were considered, the results would look even worse as transaction costs would have to be subtracted; the negative impact of the taxes generated by all of the trading activity would have to be considered; and, adding insult to injury, the cost of the newsletters themselves would have to be subtracted from returns. Perhaps most telling is that only 5.5 percent (13 of 237) of the newsletters survived the entire period. How would an investor, at the start of the period, have known which thirteen would survive?[23]

The Bottom Line

The next time you are watching CNBC or reading some financial publication and are tempted by the forecast of the latest guru, before acting on that temptation you would be well advised to remember the following words of wisdom. It is a summary of author Howard Kurtz's discussion with CNBC's Mark Haines: Anyone who invests based on CNBC's *Squawk Box* appearances is acting stupidly and will undoubtedly lose money. They are gambling pure and simple. It's like feeding coins into a slot machine. What is baffling is that anyone pays attention to these gurus. Of course CNBC makes them famous by putting them on the air and giving them credibility.[24]

On an amusing note, it seems that weather forecasters have wrongly borne the brunt of criticism on their inability to make accurate forecasts. In addition to studying the predictive ability of investment experts, William Sherden studied the performance of six other forecasting professions: meteorology, technology assessment, demography, futurology, organizational planning, and economics. He concluded that while none of the experts were very expert, the folks we most often make jokes about—weathermen—actually had the best predictive powers.[25]

Sherden offers the following advice to investors: "Avoid market timers, for they promise something they cannot deliver. Cancel your subscription to market-timing newsletters. Tell the investment advisers selling the latest market-timing scheme to buzz off. Ignore news media predictions, since they haven't a clue. Stop asking yourself, and everyone you know, What's the market going to do? It is an irrelevant question, because it cannot be answered."[26]

Investors should also listen carefully to the words of fund manager Ralph Wanger. Apparently, he agrees with Sherden.

For professional investors like myself, a sense of humor is essential. We are very aware that we are competing not only against the market averages but also against one another. It's an intense rivalry. We are each claiming that "The stocks in my fund today will perform better than what you own in your fund." That implies we think we can predict the future, which is the occupation of charlatans. If you believe you or anyone else has a system that can predict the future of the stock market, the joke is on you.[27]

Even *Fortune,* a publication that recommends when to buy and sell stocks and glorifies the latest guru, had this to say about the value of market forecasts: "Let's say it clearly: No one knows where the market is going—experts or novices, soothsayers or astrologers. That's the simple truth."[28]

Finally, here is advice from Jonathan Clements of the *Wall Street Journal:* "Read the opinions of the investment gurus who are quoted in the *Wall Street Journal*'s market-commentary stories. And as you read, laugh. We all know that the pundits can't predict short-term market movements. Yet there they are, desperately trying to sound intelligent when they really haven't got a clue."[29]

To summarize, unfortunately for investors who rely on the forecasts of market analysts and strategists, such forecasts are only likely to produce yachts for the forecasters themselves, not for their clients. Steve Forbes, publisher of the magazine that bears his name, obviously agrees, quoting his grandfather, who founded the magazine eighty years ago: "You make more money selling the advice than following it."[30] I agree with Peter Lynch's conclusion: "To the rash and impetuous stockpicker who chases hot tips and rushes in and out of his equities, an 'investment' in stocks is no more reliable than throwing away paychecks on the horse with the prettiest mane, or the jockey with the purple silks. [But] when you lose [at the racetrack, at least] you'll be able to say you had a great time doing it."[31] To conclude, here is a bit of forecasting wisdom from which you can actually benefit. Remember that there are only three types of market forecasters: those who don't know, those who don't know they don't know, and those who know they don't know but get paid a lot of money to pretend that they do.

TRUTH 11

◆

Taxes Are Often the
Largest Expense Investors Incur

The SEC requires mutual fund prospectuses to provide a great deal of information so that investors can make educated decisions. Among the information required is investment philosophy, expenses, and past performance. Unfortunately, information regarding the impact of taxes on returns did not become an SEC requirement until 2002 (although better late than never).

Whenever a fund realizes gains, it must distribute them to investors. Because dividend and realized capital-gains distributions are subject to state, local, and federal taxation, for taxable accounts after-tax returns are the only returns that matter. It is the greater turnover of actively managed funds that makes them tax inefficient relative to passively managed funds. I believe that most investors will be surprised to learn what several academic studies have all concluded: Taxes are the biggest expense most investors face—greater than management fees or commissions. These studies also conclude that mutual fund returns are far more dependent on the risks assumed (asset class allocation) and taxes than on the stock-selection or market-timing skills of the fund managers.

As you will see, there is an overwhelming body of evidence that the impact of taxes on returns is devastating—when the investment horizon is long enough (twenty-five to thirty years), taxes and the "black magic of decompounding" can reduce pretax returns by as much as 60 percent. The average turnover of actively managed funds is close to 100 percent per annum. Yet studies have found that in order to materially reduce the negative impact of taxes on returns, turnover must be reduced to 20 percent or less. Investors are suffering from a case of "taxation without representation." The reason this occurs is that there is a conflict of interest: In order for active managers to continue to collect their large fees, they need investors to continue to ignore the tax implications of active management. Listen to Ted Lux, an ex-stockbroker: "While I was at Morgan Stanley Dean Witter, I never once came across a broker talking to a client about the problems turnover creates with mutual fund investing. Nor capital gains tax. Nor the effect the tax has on lowering the investor's true rate of return. Simply put, the idea or notion of after-tax returns was shoved aside and under the rug."[1]

It is worth noting that in 2000 Vanguard announced that it would begin reporting mutual fund returns on both a pre- and after-tax basis. The SEC quickly followed suit and began requiring mutual funds to disclose after-tax returns as well as pretax returns. Perhaps with this disclosure requirement investors will begin to pay more attention to the critical issue of tax efficiency—the impact of taxes on returns.

Many investors learned an expensive capital-gains lesson in 2000 when mutual funds distributed a punishing $345 billion in capital gains, way up from 1999's $238 billion.[2] According to a study by Wiesenberger, a fund-tracking firm, the average equity fund had a taxable capital-gains distribution equivalent to 9.2 percent of its net asset value, up from 6.4 percent in 1999. Investors, however, appeared to continue to ignore the problem as, according to fund-flow tracking firm Strategic Insight, tax-managed funds had net inflows of only $4.4 billion in 2000, down from $9.6 billion in 1999 and $8.5 billion in 1998.[3]

After concluding this section, hopefully you will agree with the conclusion drawn by one study on the retail mutual fund industry: "The preponderance of evidence is so convincing we conclude that the typical approach of managing taxable portfolios as if they were tax-exempt is inherently irresponsible, even though doing so is the industry standard."[4]

Investor Focus

Despite the fact that investors in taxable accounts don't get to spend pretax returns, only after-tax returns, most investors focus on the pretax returns of their investments. Most investors are simply not aware of just how devastating an impact taxes can have on returns. One reason that investors don't focus on taxes is that they are subject to what is called mental accounting: The returns earned go into one pocket, but come April fifteenth, when their accountant hands them their tax bill based on IRS form 1099 distributions, they pay the bill from a different pocket, never tying the two together. Let's see just how large a role taxes play in determining after-tax returns.

The Devastating Impact of the Stealth Attack on Returns

Although the effect of paying taxes may be minimal in any one year, it becomes substantial over protracted periods. A study commissioned by Charles Schwab demonstrated how great an impact this stealth attack has on returns. Schwab measured the performance of sixty-two equity funds for the period 1963–92 and found that while each dollar invested would have grown to $21.89 in a tax-deferred account, a taxable account would have produced only $9.87 for a high-bracket investor. Taxes cut returns by 57.5 percent.[5] For high-tax-bracket investors, the study also found that for the ten-year period ending December 1992, Vanguard's S&P 500 Index Fund would have outperformed 92 percent of actively managed funds after taxes.[6]

A simulated study covering the twenty-five-year period ending in 1995 examined the effects of expenses and taxes on returns. This study assumed that a hypothetical fund (1) matched the performance of the S&P 500 Index (the average actively managed fund underperforms by almost 2 percent per annum); (2) had a turnover of 80 percent; and (3) incurred expenses of 1 percent (the average actively managed fund has expenses of about 1.5 percent). The study found that the typical investor received only 41 percent of the preexpense, pretax returns of the index. The federal government took 47 percent of the returns, even without considering state and local taxes or if the investor were subject to the highest tax brackets. The fund sponsor received 12 percent of the returns. This study also found that reducing expenses to just thirty basis points would have raised the investor's share of returns from 41 to 45 percent. The study also examined the effect of reducing the turnover rate to the same turnover as the S&P 500 Index. By reducing turnover to 3 percent, the share of returns realized would have increased to 64 percent, increasing investor returns by 56 percent.[7]

Let's look at several studies that cover shorter investment horizons. Robert Jeffrey and Robert Arnott demonstrated the impact of taxes on returns in their study of seventy-one actively managed funds for the ten-year period 1982–91. They found that while fifteen of the seventy-one funds beat a passively managed fund on a pretax basis, only five did so on an after-tax basis.[8]

Morningstar studied the five-year period 1992–96 and found that diversified U.S. stock funds gained an average of 91.9 percent. Morningstar then assumed that income and short-term gains were taxed at 39.6 percent and long-term capital gains at 28 percent—after-tax returns dwindled to 71.5 percent, a loss of 22 percent of the returns.[9] As you can see, even over short-investment horizons, taxes can destroy returns.

A study by the Schwab Center for Investment Research examined the historical tax efficiency of 576 large-cap actively managed funds and 44 large-cap index funds for the three-year period ending December 1997.[10] The study calculated the tax efficiency of each fund by dividing its pretax return by its after-tax return. The study assumed a ten-thousand-dollar investment and that the cash to pay the taxes was generated by selling shares. Tax rates of 39.6 percent for short-term gains and ordinary income and 28 percent for long-term gains were assumed. The center concluded:

- The average large-cap fund was approximately 86 percent tax efficient, losing 14 percent of its returns to taxes.
- The average large-cap index fund was approximately 94 percent tax efficient, losing only 6 percent of its returns to taxes.

It is important to note, especially for investors residing in high-tax areas, that state and local taxes were not considered.

The study also examined the amount of dollars that would have been lost to taxes over five-, ten-, and fifteen-year holding periods. The results are shown in the following table.

Dollars Lost to Taxes, Assuming a $10,000 Initial Investment and a 10 Percent Pretax Return		
Holding Period (years)	Actively Managed Funds	Index Funds
5	$ 999	$ 434
10	$3,118	$1,381
15	$7,302	$3,290

The Impact of Turnover on After-Tax Returns

A State Street Research study took a specific look at how turnover impacts after-tax performance.[11] They made the following assumptions:

- The investor makes a twenty-five-thousand-dollar investment for a thirty-year period.
- Both funds earn 10 percent pretax.
- The high-turnover fund had a turnover rate of 81 percent (typical of an actively managed fund) and the low-turnover one had a turnover rate of 8 percent (typical of a passively managed fund).
- Fifty percent of the distributions would be taxed as ordinary income at 39.6 percent and 50 percent taxed as long-term capital gains at 20 percent. State taxes were ignored.

- Taxes due were paid out of distribution proceeds and the remainder reinvested.
- All shares were sold at the end of thirty years.

The high-turnover fund turned the $25,000 original investment into $187,888. The low-turnover fund grew to $335,930. The benefit of low turnover produced almost 80 percent more after-tax dollars. Kennard "Pete" Woodworth, portfolio manager of the State Street Research Legacy Fund, concluded: "Taxable investors can no longer afford to overlook how taxes are affecting their investment performance."

The Odds Against Active Management Overcoming the Impact of Taxes

The study titled "How Well Have Taxable Investors Been Served in the 1980s and 1990s?" investigated:

- The pre- and after-tax efficiency of actively managed funds.
- The likelihood of pre- and after-tax outperformance.
- The relative size of outperformance vs. the relative size of underperformance.

The study included all funds with over $100 million in assets. Here is a summary of its findings:[12]

- For the ten-year period 1982–91, on a pretax basis, 21 percent of the funds outperformed their benchmark, Vanguard's

S&P 500 Index Fund. The average outperformance was 1.8 percent per annum. The average underperformance was a similar 1.9 percent. On an after-tax basis, however, only about 8 percent of the funds managed to beat their benchmark. The average outperformance was now just 0.9 percent, while the average underperformance increased to 3.1 percent. Keep this in mind: The ratio of about 3.5:1 (the 3.1 percent underperformance divided by the 0.9 percent outperformance) in favor of the underachievers is made all the more significant because there were about eleven times as many losers as winners. Thus we find that, not only are there far more losers than winners, but also the average size of the underperformance is far greater than the size of the outperformance. Therefore we need to look at the risk-adjusted odds of outperformance. We can calculate this by multiplying the odds of outperformance by the ratio of underperformance to outperformance. Doing so gives us risk-adjusted odds against outperformance of about *thirty-eight to one.*

- For the ten-year period 1989–98, on a pretax basis, just 14 percent of the funds outperformed, with the average outperformance being 1.9 percent. The average underperformance was 3.9 percent. On an after-tax basis, only 9 percent of the funds outperformed. The average outperformance was 1.8 percent. The average underperformance was 4.8 percent. The risk-adjusted odds against after-tax outperformance are about *twenty-eight to one.*

- For the full twenty-year period 1979–98, 22 percent of the funds beat their benchmark on a pretax basis. The average outperformance was 1.4 percent, with the average underperformance being 2.6 percent. On an after-tax basis, just 14 percent of the funds outperformed. The average after-tax outperformance was 1.3 percent, while the average after-tax underperformance was 3.2 percent. The risk-adjusted odds against outperformance are about *seventeen to one.*

- For the full twenty-year period 1979–98, the average fund underperformed its benchmark by 1.75 percent per annum before taxes and by 2.58 percent on an after-tax basis.

- For the entire time frame, only about 3 percent of active funds paid less capital-gains taxes than did their benchmark. Only about 10 percent of funds paid lower total taxes.

The story is actually worse than it appears, because the data above contains survivorship bias. For example, for the full twenty-year period, the average fund underperformed its benchmark by about 1.75 percent per annum on a pretax basis and by 2.58 percent on an after-tax basis. However, thirty-three funds disappeared during the time frame covered by the study. When we adjust for survivorship bias, the underperformance increases to 2.12 percent and 2.82 percent, respectively. Thus, the risk-adjusted odds of outperformance are even lower than the dismal figures previously presented. One more point on survivorship bias: Since the study only covered funds with more than $100 million in assets, it is likely that the survivorship bias is understated. Funds that have successful track records tend to attract assets. Funds with poor records tend to lose assets or are "put to death," never reaching the $100 million threshold of the study. So it seems logical to conclude that if the study covered all funds, instead of just those with assets over $100 million, the survivorship bias would have been even greater. We do know that far more than thirty-three funds disappeared during the period covered.

Individual investors are beginning to awaken to the important role that fund distributions play in after-tax performance. This has been one of the driving forces behind the rapid growth of index and other passively managed funds. Recently, many fund families, including DFA, Charles Schwab & Co., and the Vanguard Group, have taken this issue to the next level by creating passively managed funds that are also tax managed. These tax-managed funds strive both to minimize fund distributions and to maximize the percentage of distributions that will be in the form of long-term capital gains. They accomplish this by implementing the following strategies:

- Maintaining low turnover.
- Attempting to avoid realization of short-term gains.
- Harvesting losses by selling stocks that are below cost in order to offset gains in other securities.
- Selling the appreciated shares with the highest cost basis.
- Trading around dividend dates.

KPMG Peat Marwick studied the benefit that such a tax-managed fund might provide.[13] To understand the impact of taxes on returns, the firm examined the hypothetical performance of ten thousand dollars invested in two funds, one a tax-managed fund and the other an actively managed fund, both having pretax returns of 10 percent. The example assumed that short-term gains and ordinary income would be taxed at 39.6 percent and long-terms gains at 20 percent, and the funds would be liquidated after twenty years. The following table lists the study's other assumptions.

	Tax-Managed Fund (%)	Actively Managed Fund (%)
Income and short-term distributions	0.0	3.0
Long-term distributions	1.0	4.0
Price appreciation (unrealized gains)	9.0	3.0
Total annual returns	10.0	10.0

After twenty years, the tax-managed fund would grow to $54,792, or 25 percent greater than the $43,941 produced by the actively managed fund. The difference in after-tax returns was 8.9 percent versus 7.7 percent. Taxes cost the tax-managed fund 11 percent of its pretax returns, as compared to 23 percent for the actively managed fund. Another way to look at it is that the pretax return of the actively managed fund would have had to be 11.6 percent (or 16 percent greater) just to match the after-tax return of the tax-managed fund. Given that the average actively managed fund has underperformed its benchmark on a *pretax* basis by almost 2 percent per annum, the extra burden of taxes would seem to create an almost insurmountable hurdle.

KPMG took their study one step further. They considered what would happen if instead of liquidating the funds after twenty years, the investor either transfers them to his/her estate at death or gifts them to a charitable institution. In either case, the capital-gains taxes that were otherwise due on sale could now be avoided. In this case, the $10,000 would have grown to $64,870 in the tax-managed fund, 39 percent greater than the $46,690 produced by the actively managed fund. The after-tax returns were 9.8 percent and 8.0 percent, respectively. The actively managed fund would have had to generate almost 23 percent per annum greater pretax returns in order to match the after-tax returns of the tax-managed fund.

Using data from Morningstar, KPMG found that over a ten-year period the median actively managed fund lost 16 percent of its pretax returns to taxes on an annual basis, with some funds losing as much as 40 percent of their pretax returns to taxes. This result was not all that different from the hypothetical example they created.

The Really Dirty Secret

Before concluding, I would like to relate the following story. It is a highly unusual one, as you will see. Aronson + Partners is an actively managed institutional fund that, as the plus sign in its name suggests, uses a quantitative (mathematically based rules as opposed to subjective judgment) approach to stock selection. The main variables they use to select stocks are value driven: price-to-book, P/E, and price-to-sales ratios. They then use a factor for momentum (the tendency for a stock to continue to move in the same direction) and management (Is management buying its own stock?). Their strategy leads to an annual turnover of about 100–120 percent per annum.

In an interview with *Barron's,* Theodore Aronson made some very interesting statements:[14]

- "I never forget that the devil sitting on my shoulder [is the] low-cost passive funds. They win because they lose less."

- "None of my clients are taxable. Because, once you introduce taxes *active management probably has an insurmountable hurdle.* We have been asked to run taxable money—and declined. The costs of our active strategies are high enough without paying Uncle Sam."

- "Capital gains taxes, when combined with transactions costs and fees, *make indexing, profoundly advantaged,* I am sorry to say."

- "All of the partners are in the same situation—our retirement dough (tax deferred accounts) is here. But not our taxable investments."

- "If you crunch the numbers turnover has to come down, not low, but to super-low, like 15–20 percent, or taxes kill you. That's *the real dirty secret* in our business: *Mutual funds are bought with and sold with virtually no attention to tax efficiency.*"

- "My wife, 3 children and I have taxable money in 8 of the Vanguard index funds."

In an interview with Jason Zweig, a columnist for *MONEY,* Aronson was asked: "You're an active fund manager, and most of your money is in index funds?" He responded: "Personally, I think indexing wins hands-down. After tax, active management just can't win."[15] Investors can learn from Aronson, whose honesty is refreshing in an industry known for its focus on self-interest. Aronson could generate increased fees by just doing what his clients ask him to do—manage their taxable accounts. He refuses to do that because he doesn't believe that for taxable accounts he can outperform passive asset class funds of similar style. In other words, he is putting his clients' interests ahead of his own.

Conclusion

The impact of taxes on returns is so great that Joel Dickson, who wrote his doctoral dissertation on mutual fund taxes, made the following recommendation for individuals considering investment choices: "Taxes and expense ratios are probably the most important things, after a well-diversified portfolio."[16] Now listen carefully to the advice of Jonathan Clements, columnist for the *Wall Street Journal:* "If index funds look great before taxes, their performance is almost unbeatable after taxes, thanks to their low turnover and thus slow realization of capital gains."[17] In light of all of the evidence, a logical conclusion for investors is that for taxable accounts the already low probability of actively managed funds outperforming a passive alternative are dramatically reduced.

Ignoring the impact of taxes on the returns of taxable accounts is one of the biggest mistakes investors make. You can avoid this mistake if you keep the following points in mind:

- Because of the important impact of taxes on returns, passively managed funds that are also tax managed should be the investment vehicles of choice for taxable accounts.
- Exchange-traded funds are also appropriate vehicles as their structure enables them to be highly tax efficient.
- If you do choose to use actively managed funds, they are best held in a tax-deferred account, where their tax inefficiency won't impact after-tax returns.

TRUTH 12

◆

Knowledge of Financial History Is Critical to Successful Investing

In calm water every ship has a good captain.

—Swedish proverb

To paraphrase a famous line by Spanish-born U.S. philosopher George Santayana, those who cannot remember their financial history are condemned to repeat it. The history of financial markets is filled with instances when investors allowed the very human emotions of greed and envy to overcome all rational thought. Once prudent investors will abandon well thought-out investment strategies to chase the latest mania. Ignorance of financial history also leads to the loss of patience, resulting in the loss of discipline (and, too often, the loss of one's savings shortly thereafter). Even investors who believe that a buy-and-hold strategy is the one most likely to allow them to achieve their financial goals will find themselves selling assets that have performed poorly in the very recent past and buying the recent winners.

As I hope you will learn, there is really nothing substantially new in financial markets, only the history you don't know. By taking a brief tour of some episodes of financial folly, I hope to provide you with a road map that will allow you to avoid disastrous detours to interesting investment "opportunities." We will begin our tour with the most recent example of what Federal Reserve Board chairman Alan Greenspan called "irrational exuberance."

Irrational Exuberance

On December 5, 1996, Alan Greenspan, arguably the most influential man in terms of the capital markets, described the state of the U.S. stock market as "irrationally exuberant." His comment reflected what he felt was a market that had risen to an irrational level, one that could not be justified by fundamental economic conditions.

The DJIA (Dow Jones Industrial Average) had risen from around thirty-six hundred in early 1994 to around seven thousand when Greenspan made his famous remark. Ignoring his comment, the market continued to skyrocket, passing eleven thousand in early 2000. However, knowledgeable investors were noting that over the same period, while the market was tripling, U.S. personal income and GDP (gross domestic product) rose less than 30 percent and corporate earnings rose less than 60 percent. This degree of "disconnect" between the real economy and the financial markets had never been experienced—not even prior to the crashes of 1929 or 1987. P/E ratios far exceeded anything that existed before those famous crashes. What accounted for this irrational exuberance?

The Internet Bubble

The end of the last millennium saw financial markets witness some truly amazing phenomena. Among them were the astronomical and seemingly inexplicable rise of Internet stocks, the "birth" of day trading with thousands of otherwise normal individuals abandoning their chosen professions to speculate on minute-to-minute pricing of securities, and the push for extended trading hours. New technology, especially the Internet, provided the fuel for all of them. Were these new phenomena, or had we already "been there and done that"? We will address each of these issues, beginning with describing why investors should have easily been able to identify the Internet craze as a bubble.

The prices of Internet stocks, and technology stocks in general, rose to levels that could not be justified by any traditional valuation measure. In order to justify the unjustifiable, analysts were forced to come up with new metrics to "properly" value these stocks. Metrics such as the ratio of the number of Web-site page views-to-market capitalization were created—despite the fact that no one had yet figured out how to convert a page view into financial profits. By March 2000, the P/E ratio of the overall market had reached levels never before experienced. The NASDAQ P/E ratio was about 250. The only question seemed to be when, not if, the bubble would burst. The reason was that despite investors believing otherwise, there was nothing really new happening that could justify such valuations. Neither corporate earnings nor the GNP overall were growing at unprecedented rates. And despite all the talk about technology, productivity was growing no faster than it had in the 1920s.

Many long-time professionals and academics were crying out that investors should come to their senses before it was too late as this was just another in the long line of financial bubbles that would eventually burst. Investors might even have avoided the eventual collapse if they had just studied what returns had been after previous periods of similarly very high valuations in the twentieth century. The first, coincidentally, also occurred at the turn of a century. Prices had exploded as real earnings growth boomed. Corporate profits had doubled over the previous five years. The future was certainly optimistic, fueled by the dawning of a new era—a high-tech future. What actually occurred? By June 1920, the stock market had lost two-thirds of its real June 1901 value.

The second occurrence of high valuations occurred in 1929, when a spectacular bull market had sent P/E ratios far above previous peaks. By June 1932, the market had fallen over 80 percent in real terms. The real return for the full fifteen-year period ending in 1943 was 0.5 percent per annum.

The third instance occurred in the late 1960s. There was a group of stocks called the Nifty Fifty—roughly fifty large-cap growth stocks with P/E ratios of about fifty or more. They were mostly high-tech stocks like IBM, Sperry Rand, NCR, CDC (Control Data Corporation), Xerox, Honeywell, Polaroid, and so on. Like today's Ciscos, they were called one-decision-just buy-at-any-price-and-hold-forever stocks. Investors were led to believe that the price they paid simply didn't matter, and that companies would grow earnings fast enough to justify any valuation. However, reality set in and within two years many of them had fallen by 80 to 95 percent. By December 1974, real stock prices fell 56 percent and would not return to their January 1966 level until May 1992.[1] And not a single stock of that Nifty Fifty group that sold above a fifty P/E ratio was able to match the performance of the S&P 500 Index over the next twenty-five years.

What caused investors to get caught up in the seemingly obvious Internet bubble? Was it just ignorance of how securities are valued and the lessons a simple review of historical returns would have provided? Or are there other explanations?

Behavioral Explanations

Writing during the era of the most recent tech bubble, Robert J. Shiller, a behavioral economist, observed a number of behavioral and societal explanations for why investors ignore the warning signs of a bubble. His book, *Irrational Exuberance,* summarized them as follows:

1. The arrival of the Internet. Its pervasiveness gives a much greater impression of the impact of technology than anything ever experienced. The impression, however, is not aligned with the reality.

2. The triumph of American capitalism and the decline of foreign rivals. Merrill Lynch's "We're Bullish on America" sums it up.

3. Cultural changes favoring business success. Increased materialism fueling demand for stocks.

4. Change in political climate favoring business and investing. A Republican Congress and capital-gains tax cuts.

5. The baby boom and its perceived effect on the market. Demographics will lead to more savings, more investment in the market, more demand for health care, etc.

6. Dramatic expansion of media coverage on financial markets. This creates portfolio envy for those "missing the boat."

7. Overly optimistic analyst earnings forecast. In late 1999, 70 percent of stocks had buy recommendations, but only 1 percent had sell recommendations.

8. Expansion of deferred compensation plans, providing many more equity opportunities than were previously available to

the general public—creating *interest value* or *curiosity value* not based on rational decision making

9. The growth of mutual funds—and all the advertising that accompanies them. By 2000, the number of mutual funds was competing with the number of stocks!

10. The decline of inflation and the effects of money illusion. Stock indices are not inflation adjusted, giving the illusion of greater real returns.

11. Explosion of day traders, discount brokers, and twenty-four-hour trading—all making trading more accessible.

12. The rise in gambling opportunities, contributing to a speculative environment.

Shiller adds one more factor—what he calls a Ponzi scheme. The *scheme* begins like this. Investors witness stock prices rising rapidly over a sustained period. Buoyed by rising prices, investors become more confident, thereby enticing more money into the market, and the process repeats itself in a *feedback loop*. The investing public seems to have learned that the market only goes up, so they should buy on any declines since they will be temporary. (History, however, provides a very different lesson.) *Perceived* long-term risk is down. And since risk and reward are related, investor expectations of returns should also be down. However, despite the high-flying market, return expectations have not fallen.

Investors would be well served to never forget that stocks are nothing more than financial instruments whose value is based on future earnings, the rate on riskless instruments, and a discount for risk. Stock returns in the long run cannot defy the laws of mathematics. High prices must invariably lead to low returns. Shiller's book is a very worthy contribution to our understanding of financial markets and the impact human behavior can have on markets.

Let's now examine the illustrious history of financial bubbles. I hope you will be convinced that there really was nothing new in each of the "New Age" phenomena mentioned earlier: the "birth" of day trading, otherwise normal individuals abandoning their chosen professions to speculate on minute-to-minute pricing of securities, and the push for extended trading hours. You will see that the history of financial markets is filled with financial bubbles that eventually burst.

History's Lessons

The most famous bubble is the tulip bulb mania that occurred in Holland in the 1630s. "Tulip prices rose as much as 1,000 percent over a three-year period. At a time when the average annual wage was between two and four hundred guilders and a small house cost about three hundred guilders, tulip bulb prices reached as high as six thousand guilders for the most prized bulb."[2] Prices went up because they were going up as speculators bought on the assumption that there would always be a greater fool to buy at ever-higher prices. Unfortunately for some investors, the greater fool was staring at them in the mirror when prices suddenly collapsed and there were no buyers to be found at any price. It is worth noting that the fad of momentum investing is just another version of the greater fool theory—buy because the price has gone up. More recent examples of bubbles are the conglomerate craze of the 1960s, the biotech craze of the late 1980s, and the casino stock craze of the early 1990s. Inevitably, all of these bubbles eventually burst.

Let's turn to the birth of day trading. When the South Sea Company was formed in England in the early 1700s, another financial bubble appeared. The English company received a monopoly on the trade with the Spanish colonies of Latin America. When the king of England personally invested in the South Sea Company stock, the price of its shares bloomed in a manner strikingly similar to the rise of tulip bulb prices. Speculation ran rampant. A Dutch newspaper reported that the level of speculation soared to such a level that "trade has completely slowed down, that more than 100 ships moored along the river Thames are for sale, and that the *owners of capital prefer to speculate on shares than to return to work at their normal business.*"[3] Sir Isaac Newton was reported to have said: "I can calculate the motions of heavenly bodies, but not the madness of people."[4] In due course prices collapsed and everyone went back to business (at least those who still had businesses to go back to).

Let's now turn to the latest craze for extended trading, another new phenomenon—NOT. A combination of events led to a burst of speculative activity in the United States in the 1860s: the expansion of the rail system; the advent of the telegraph, which allowed information to travel at previously unimaginable speeds (sound familiar?); and the Civil War. The prices of gold and silver mining stocks rose and eventually crashed in true tulip bulb fashion. Speculation on the price of that new commodity, oil, was so rampant that the price of crude rose ninefold in just a few months, reaching a level in real terms that it has never again reached.[5] By 1864, trading had reached such a feverish peak that after-hours trading was moved from the Exchange to the basement of the Fifth Avenue Hotel, where it continued until nine o'clock in the evening.[6] The introduction of the "ticker" in 1867 further fueled the frenzy of speculation. It got so bad that ordinary clerks formed investment clubs to pool their limited resources. (The Beardstown Ladies had nothing on these folks.)[7]

Another new phenomenon related to the Internet craze is the trend toward bringing public only a very small offering. The idea is to create a scarcity value to the shares of newly public companies. The scarcity of shares is also intended to prevent short sellers from speculating in "overvalued" stock for fear that they might not be able to buy shares back. In the 1840s, British railway companies were being created with about as great a frequency as Internet companies were being created in 1999. Each offering was for only a very few shares, with the issuers retaining a large allocation for themselves. The stock would be hyped to speculators. When the stocks rose, on very thin trading of course, the promoters would sell their retained stock at a big profit, and, of course, the stocks would collapse.

Of Fashions and Markets

Henry Fielding, author of *The True Patriot,* observed: "Fashion is the great governor of this world; it presides not only in matters of dress and amusement, but in law, physic, politics, religion, and all other things of the gravest kind; indeed, the wisest of men would be puzzled to give any better reason why particular forms in all these have been at certain times universally received, and at other times universally rejected, than that they were in or out of fashion."[8] What does fashion have to do with the stock market? Unfortunately, it can play a large and often destructive role.

Investing, especially in speculative assets (such as tulip bulbs, technology stocks, biotech stocks, etc.), is often a social activity. Investors often spend much of their nonworking hours online, reading, discussing, or simply gossiping about their investments. Of course they discuss their successes with far greater frequency than they do their losses—contrary to the behavioral theory that misery loves company. How can fashion be destructive? Let's see.

Fashions, like the length of a skirt or the width of a tie, seem to come in and go out of favor for no apparent reason. Perfectly rational people can be influenced by nothing other than a herd mentality, a desire to be like others and part of the "action" or "scene." This is especially true of investing, where the potential for large financial rewards exists and can play on the human emotions of both greed and envy. Fluctuations in attitudes often spread widely without any apparent logic. Once-conservative investors start betting huge sums on investments about which they may know little or nothing, nor would have even previously considered. They forget simple principles such as risk and reward and diversification (not putting all your eggs in one basket). It is what I call the "Aunt Sally" syndrome: If Aunt Sally can make all that money owning Priceline, E-LOAN, and Amazon, why can't I? I am certainly at least as smart as she is.

While it doesn't happen that often, perhaps once every generation or so (just long enough for people to forget the last bubble and for a new generation of "suckers" to become of investment age), bubbles do seem to appear with regularity. The most recent technology, the dot.com bubble was not unique. In the 1960s, for example, instead of a dot.com bubble we had a "tronics" bubble. Any stock with *tronics* as a suffix soared to heights never even imagined.

Since fashions affect social behavior, is it illogical to believe that they impact investment behavior as well? What has been described as the "madness of crowds" simply takes over and a new "conventional wisdom" quickly forms. "Anyone taken as an individual is tolerably sensible and reasonable—as a member of a crowd, he at once becomes a blockhead."[9] And in mass, block-heads can play a major role in the stock market. They can create bubbles and, unfortunately, the devastating impact that results from the bursting of those bubbles.

For rational investors who are able to avoid the madness of crowds, there does not seem to be a way to systematically exploit the madness of crowds. The reason is that there is no way to predict just how irrational prices might get. For example, in hindsight Amazon may have looked irrationally priced at fifty, tempting rational investors to short the stock. Unfortunately, it became even more "irrationally" priced, reaching over one hundred. A "rational" investor shorting the stock at fifty certainly would have been proven correct in the long term, but he might also have been long dead—margin calls might have forced him to cover his position well before the "inevitable" collapse occurred.

There is one more important point we need to cover regarding bubbles. Their existence would seem to fly in the face of the EMH. However, there is no conflict. The mistake many individuals make is confusing the concepts of *efficient* and *rational.* Markets can be highly efficient while individuals are being irrational. The reason for this seeming anomaly is that in order for a market to be considered inefficient, it must be demonstrated that investors can systematically exploit any inefficiency. And as we have seen, there is no such evidence. One reason is that as John Maynard Keynes stated: "Markets can remain irrational longer than you can remain solvent." Burton Malkiel, professor of economics at Princeton University, put it this way: "We know in retrospect that stock prices tend to overreact and valuations revert to the mean. But it's never possible to know in advance when the reversion will occur."[10]

Investors Need a Very Long Investment Horizon

Before concluding this section, there is one more important topic we need to cover. Most investors are unaware that history is filled with very long periods when one particular asset class does very poorly. Those periods are the price we pay for the greater returns we expect when we invest in equities. If those periods did not exist, there would be very little risk involved in equity investing, and equities would not provide greater expected returns than riskless instruments. Long periods of underperformance sorely test the discipline of most investors—leading them to abandon their well thought-out strategies. While there are many examples that could be used to make this point, I hope that the following is the only one necessary to convince you that in order to avoid some serious investment mistakes you need to have a *very* long investment horizon. Unfortunately, the horizon needed is far longer than most investors would believe, let alone to be a horizon during which the vast majority of investors will have the discipline to stay the course.

It is my experience that despite what investors will tell you, their typical investment horizon is three years or less (and you will see data to support my experience). It seems that just a few short years is all investors have the patience and discipline for. Yet as you will see, even twenty-three-year periods are not always long enough.

Imagine the following scenario. The year is 1966 and you are trying to decide if you should invest in equities or in riskless bank CDs. Being a conservative investor, you are leaning to CDs. However, a friend shows you the history of financial returns. You note that for the period 1926–65, the S&P 500 has returned over 10 percent per annum. It also provided real returns of 9 percent per annum while outperforming riskless one-month Treasury bills by virtually the same amount. You decide that since you have a long investment horizon you can accept the risk of owning equities. But being conservative you decide to invest in the safest stocks, large-cap growth stocks. Fast forward to the end of 1974. You have just suffered two consecutive years of losses of 20 and 30 percent. And since your average return for the nine years is a negative fifty basis points per annum, you have less than you started out with. To make matters worse, since inflation averaged 5.6 percent per annum, each dollar you started out with is worth less than fifty-seven cents in real terms. Even more aggravating is that if you had invested in those safe one-month CDs, you would have earned 6.7 percent per annum and slept a lot better, too. Despite the terrible unexpected outcome, you decide to stay the course. After all, you knew that equities entailed risk, and it has "only" been nine years.

Flash forward now to 1984. You now have *nineteen* full years of evidence. Here is what you find. Large-cap growth stocks have returned less than 6 percent per annum, providing negative real returns as inflation averaged almost 7 percent per annum. And by the way, those riskless bank CDs returned over 8 percent per annum. Even after a full twenty-three years (1966–88) large-cap growth stocks would still have underperformed riskless one-month CDs by close to 1 percent per annum. How much patience do you have? How many investors would wait a full twenty-three years before deciding that their strategy was wrong?

Investors who decided that after twenty-three years "enough was enough" and abandoned their belief and the logic that large-cap growth stocks are likely (not certain) to provide higher returns than riskless instruments missed out on the greatest rally for large-cap growth stocks in history. For the period 1989–99, they returned over 20 percent per annum while one-month CDs returned just over 5 percent per annum. For the entire thirty-four-year period 1966–99, large-cap growth stocks outperformed one-month CDs by over 4 percent per annum. Investors who abandoned their strategy after twenty-three years were basically abandoning their belief that markets reward for risk. They would have suffered through a very long period with very poor returns and then missed out on the bull market that followed.

Unfortunately, the evidence is that investors abandon asset classes after periods of underperformance as short as one or two years. For example, for the period 1998–99, growth stocks, especially technology-related stocks, dramatically outperformed value stocks. While the S&P 500 (a large-cap growth-oriented index) returned almost 25 percent per annum, large-value stocks returned just over 8 percent per annum, and small-value stocks returned just 4 percent per annum. How did investors react?

In the first three quarters of 2000, there were over $60 billion of redemptions from value funds. On the other hand, over $160 billion poured into growth funds and over $40 billion poured into tech funds.[11] Of course, 2000 and 2001 witnessed an almost complete reversal with both value- and small-cap stocks dramatically outperforming large-cap growth stocks, and technology stocks in particular. Investors chasing recent events were ignoring the historical evidence that value stocks have provided greater returns over the long term. It is also worth noting that in 1999, with the NASDAQ soaring to record heights, there were net redemptions of $8 billion of bank small CDs. Small CDs are those with a face value of less than $100,000. Investors were redeeming their safe CD investments, presumably to invest in NASDAQ and other growth stocks.[12]

I hope you are now convinced that a very long horizon and the discipline to stay the course are key ingredients of the winning investment strategy.

Summary

Knowledge of financial history, an understanding of human behavior, and the discipline to avoid the temptation of following the crowd and the noise of the moment are all very important ingredients of a winning investment strategy. Unfortunately, because our education system has failed investors, most are ignorant of the lessons with which history provides us. This leaves them far too susceptible to the emotions of greed and envy. Investors would also be well served if they simply remember that the four most dangerous words in the English language are THIS TIME IT'S DIFFERENT.

It seems that it is very hard for human beings to stand still (even when we know it is in our best interests to do nothing) when all around them are taking action. Perhaps Warren Buffett said it best: "Inactivity strikes us as intelligent behavior."[13] The winning strategy is to ignore the latest investment fads. Students of investment history know that the best way to achieve their financial objectives is to build a globally diversified portfolio of index or passive asset class funds that reflect their unique risk tolerance, investment horizon, and financial goals and to have the discipline to stay the course. Remember, the goal of investing is not to achieve the highest return. Instead, it is to have the highest likelihood of achieving your objectives. Passive investing may not be as exciting as active investing, but the results are far more likely to be rewarding.

TRUTH 13

◆

Adding International Assets to a Portfolio Reduces Risk

Effective diversification depends not only on the number of assets in a trust portfolio but also on the ways and degrees in which their responses to economic events tend to reinforce, cancel or neutralize one another.
—The American Law Institute, 1992 Restatement
of the Prudent Investor Rule

When AT&T was broken up, shareholders were given shares in each of what were called "the Baby Bells." A study done a short while later found that the residents of each region held a disproportionate number of shares of their local regional Bell. Each group of regional investors was confident that their regional Baby Bell would outperform the others. How else can you explain each investor having most of his/her eggs in one baby basket? Another example of "familiarity breeding invest-ment" is a study observing that Georgia residents own 16 percent of all Coca-Cola stock, and people in Rochester tended to own stock in Kodak and Xerox.[1] This story is a good analogy for the way domestic investors view nondomestic assets.

It seems to be a global phenomenon that most investors hold the vast majority of their wealth in the form of domestic assets. Although the following data is a bit dated, not that much has changed. In 1990, the domestic ownership shares of the world's five leading stock markets were: United States 92 percent, Japan

96 percent, United Kingdom 92 percent, Germany 79 percent, and France 89 percent.[2] With the relative freedom of capital to travel around the world, the lack of global diversification cannot be explained by capital constraints. The only explanation is that investors in each country believe that their domestic market provides the best/safest investment opportunities. Investors in all five countries were taking the unnecessary risk of having almost all their eggs in their domestic basket, without any rational reason for doing so. It is simply a behavioral issue.

A 1991 study found that the expected real return to U.S. equities was 5.5 percent in the eyes of U.S. investors, but only 3.1 percent and 4.4 percent in the eyes of Japanese and British investors, respectively. Similarly, the expected return on Japanese equities was 6.6 percent in the eyes of Japanese investors, but only 3.2 percent and 3.8 percent in the eyes of U.S. and British investors, respectively.[3] Familiarity breeds overconfidence, or an illusion of safety, and lack of familiarity breeds a perception of high risk.

Many investors avoid adding international investments to their portfolios because they believe international investing is too risky. Is this perception accurate? A 1996 study found that portfolio allocations by U.S. investors to foreign and domestic securities are consistent with the belief by investors that the standard deviations of foreign securities are higher by a factor of 1.5 to 3.5 than the historical evidence suggests.[4] Behavioral finance explains this phenomenon in the following way: "The distinction between foreign stocks and domestic ones is an illustration of the distinction between risk, where probabilities are known, and uncertainty, where probabilities are not known. Familiarity with a security brings the situation closer to risk than to uncertainty. Uncertainty averse investors prefer familiar gambles over unfamiliar ones, even when the gambles have identical risk."[5] For example, a study found that people who identify themselves as being familiar with sports but not politics prefer to bet on sports events rather than on political events. This preference exists even when subjects judge the odds in sport bets as identical to the odds in political bets.[6]

To make clear the difference between risk and uncertainty consider the following. Risk is when the odds of an event occurring can be calculated. A good example is that we can calculate the odds of any set of numbers being thrown with a pair of dice. Uncertainty is when the odds of an event occurring cannot be calculated. They may not even be able to be estimated with any degree of confidence. Being more familiar with domestic equities than foreign equities, individuals think of an investment in domestic stocks in terms of *risk,* while they consider an investment in international stocks in terms of *uncertainty.* Since investors prefer situations where they believe they can calculate the odds with a high degree of confidence, they seek familiar risks and avoid unfamiliar ones. This distinction between risk and uncertainty is what leads many investors to avoid investing internationally.

Academics recommend that investors add international assets to their portfolios because they actually *reduce* risk. International equities do not move in perfect tandem with domestic equities. Therefore, the addition of international stocks to a portfolio should reduce the volatility (risk) of the *overall* portfolio.

A study published in the fall 1998 issue of the *Journal of Investing* sought to determine whether international equity diversification actually provided that theoretical risk-reduction benefit. The study covered the period 1970–96. David Laster of the Federal Reserve Bank of New York examined the performance of portfolios with varying allocations to the S&P 500 Index and the EAFE Index.[7] The study looked at portfolios with allocations of

10 percent S&P 500 and 90 percent EAFE, 20 percent S&P 500 and 80 percent EAFE, and so on. At the end of each year, each portfolio was rebalanced, correcting for market movements, to its original allocations. Using a statistical method called "bootstrapping" (creating a series of monthly returns using randomly selected subperiods from the entire period), the study was able to effectively examine far more five-year holding periods than its twenty-seven-year period contained. Before reviewing the results of the study, it is important to note that during this period the S&P 500 Index outperformed the EAFE Index by thirty basis points per annum. In addition, the correlation of returns between the two indices was 0.48, a very low figure. The study concluded:

- Any combination of the S&P 500 Index and the EAFE Index outperformed either index individually—a result of the low correlation.

- Increasing the international allocation to as much as 40 percent *increased* returns and *reduced* risk as measured by standard deviation (volatility).

- An allocation of 40 percent international produced the highest Sharpe Ratio—a measure of the amount of excess return (above the rate on riskless short-term U.S. Treasury bills) for a given level of risk (with risk being defined as the standard deviation of returns).

- Increasing the international allocation from 0 to just 20 percent reduced the likelihood of negative returns by one-third.

- Investors with a 10 percent international allocation could be 98 percent confident that they would reduce risk by raising the international allocation.

- Investors with an allocation as high as 22 percent could be 90 percent confident that they would reduce risk by raising their international allocation.

What is likely to surprise most investors is that adding international assets to a portfolio during a period when they underperformed actually resulted in higher returns and lower risk.

David Blitzer, S&P's chief investment strategist, provided further evidence on the wisdom of international diversification. Blitzer constructed a portfolio that was 60 percent U.S./40 percent international.[8] The international portion consisted of an equal 8 percent weighting of five major countries: France, Germany, Japan, Switzerland, and the United Kingdom. He used the MSCI (Morgan Stanley Capital International) country indices for his data and rebalanced the portfolios annually. The result of his study, which covered the period from January 1970 to February 2000, was that no single country produced a higher return than did the overall portfolio, and the standard deviation (measure of volatility) of the portfolio was below that of any single country. Thus, by diversifying, investors earned higher returns while experiencing lower volatility than they could have done by investing either in the United States alone or in any other country alone. Of course, to obtain that benefit an investor would have had to have the discipline to regularly rebalance to an equal weighting, selling some of the recent winners and buying more of the recent losers.

	Annualized Return (%)	Standard Deviation (%)
Portfolio	14.2	14.0
United States	13.1	15.3
France	13.8	23.0
Germany	13.4	20.5
Japan	14.2	22.9
United Kingdom	13.4	24.0
Switzerland	13.5	19.1

Another study, "Total Investment Returns to International Stock Portfolios 1925–1998," by Brian Taylor of Global Financial Data came to the same conclusions.[9] The country and regional weightings were based on their own design of a combination of market cap and GDP weightings.

Period	Europe (%)	U.S. (S&P 500) (%)	EAFE total (%)	Asia (%)	World (%)
1950–59	24.2	19.2	24.6	28.9	21.4
1960–69	6.4	8.9	7.6	14.0	7.7
1970–79	9.3	5.8	11.1	17.3	9.0
1980–89	17.6	17.6	22.0	27.8	20.3
1989–98	15.1	19.2	7.1	−5.9	11.4
1950–98	14.2	13.4	14.0	15.8	13.2
Standard Deviation (1925–98)	22.2	20.3	22.1	27.4	18.1

Note that over the long term returns around the world have been strikingly similar. The only decade with a significant difference in returns between the world and the U.S. market was the 1990s, with

U.S. markets outperforming the world markets by almost 8 percent per annum. Over the entire forty-nine years, however, there was virtually no difference in returns between the two. However, this should come as no surprise. Given the freedom of capital to travel most anywhere among the developed-country markets in search of the best returns, we should expect to see similar returns. If investors perceived one market to have greater prospects than another, that information would already be incorporated into market prices. The important question is: What, if any, implication does this similarity in returns have for investors making portfolio decisions?

The skeptics argue that if international diversification provided no higher returns, why take the "risk" of diversifying internationally? However, if the question is framed in a different manner, a different answer becomes obvious. Individuals are fully aware of the adage: "Don't put all your eggs in one basket." The investment equivalent is diversification. In order for diversification to be effective, however, you must own assets with nonperfect correlation—and the lower the correlation the better. Low-correlating assets serve to reduce the risk of the portfolio. As one can see in the above table, there may be long stretches when one asset class or region outperforms others. Diversification reduces the risk of holding only the losing asset class. It also reduces the risk of only owning an asset class that experiences a financial bubble (e.g., Japan in the late 1980s).

The half-empty argument is that if you don't get higher returns, why take the risk of international diversification? The half-full argument is:

- A United States–only investor did not receive any greater return over a very long period, yet he/she took the risk that the United States would provide lower returns. The risk went uncompensated.

211

- Given the efficiency of global markets, there is no logical reason to believe that U.S. investments should provide higher expected returns.

- If investors received no greater return, and have no logical reason to expect to receive greater returns, why put all your eggs in one basket?

Is the United States a Safer Place to Invest?

One of the most common arguments against international investing is that the regulatory environment created by the SEC makes the United States a safer place to invest. Even if you fully agree, before believing that you can benefit from this information you must ask yourself if you are the only one who knows it. Obviously the market is aware of this information, and security prices around the world surely reflect it. Here is something else to think about. Perhaps one of the contributing factors to the strong returns U.S. stocks have provided over the last fifty years is the improvement to U.S. capital markets that the SEC has made by its oversight. It seems logical to conclude that this improvement has contributed to the lowering of the perception investors have of the risks of equity investing in the United States. The result was a lowering of the risk premium investors demand. That resulted in a *one-time* capital gain and lower future expected returns (reflecting the now lower perceived risk). Now, applying that analysis to foreign stocks, you might draw the following conclusions: The market knows that foreign stocks are riskier because of their more lax regulatory environment. The market therefore prices for that risk, and you get higher expected returns as compensation. Let's now speculate on the following possible, if not likely, scenario.

The world has learned much about economic growth over the past fifty years as capitalism has triumphed. Countries need access to capital in order for their economies to grow. If a country does not have adequate disclosure laws, investors won't provide capital. Therefore, is it not logical to conclude that the rest of the world will be moving to replicate U.S. regulatory standards? In fact, many foreign companies are already adopting U.S. accounting standards, as they want access to the U.S. capital markets. As more international companies and foreign markets adopt U.S. regulatory standards, the risk premiums demanded for international stocks might fall as investors recognize the change and lower their required risk premium. Investors in international stocks would then realize a capital gain from the fall in the risk premium.

Let's assume that you believe that the United States is safer because the economic and/or political prospects are better (keeping in mind that investors in other countries also appear to believe that their own domestic market is safer). You should then conclude that the United States has lower expected returns. If you believe that U.S. companies have higher returns, then you must also believe that U.S. companies have higher costs of capital (the flip side of higher returns). This does not sound very logical, safer investments having higher costs of capital. It is illogical to believe that the United States is a safer place to invest while also believing that the United States will provide higher returns. Risk and expected reward should be related.

There are other arguments for including international asset classes in a portfolio. U.S. investors have all of their intellectual capital in the domestic market. Their ability to generate income from employment is tied to U.S. economic conditions. They also might own a home, which may constitute a large percentage of their assets. Owning international assets provides diversification from the risks these assets entail.

Currency Risk

A frequently heard reason for avoiding owning international equities is that they entail currency risk—the risk that foreign currencies will fall in value. It is true that this risk exists. However, currency risk is not a bad risk. It is a different type of risk than equity risk or small or value risk (which have expected risk premiums as compensation). Currency risk has no expected return and therefore has no risk premium. But the addition of currency risk reduces the volatility of the portfolio since you are adding a nonperfectly correlating asset. Thus you reduce volatility without reducing expected returns. Hence, it is a good thing to have currency risk, not a bad thing. But the more important issue is the following one: Most investors don't seem to understand that U.S. investors only investing in domestic companies are taking a very serious currency risk—it is just that they don't know it. The risk is that the dollar will fall in value, deteriorating their standard of living. A falling dollar will not only lead to rising import costs, but also to rising prices from domestic competitors who are no longer faced with competing with cheap imports. This can also lead to rising inflation overall. In fact, this is exactly what happened in the 1970s and early 1980s, and, of course, it can happen again. Owning international assets diversifies currency risk. Owning only U.S. stocks does not avoid currency risk—the risk is still there, only in a different form. If the dollar rises in value, it is likely that foreign equities will underperform. However, if the dollar falls in value, the cost of maintaining your lifestyle will rise. The difference is that in the first case (rising dollar) the risk shows up on your balance sheet. In the latter case (falling dollar) it doesn't. However, the risk is there nonetheless. The lack of visibility is one reason currency risk is misunderstood. I hope that you are now convinced that currency risk is a two-way street, and there is no free lunch.

An Insurance Policy

Allocating a significant portion of your portfolio to international asset classes will provide an insurance policy against potential problems in the United States. Since we don't have a clear crystal ball, diversification of risk is an important element of the winning strategy. If you need any more evidence of this, just think about Japanese investors in 1989. Like U.S. investors in 2000, they may have seen no reason to diversify internationally. Their economy was king. Their technology was dominating the world. Their managed-capitalism system was clearly superior to our more market-oriented system. And the Japanese stock market had far outperformed the United States and other global markets. As we ended 2002, the Nikkei Index was still down approximately 75 percent from its level of over thirteen years ago. (Those who do not learn from history are doomed to repeat the same mistakes.)

In evaluating the risks of international investing, it is worth considering these additional points. First, it is useful to remember that the United States was once an "emerging market." Many European investors lost fortunes in perfectly legitimate enterprises, such as canals, railways, toll roads, and so on. There were also many incidents of fraud and defaults on debt obligations. Is it not logical to assume that many European investors swore off investing in a nation populated by such swindlers? Of course, fortunes were also made by those who continued to invest in the United States. Second, many investors point out the political risks of investing overseas, including the risk of confiscation of property. While neither dismissing nor denying those risks, restricting investments to the United States does not eliminate that risk. How do you think investors in such companies as Philip Morris or Johns Manville (producer of asbestos-based insulation materials) felt about having their wealth effectively transferred by the U.S. court system to well-compensated attorneys and their plaintiffs? Is that not simply another form of expropriation?

Hopefully, you have been convinced of the logic of including in your equity portfolio a significant allocation to international stocks. The next question is: What is the best way to achieve international diversification? Is it through international large-cap stocks or small-cap stocks? And should emerging markets be one of the portfolio's building blocks? Or, can you gain all the international exposure you need by investing in U.S. multinational companies?

The Case Against Using U.S. Multinationals

Some investors argue that you don't need to add international stocks to effectively diversify. The logic is that you can gain all the international exposure you need by investing in U.S. large-cap stocks as they are mostly multinational companies with plenty of international exposure. The problem is that U.S. multinational stocks, while having exposure to foreign economies, trade mostly like U.S. stocks. They don't trade like foreign stocks. If they did, then the Fama-French three-factor model would not predict their returns. In addition to the exposure to equities and the size and value effect, a fourth factor would be needed. This, however, is not the case.

International Diversification: The Case for Small-Cap Stocks

Both the evidence and the logic suggest that while owning international large-cap stocks provides significant diversification benefits, international small-cap stocks make for better portfolio building blocks.

Let's look at some of the evidence. For the period 1975–2002, the monthly correlation of the EAFE Index to the S&P 500 Index was 0.5. This is far lower than the correlation of the S&P 500 to U.S. large-value stocks (0.9) and to U.S. micro-cap stocks (0.7). Since the lower the correlation the more effective the diversification, large-cap international stocks have proven to be excellent diversifiers. However, the correlation of international small-cap stocks to the S&P 500 was significantly lower—less than 0.4.[10] Thus we can conclude that international small-cap stocks have proven to be a more effective diversifier than international large-cap stocks.

The logic for the lower correlation is clear and simple. Many large companies are global giants, selling all over the world. Their earnings will clearly be impacted by global conditions. On the other hand, many smaller companies are more dependent on the condition of their local economies. As an example, the performance of two giant global pharmaceutical companies like Merck (a U.S. pharmaceutical company) and Roche (a Swiss pharmaceutical company) is likely to be more highly correlated than the performance of two small-cap domestic restaurant chains or drug store chains from two different countries.

Some investors may also be attracted to international small-cap stocks due to the small-cap premium. Small-cap companies are riskier and thus provide higher expected returns. For example, for the period 1975–2000, international small-cap stocks outperformed the large-cap EAFE Index by almost 4 percent per annum. It is also important to note that some of the incremental risk of owning international small-cap stocks is mitigated by the very low correlation between international small-cap stocks and U.S. equities in general.

One of the tenets of MPT is that by adding risky assets to a portfolio an investor can actually reduce the overall risk of the portfolio—as long as the assets are not perfectly correlated. And the lower the correlation, the greater the benefit in risk reduction. The data shows that international small-cap stocks have a low correlation with international large-cap stocks and also with both U.S. large-cap stocks and U.S. small-cap stocks. Therefore, in terms of building efficient portfolios, international small-cap stocks have offered better diversification for investors in U.S. large-cap stocks than either international large-cap stocks or U.S. small-cap stocks.

The Case for Emerging Markets

Before concluding this section, let's discuss the potential inclusion of emerging-market equities in a globally diversified portfolio. Many investors shy away from investing in emerging markets because of the perception of high risk. It is true that investing in emerging markets is risky when viewed in isolation, but considering adding them to a portfolio is worthwhile for two reasons: First, since markets are efficient at pricing for risk, the greater risk of investing in emerging markets should be accompanied by higher expected returns. Second, emerging markets are excellent diversifiers as they have low correlation with both the S&P 500 and the EAFE Indices. The following example will illustrate the point.

To see the impact of adding emerging markets to a portfolio, I assumed a 10 percent emerging-market allocation being added to an S&P 500 fund to create a 90 percent S&P 500/10 percent emerging-markets portfolio that would be rebalanced annually.

Annual Returns and Standard Deviation 1988–2002	
	Percent
Emerging Markets*	14.6/46
S&P 500	11.5/19
10% Emerging Markets/ 90% S&P 500 portfolio	12.3/19

*Emerging-markets returns represent the live DFA Emerging Markets Fund and simulated returns prior to its going live in April 1994.

Note the very similar standard deviation of the portfolio as compared to the S&P 500, despite the very high standard deviation of the emerging-markets asset class. Also note that with a 90/10 allocation, the weighted-average return of the asset classes (without rebalancing) was 11.8 percent. Despite emerging markets making up just 10 percent of the portfolio, rebalancing added

0.5 percent per annum to returns. This is due to the low correlation of returns between the two asset classes and the high volatility of returns of emerging markets.

Investing in international equities surely involves risk, but so does investing in domestic equities. And the evidence suggests that including international equities within a portfolio reduces the overall risks of the entire portfolio. The evidence also suggests that the most effective way to diversify internationally is to add the asset classes of international small-cap stocks and emerging markets. In conclusion, diversification is a form of insurance. And we only insure against bad things not good things. International diversification provides us with insurance in case the U.S. capital markets and the dollar perform poorly.

TRUTH 14

◆

There Is No One Right Portfolio, but There Is One That Is Right for You

If you don't know where you are going, you might end up somewhere else.
                                                              —Yogi Berra

U nfortunately for investors there is no such thing as the perfect portfolio, at least not the same perfect portfolio for all
investors. The allocation of a portfolio's assets is not only the
most important decision an investor will make (as it is the overwhelming determinant of risk and expected reward), it is also a
multidimensional one. The first decision is how much to allocate
between equities and fixed income. There is no right answer, just
a right answer for each individual given his or her own set of
unique circumstances. But this is only the beginning of the
decision-making process.

On the equity side alone, decisions must be made on allocating
between: domestic and international, value and growth, small and
large, and whether or not to invest in the asset classes of real
estate and emerging markets. On the fixed-income side, decisions
must be made as to maturity (long or short term), taxable or
municipal instruments, and whether or not to invest in inflation-
hedged securities such as TIPS and I bonds. Once again there is
no right answer, just the right answer for each individual.

Having made those decisions, we are still not finished.
Investors must decide which asset classes to allocate to their tax-

able accounts and which to allocate to tax-deferred accounts. There are even different answers for IRAs and 401(k)s (and other similar tax-deferred accounts such as 403(b)s) vs. Roth accounts, since no taxes are due on Roth account withdrawals, while for IRAs and 401(k)s the tax is only deferred until withdrawal.

Ability, Willingness, and Need to Take Risk

Let's begin our tour of the process by examining the issues that should be considered when making the equity to fixed-income decision. In order to make that decision an analysis should be done to determine the investor's ability, willingness, and need to take risk. An investor's ability to take risk is determined by two things: his/her investment horizon and the stability of his/her earned income. The longer the horizon, the greater the ability to wait out the almost inevitable bear markets. The greater the stability of earned income, the greater the ability to take the risks of equity ownership. For example, a tenured professor has a greater ability to take risk than either a worker in a highly cyclical industry where layoffs are common or an entrepreneur who owns his/her own business. The self-employed owner not only must be prepared to meet unexpected calls for capital from the business but also probably has much of his/her assets in an illiquid investment. The willingness to take risk measures the investor's risk tolerance, his/her ability to sleep well during bear markets and not panic and sell. An investor's need to take risk is determined by financial goals—what rate of return is required to achieve them. The following tables provide guidelines for each of these considerations.

THERE IS NO ONE RIGHT PORTFOLIO

Ability to Take Risk

Investment Horizon (Years)	Maximum Equity Allocation (%)
0–3	0
4	10
5	20
6	30
7	40
8	50
9	60
10	70
11–14	80
15–19	90
20 or longer	100

Willingness to Take Risk

Willingness Maximum Tolerable Loss (%)	Maximum Equity Exposure (%)
5	20
10	30
15	40
20	50
25	60
30	70
35	80
40	90
50	100

Need to Take Risk

Financial Goal (Rate of Return Required, %)	Equity Allocation (%)
2.0	0
3.0	20
4.5	40
6.0	60
7.5	80
9.0	100

The following should be noted regarding the above tables. This is not a science. The tables are, however, based on historical evidence and some judgment on my part. They should serve as good guidelines. More risk-tolerant investors might want to be more aggressive. However, I would not recommend straying too far from the above guidelines without a lot of thought going into the process. Also, note in the "Need to Take Risk" table the 2 percent goal for the 0 percent equity allocation should be adjusted to whatever the current rate is on one-month Treasury bills, and adjust all other figures accordingly. The table also assumes a broadly diversified by asset class portfolio, including significant exposures to the asset classes of small and value. A more market-like portfolio (like a portfolio that consisted solely of either an S&P 500 Index fund or a total stock market fund) would have somewhat lower expected returns. Also note that the expected return on equity investments is not constant. When market valuations are high (P/E ratios are high), expected returns are low, and vice versa. Thus some adjustment to the table (lower expected returns if valuations are higher than the historical average, and higher expected returns if valuations are lower than the historical average) may be needed based on current valuations.

In regard to the above tables, sometimes there are conflicts that must be resolved. For example, an investor might have a long investment horizon (giving him/her the ability to take risk) and the need to achieve high returns to meet his/her financial objectives, but a very low risk tolerance. This conflict must be resolved by determining which priority takes precedence (the "sleep well or eat well" decision). Once the equity-to-fixed-income decision is made, the investor can then move on to the decision on how much to allocate to the various equity asset classes. Once again, there is no right answer, just the right one for each person. There are, however, some general guidelines that apply to all investors. First, diversification is the prudent strategy. It is an issue of prudent risk management—not having all your eggs in one basket. Therefore, all investors should consider building a globally diversified portfolio across many asset classes. Our discussion on the various building blocks of a portfolio begins with the asset class of fixed income.

Fixed Income

Let's begin by discussing the role of fixed-income assets in a portfolio. Are fixed-income assets expected to generate income that is needed to meet living expenses? Or are fixed-income assets being used to reduce the risks of an equity portfolio? For the vast majority of investors (with the exception of retired individuals), the overriding motivation for including fixed-income assets is usually risk reduction. Assuming that current income is not the primary reason for holding fixed-income assets, we can determine the strategy that is most likely to produce the desired results. We begin with the following facts.

- Academic research has found that over long periods of time, while investors have been compensated for accepting the risk of owning longer maturity fixed-income assets, on average this relationship has broken down beyond two to three years. Therefore, if a fixed-income investor is seeking the highest expected return over a thirty-year period, he should buy a two- to three-year note and continually roll it over (instead of buying a thirty-year bond).[1]

Research on the relationship between risk and return has shown that:[2]

- Holding one-month short-term U.S. Treasury bills provides what is considered a risk-free rate of return (historically about 6.3 percent) and has a standard deviation of just over 1 percent per annum.

- Extending the maturity to one year increases returns above the risk-free rate by about 1 percent while increasing the standard deviation to about 2 percent.

- Extending the maturity to five years adds only another 0.4 percent (total premium above the risk-free rate of about 1.4 percent) to returns, yet the standard deviation increases by more than two-thirds to 6.3 percent. Extending the maturity to twenty years causes returns to *fall* 0.2 percent (total premium above the risk-free rate of about 1.2 percent), yet the standard deviation almost *doubles* again to 11.1 percent.

There is another reason not to hold long-term fixed-income instruments. As was stated earlier, the main reason for holding fixed-income assets is to provide a ballast to anchor your portfolio during bear markets. The more stable fixed-income part of your portfolio allows you to stay disciplined. Unfortunately, long-term bonds can have high correlation with the equity portion of your portfolio at just the wrong time. There may be times when interest rates rise, bond prices fall, and the stock market falls at the same time. Just when you need low correlation, you may get high correlation. The following are the correlations between government instruments of various maturities and the S&P 500 and EAFE Indicies.[3] Note that the lower the correlation, the more effective the diversification and the lower the overall risk of the portfolio. Note also the low correlation between short-term maturities and both U.S. and international equities.

Quarterly Correlation Data		
Maturity	Correlation with S&P 500 Index 1964–2001	Correlation with EAFE Index 1969–2001
One month	-0.08	-0.13
Six months	0.01	-0.04
One year	0.05	-0.01
Five years	0.22	0.17
Twenty years	0.30	0.22

As the above figures demonstrate, the risk of having high correlation between equities and fixed-income instruments can be avoided by buying short-term fixed-income instruments—they have essentially no correlation with equities.

With the preceding information, we can now determine the winning strategy for the fixed-income portion of our portfolio. For the vast majority of investors using fixed-income assets to reduce the risk of an equity portfolio, the winning strategy seems obvious: own only very short-term fixed-income assets. Here's why.

Since the main purpose of fixed-income assets is to reduce the volatility of the overall portfolio, investors should include fixed-income assets that have low volatility. Short-term fixed-income assets have both low volatility and low correlation with the equity portion of the portfolio. By limiting the maturity of the fixed-income portion of the portfolio to just one year, we get most of the yield benefit and accept only moderate risk (a standard deviation of only 2 percent). The benefit of lower volatility of the asset class itself combined with the benefit of the reduced volatility of the overall portfolio seems a small price to pay for giving up an extra thirty basis points in per annum returns that could be gained by extending the maturity of the fixed-income assets to five years. Remember, in a 60 percent equity/40 percent fixed-income portfolio, that extra thirty basis points (0.3 percent) becomes only a twelve basis point per annum (0.3% × 40%) added return on the overall portfolio.

We can further improve on this scenario by including international short-term fixed-income assets within the fixed-income allocation, as long as these assets are fully hedged against currency risk. The reason is that their inclusion should further reduce volatility, since not all international fixed-income markets fluctuate in the same direction at the same time and/or by the same amount. The lack of perfect correlation will reduce the overall volatility of the fixed-income portion of the portfolio.

Inflation-Protected Securities

We need to cover two other points related to fixed-income investing. The first is that with the recent introduction of inflation-protected securities, investors, particularly those for whom inflation is a great risk, now have other good fixed-income alternatives in the form of TIPS and I bonds. Both provide a guaranteed real rate of return plus an inflation adjustment. Both investments should be considered as appropriate fixed-income options. Note, however, that short-term fixed-income investments offer almost the same inflation protection. The reason is that their short maturity results in their yields adjusting rapidly to current rates (which rise in inflationary environments). The difference is that with TIPS and I bonds you are locking in, or guaranteeing, the real rate of return that will be earned. With short-term fixed-income instruments, the real rate will fluctuate with economic activity. The real rate will rise when economic activity is strong (as the demand for funds is strong) and will fall when it is weak.

There is also an important tax distinction between short-term instruments and inflation-protected instruments. Because taxes are due on the inflation adjustment of TIPS instruments, while the adjustment itself is not paid out until maturity, they are more appropriate for tax-deferred accounts; and I bonds, because no taxes are due until maturity, are more appropriate for taxable accounts.

Municipal Bonds

The other fixed-income area we need to address is the municipal bond market. Their tax-exempt status makes them the preferred candidate for taxable accounts. This is generally true for investors in all but the lowest tax bracket. It is important to note that because of two issues (the risk of the loss of tax exemption and credit risk), the municipal bond yield curve is generally steeper than the Treasury yield curve. For example, if a five-year municipal bond was trading at 80 percent of a Treasury note with the same maturity, a ten-year municipal bond might trade at 85 percent and a twenty-year municipal bond might trade at 90 percent. The result is that the risk/reward relationship for extending the maturity of an investment is better in the municipal bond market. Therefore, generally (depending on the shape of the municipal bond yield curve at the time the investment decision is made) it is appropriate to extend the maturity of municipal bonds to an average of about five to seven years (vs. the one to two years for taxable instruments). Also note that because of their tax exemption municipal bonds are generally less volatile than U.S. Treasury instruments of the same maturity.

We need to discuss a few other issues related to municipal bond investing. First, only invest in the highest investment grade, AA or better. Second, don't buy municipals from a retail broker unless they are a new issue—that is the only way you can be sure you are receiving a fair price. Brokers will sell bonds out of their firm's inventory, often with a large markup, thus hiding their "commission" in the price. Finally, another advantage of municipal bonds is that instead of having to hold taxable fixed-income in a tax-deferred account, an investor can free up room in that account (to hold a less tax-efficient asset class such as real estate) by instead holding their fixed-income allocation in a taxable account in the form of municipal bonds.

We can now turn to the issues related to equity investing. We begin by deciding on the appropriate allocation between domestic and international equities.

Diversification and Global Investing

Many people make the mistake of avoiding international investing because it is risky. As we discussed in truth 13, this is a mistake for many reasons, including considering the asset class of international equities in isolation and not how the addition of international assets can impact the overall risk of a portfolio. It is also important to remember that the most risk reduction comes from owning international assets that are not hedged against currency risk, as hedging will increase the correlation of returns between U.S. and international markets. This goes contrary to the strategy of owning low-correlating asset classes.

The bottom line is that it is prudent to consider allocating a significant exposure to international equities in a portfolio. A prudent allocation might range from a minimum of 20 percent to as high as 40 percent, or even 50 percent. Investors should also consider diversifying their international exposure across small and large companies, value and growth companies, and also emerging-market companies. How much to allocate to each asset class is, once again, a personal decision, depending on the investor's risk tolerance. Further guidance in making this decision will be provided as we now turn to the allocation decision on domestic equities.

Domestic Equities

Once again we begin with the prudent strategy being to not have all our eggs in one basket, no matter how large or diversified that basket might seem. Thus all investors should consider allocating at least some of their domestic equity exposure to each of the five major asset classes of large cap, small cap, large value, small value, and real estate. There are several issues we need to address in the decision-making process. Let's begin with what is called the issue of "tracking error."

While diversification across asset classes is the prudent strategy, once an investor diversifies across many asset classes, then his portfolio will no longer likely look like, and therefore will not perform like, "the market"—with "the market" being defined in most investors' minds by a popular index such as the S&P 500. This index, while reported by the press on a daily basis, is narrowly focused on the asset class of large-growth stocks. Thus the performance of a diversified portfolio will not "track" the performance of this popular index. In periods like 1998 and 1999, when large-cap growth stocks dominate the performance charts, investors in diversified portfolios might become subject to such emotions as performance envy and greed and thus become subject to losing the discipline to stick with their well thought-out strategy. Of course, the reverse will be true in years like 2000 and 2001, when value stocks and small-cap stocks are dominating the performance tables. Investors subject to tracking-error regret should consider building a portfolio that looks more like the market. Thus while they should still include some exposure to small and value stocks, they might want to tilt their portfolio (have a large allocation) to the large-cap asset class (an S&P 500 Index or a total stock market mutual/exchange-traded fund being good choices).

Value and Growth

Now let's turn to the issue of the allocation between value and growth. As we have discussed, value stocks are riskier investments, with higher *expected* returns as compensation for that risk. Among the common characteristics of value companies are both high leverage and high volatility of earnings—a very risky combination if both characteristics are present. Logically, the risks of value companies show up in recessions and deflationary periods. A perfect example of this is the period from 1929 through 1932. During this period, while the S&P 500 Index fell 22.7 percent per annum, risky large-value stocks fell 33.9 percent per annum. The even riskier small-value stocks fell 38.7 percent, underperforming the S&P 500 Index by almost 16 percent per annum for four years. It is important to point out that the risk of value stocks does not show up in all recessions. While value stocks underperformed growth stocks in the severe depression/deflation of 1930–31 (the value premium was negative 15 percent and negative 17 percent, respectively), the risk of value stocks did not appear in the recession of 1973–74. During this period, while the S&P 500 Index fell 20.8 percent per annum and small-value stocks fell 22.2 percent per annum, large-value stocks fell just 12.3 percent per annum. Why did the risk of large-value stocks not show up in this recession? The answer may be that the 1973–74 recession was an unusual one in that inflation actually rose during this period. The CPI (consumer price index) rose from 3.4 percent in 1972 to 8.8 percent in 1973. It rose again in 1974 to 12 percent. This leads us to the issue: Do value stocks provide greater protection against the risks of inflation than do growth stocks?

The Value Premium, Inflation, and Portfolio Risk

As you will see, while the relationship between inflation and the value premium is quite complex, there is evidence that value stocks provide greater returns than growth stocks in inflationary periods—and there is no reason to believe that this relationship should change. Therefore, this relationship should be an important consideration for investors when developing their asset-allocation plan.

As noted earlier, the average value stock is highly leveraged, and inflation reduces the real cost of debt. Thus, in general, it seems logical that value companies will benefit from rising inflation. The flip side is that deflation increases the real cost of debt, increasing the risk of value companies. Keep in mind that deflation is generally associated with severe recessions or depressions—when the economic-cycle risk of value companies would be expected to show up. Thus inflation/deflation risk and the economic-cycle risk are related and impact the value premium, as we shall see.

An important point to note is that the longer the maturity of the debt, the greater will be the impact of a changing inflation rate. While the credit rating of many value companies prevents them from issuing long-term debt, they are often effectively able to create long-term debt by locking in current interest rates through what is known as the swap market (swapping their floating-rate debt payments for the fixed-rate debt payments of higher rated companies, with a bank typically acting as the middleman). In addition, the junk bond market has historically consisted of the long-term debt (backed by pledged or secured assets) of value companies. (The tech bubble of the late 1990s allowed growth companies, with little to no hard assets to pledge as security, to issue junk debt.) The bottom line is that we would logically expect that the risk of value companies would decrease during inflationary periods and increase in deflationary periods. Unfortunately, the relationship is not that straightforward. In fact, the correlation between the value premium and inflation between 1964 and 2000 was effectively zero (0.05). The reason is that due to the economic-cycle risk of value stocks, the correlation of inflation to the value premium is nonlinear. Let's explore this issue.

It is very clear that the risk of value stocks shows up in deflationary times. There have been eight years since 1928 when inflation was negative. The value premium for those eight years averaged a *negative* 2.9 percent, more than 7 percent below its historical average. In only two of those years was the value premium positive. Nineteen fifty-four and 1932 are the two real exceptions as the value premium exceeded 18 and 23 percent, respectively, during years of deflation. However, in 1954 the inflation rate was barely negative at minus 0.5 percent.

Periods of low-to-moderate inflation are generally associated with good economic times. During such periods the economic-cycle risk associated with value stocks rarely shows up. Thus the value premium has been large and persistent during such periods. Also note that higher rates of inflation are *generally* associated with a higher value premium. For example, for the period 1928–2002, in years when inflation averaged less than 3 percent, the value premium was just 2.8 percent. However, when inflation was greater than 3 percent, the value premium averaged 5.8 percent. When we raise the breakpoint to 4 percent, the value premium is 3.0 percent when it is below the breakpoint and 7.3 percent when it is above. A good illustration of this is the period from 1968 through 1981. In 1968, inflation crossed the 4 percent level for the first time since 1951. It rose to over 13 percent in 1979 and stayed at a very high level until 1982. (In late 1981 the Federal Reserve finally tightened monetary policy sufficiently to break the back of inflation.) This is the only period of sustained high inflation in the United States in the twentieth century. During this period the value premium was 6.5 percent, a 50 percent greater premium than the long-term historical average of about 4.3 percent.

However, it is important to note that high inflation carries with it significant economic risks. A high rate of inflation has historically led the Federal Reserve to eventually tighten monetary policy. While tight monetary policy will cure inflation, it will also depress economic activity as it raises the real cost of money. This will raise the economic-cycle risk for value stocks. If we have high inflation with no monetary tightening, we would expect the value premium to generally be high. However, at some point the Federal Reserve will likely tighten monetary policy and the value premium will not only shrink, but it is highly likely to turn negative (depending on the degree of tightening). For example, in late 1979 the Federal Reserve altered monetary policy to place greater emphasis on combating inflation, driving short-term interest rates above 20 percent. Thus despite still very high inflation rates (monetary policy works with a lag), the value premium turned sharply negative as the economic-cycle risk increased.

The relationship between the value premium and inflation is complex because there are also other factors at work (inflation is clearly not the only factor impacting the size or existence of the value premium). Whenever there are shocks to the economic system that lead to a "flight to quality," investors tend to: flee lower quality debt instruments for the safety of U.S. government debt, flee equities for the safety of fixed-income instruments, and flee value stocks for the safety of growth stocks. Thus in periods of crisis, particularly if the crisis increases the risks to the banking (credit) system, the value premium will not only disappear, but it will likely turn sharply negative. Three good examples of this are:

- In the period 1990–91, the United States experienced a crisis focused on the S&L and banking industries. Since value stocks are highly dependent on credit, they are more vulnerable to being cut off from liquidity sources. During these two years the value premium was minus 12.4 percent and minus 11.0 percent, respectively.

- In 1998, the "Asian Contagion" threatened to spread around the world. In 1998 and 1999, the value premium was negative 15.3 percent and negative 30.1 percent, respectively.

- In the immediate aftermath of the events of September 11, 2001, growth stocks outperformed value stocks. Once it appeared that this crisis would likely be contained from a military standpoint, and the Federal Reserve acted quickly to provide liquidity and lessen the risk of recession by lowering rates, value stocks quickly recovered.

It is important to note that there is bias in the data on inflation and the value premium. We do know with hindsight that the Federal Reserve has eventually always tightened when high inflation threatened the economy. However, there is no guarantee that they will do so in the future. And the longer they delay their action, the greater the value premium is likely to be (as inflation reduces the real cost of debt for value companies).

As you can see, there are many factors that influence the size of the realized value premium, including, but not limited to, economic-cycle risk, inflation, and crises that lead to a flight to quality. *None of these have proven to be forecastable.* Thus it is not likely that an investor will be able to alter asset allocations in a way that will generate persistently greater returns. If these events were forecastable, active managers would anticipate them and benefit from shifting allocations. We have no evidence of any such skill. However, we can make more prudent investment decisions regarding asset allocation if we understand the nature of the correlation of value stocks and economic-cycle and inflation risk.

First, since the value premium is highly correlated with economic-cycle risk, investors whose earned income is also highly correlated with economic-cycle risk (likely to see their earned income fall, or disappear entirely, in a recession) should consider limiting their exposure to the value factor. They should also consider limiting their exposure to equities in general. For example, government employees and those working in the field of health care generally have a low correlation of their earnings to the economic cycle. Thus the risks of value stocks have low correlation to their intellectual assets. They are unlikely to face a job layoff or reduced income at a time when their value stocks are doing poorly and might have to be sold (at the worst possible time). Thus they have a greater ability to accept the risks of value companies. On the other hand, someone whose business or employment prospects are highly correlated to the economic cycle or whose business is highly leveraged (i.e., an owner of a construction company or a UAW [United Auto Worker] member) should consider limiting his/her exposure to value stocks.

Second, investors who have greater exposure to the risk of inflation negatively impacting their lifestyle should consider tilting their equity portfolios more to value stocks, as there is evidence that they provide greater inflation protection than do growth stocks. For example, retired investors typically have greater exposure to inflation risk, as they no longer have earned income that could be expected to increase along with inflation. In addition, they no longer have any correlation of economic-cycle risk to their earned income. For these two reasons, therefore, retirees might consider having a greater value tilt to their equity holdings.

Third, investors for whom the risk of not achieving their financial objectives outweighs the risks of value companies (they are willing to accept the risk of value stocks to earn the higher *expected* returns) may find it necessary to tilt their portfolio allocation toward value stocks.

If you are going to hold a high allocation to value stocks, you should also consider holding longer-term fixed-income instruments. The recession/deflation/flight to quality risks of value stocks have negative correlation with the risks of longer-term fixed-income instruments (which generally perform well in these types of environments). And since the evidence suggests that value stocks provide greater returns than growth stocks during inflationary periods, they offer greater protection than growth stocks against the inflation risk inherent in longer term bonds. Thus holding a value tilt not only provides greater expected returns on your equity holdings, but it also allows you to take more interest-rate risk and thus potentially earn greater returns on your fixed-income investments. Diversification of risk through the ownership of low-correlated assets is the only free lunch in investing.

Large Caps and Small Caps

Small-cap companies are riskier than large-cap companies. As with value stocks, their risks tend to show up in recession and deflationary periods. Therefore, the same issues related to value stocks (with the exception of the inflation-risk question) are applicable to the small-cap vs. large-cap allocation question.

The Role of Mid Caps

Almost inevitably, whenever I show model or sample portfolios to new or potential clients, I am asked, Why do you recommend investing in small caps and large caps, but not mid caps? Before explaining why they are not needed as part of a diversified port-folio, it is important to note that there is nothing wrong with mid caps. Like other asset classes, they provide the appropriate expected returns for the risk taken. The reason that you do not have to include them is that a "barbell" approach (owning the ends and not the middle) is more effective. Let's explain why.

1. Large caps are less risky than small caps and thus logically have lower expected returns. This is exactly what the historical record shows—the smaller the market capitalization, the higher the returns. Thus mid caps should provide returns midway between large caps and small caps. Looking at the historical record, we find that even over relatively short-investment horizons, mid caps have provided returns between small caps and large caps. For periods even as short as three years (and if your horizon is less than three years then you probably should not be investing in stocks) this relationship holds true. There are twenty-four three-year periods from 1929 to 2000. If we define large caps as deciles one to three, mid caps as four to seven, and small caps as eight to ten, we find that during this timeframe:

   • Large caps were the best performer twelve times and the worst performer nine times.

   • Small caps were the best performer twelve times and the worst performer thirteen times.

   • Mid caps were the best performer just once and were the worst performer just twice.

2. When large caps are the best performer, the very largest tends to do the best and the very smallest tends to have the worst returns, and vice versa. If you are going to own large caps as part of your portfolio, the most effective diversifier is the very smallest.

3. When constructing a portfolio, we want to add low-correlating asset classes to reduce portfolio volatility. Most

investors begin with using large caps as the core portion of the portfolio around which they design their asset allocation. Thus we seek to add low-correlating asset classes to the large-cap core. With the first decile being the largest cap stocks, here are the correlations to the S&P 500 Index since 1929 from the first to the tenth decile: 0.999 (the almost perfect correlation shows that the S&P 500 performs as if it is a first-decile fund): 0.962, 0.924, 0.905, 0.905, 0.882, 0.879, 0.837, 0.813, 0.728. Note the almost perfect straight line down. While mid caps offer some diversification benefit to large caps, small caps and micro caps offer more effective diversification.

4. Mid caps, because of their high turnover (some grow to be large caps and some shrink to become small caps), are not a very tax-efficient asset class, even for passively managed funds. This is a real problem for taxable investors. In addition, there are no tax-managed passive mid-cap funds that would improve tax efficiency (though there are mid-cap ETFs).

5. Adding mid caps to large caps and small caps can increase the transactions costs of the portfolio, both at inception and when rebalancing, and for taxable accounts will likely decrease the tax efficiency when rebalancing.

The bottom line is that you can build a portfolio using just small caps and large caps with the same expected risk and returns as one that includes mid caps. However, the addition of mid caps will likely lead to greater transactions costs and for taxable accounts less tax efficiency. Thus I conclude that mid caps are not a necessary building block of a well-diversified portfolio.

Real Estate

The final domestic equity asset class to consider is real estate. When testing their three-factor model, Professors Kenneth R. French and Eugene F. Fama found that their model, while explaining almost all of the returns of equity portfolios, did not explain the returns of the real estate sector. Thus real estate must have risks that are not explained by exposures to the risk factors of size and value. Therefore, they concluded that real estate should be considered as a separate asset class. Real estate has low correlation to the other domestic equity allocations. Because of its nature as a "hard asset" and its typically high leverage, real estate has tended to perform well in inflationary environments. Real estate is also highly tied to the economic cycle. It is also highly dependent on access to the banking system and capital markets. Thus the same types of investors who should consider tilting toward value stocks should consider tilting toward real estate.

The Location Decision

Let's now turn to the final asset allocation issue, the location of the asset class in either the taxable or tax-deferred/nontaxable account. The issue is relatively straightforward. The easiest account to deal with is a Roth account. Withdrawals from such an account are tax exempt. Therefore, we should generally place within that account the asset class with the highest expected return—small value. If no small value is being held, then, in order, the choices should be: large value, emerging markets, real estate, small cap, and finally large cap.

In taxable accounts we want to place the most tax-efficient equity asset classes. This is basically a large-cap fund (like an S&P 500 Index fund), a total stock market fund, or any tax-managed fund. The least tax-efficient asset classes (value, real estate, small cap, and taxable fixed income) should be placed in tax-deferred accounts. If there is not any room inside of a tax-deferred account, and there is no tax-managed alternative available, then an exchange-traded fund can be used to gain exposure to the desired asset class (due to their operating structure, exchange-traded funds are highly likely to prove more tax efficient than their nontax-managed mutual fund counterparts).

One other point on asset location. Foreign stock holdings often entail taxes being withheld at the source. Investors can then claim a foreign tax credit that can then be used as a credit against U.S. taxes due on a distribution. However, this credit does no good if the asset is not in a taxable account. Thus if there is a choice between holding similar U.S. and international asset classes in a taxable or tax-deferred account, the international asset should be held in the taxable account. While not a major issue (the impact is likely to be less than fifty basis points per annum), every penny saved is a penny earned.

Suggested Starting Point

While diversification is the prudent strategy, there is not a set portfolio that is the correct one for every individual. Having said that, the following "coward's portfolio" is offered as a starting point from which to begin considering the appropriate asset allocation for your portfolio. The portfolio addresses only the equity side of the balance sheet. It is called the coward's portfolio because it weights equally each esset class, placing no "bet" on any one class.

One of the major reasons I suggest broad asset class diversification is that any one asset class might perform very poorly over a very long time, possibly over even an investor's entire investment horizon. That is the nature of risk. For example, as we discussed before, for the twenty-three-year period 1966–88, the asset class of large-cap growth stocks returned just 7.7 percent, underperforming even riskless one-month bank certificates of deposit by 0.6 percent per annum. However, over this same period, small-value stocks returned 17.3 percent, outperforming large-cap growth stocks by 9.6 percent per annum for twenty-three years. Of course, there are periods when large-cap growth stocks outperformed all other asset classes by wide margins (as in 1998 and 1999).

The point of broad asset class diversification is to not take the risk of having all your eggs in the wrong basket for a very long time. Most investors do not understand that the total stock market is dominated by the asset class of large-cap growth stocks. For example, as we entered the new millennium, large-cap growth stocks made up almost 70 percent of the total market's capitalization. That is a lot of eggs in just one basket. Again, it is important to remember that the coward's portfolio should not be taken as a recommendation but just as a starting point. (See table on next page.) (See appendix C for recommendations on specific investment vehicles.)

Before concluding this section, I want to add some words of caution on the subject of the "perfect portfolio." In the pursuit of the perfect portfolio, investment advisors have begun to tout the

Asset Class	Minimum Allocation (%)	Target Allocation (%)	Maximum Allocation (%)
U.S. large	10.5	14	17.5
U.S. large value	10.5	14	17.5
U.S. small	10.5	14	17.5
U.S. small value	10.5	14	17.5
Real Estate	10.5	14	17.5
Total U.S.	**65**	**70**	**75**
International large value	5.625	7.5	9.375
International small	5.625	7.5	9.375
International small value	5.625	7.5	9.375
Emerging markets	5.625	7.5	9.375
Total International	**25**	**30**	**35**

use of what are known as either efficient frontier models or portfolio optimizers. While they can be good tools in the hands of the right person, they can also be very dangerous because, as you will see, they treat investing as if it was an exact science—and it is not. Unfortunately, most investors, and even many advisors, do not understand the nature of this problem. I hope the following will make the dangers clear.

Efficient Frontier Models

NASCAR racing machines are very sophisticated, complex automobiles. In the hands of a Richard Petty, they are capable of great feats. The same machine, however, in the hands of a drunk driver is a very dangerous vehicle. The financial equivalent of racing cars is an efficient frontier model.

Harry Markowitz first coined the term "efficient frontier" almost forty years ago. He used it to describe a portfolio that was most likely to deliver the greatest return for a given level of risk. Today, there are many efficient frontier programs available. They begin by having an individual investor answer questions about his/her risk profile. The program will then generate a portfolio consisting of various asset classes that will deliver the greatest expected return given the individual's risk tolerance. Sounds like a wonderful idea. So what's the problem? The problem is understanding the nature of an efficient frontier model and the assumptions on which it relies.

Efficient frontier models, in effect, attempt to turn investing into a science, which it is not. For example, it is very logical to believe that in the future stocks will outperform fixed-income investments. The reason is that stocks are riskier than risk-free Treasury bills. Investors will demand an "equity risk premium" to compensate them for this risk. While the past may be a guide to the size of the "equity risk premium," it is not, however, a guarantee. For example, if we look at the period 1926–90, the equity risk premium for the S&P 500 was 6.4 percent. Once we include the bull market of the 1990s, the risk premium jumps over 1 percent to about 7.6 percent. As you can see, the equity risk premium is not constant. We shall see why even this seemingly small change is very important when it comes to efficient frontier models.

Efficient frontier models rely on historical data and relation-ships to generate the "perfect" portfolio. Expected returns, corre-lations, and standard deviations (measure of volatility) must be provided for each asset class, or building block, that could be used in a portfolio. Let us begin with a simple portfolio that can potentially invest in just five asset classes: S&P 500 (U.S. large cap), U.S. small cap, one-year fixed income, EAFE (international large cap), and international small cap. The table shows our assumptions regarding historical data for returns, correlations, and standard deviations. Using standard deviation as the measure of risk, let us also assume that we have designated a 12 percent standard deviation as the level of portfolio risk we are willing to accept. An efficient frontier model will then generate the "cor-rect" asset allocations.

Correlations (R)

	S&P 500	U.S. small	One-Year fixed income	EAFE Index	Int'l small
S&P 500 Index	1.0				
U.S. small	0.8	1.0			
One-year fixed in-come	0.0	0.0	1.0		
EAFE Index	0.6	0.4	0.0	1.0	
Int'l small	0.4	0.4*	0.0	0.8	1.0

Expected return (%)	12*	14	6	12	14
Standard deviation (%)	20	30	4	20*	30

The following is the recommended allocation generated by our efficient frontier model.

Case I	Percent (%)
S&P 500 Index	22
U.S. small	9
One-year fixed income	38
EAFE Index	22
International small	9

We will now make a series of minor changes to expected returns, standard deviations, and correlations in order to see how sensitive the efficient frontier models are to assumptions. Each change, indicated by an asterisk in the preceding table, will be a minor one from our original base case. In case two, we reduced the expected return of the S&P 500 from 12 percent (its return from 1934 to 1996) to 11 percent (its return from 1926 to 1996). In case three, we increased the standard deviation of the EAFE Index from 20 to 22 percent. In case four, we reduced the correlation between U.S. small caps and international small caps from 0.4 to 0.2. In each case, the efficient frontier model generated a dramatically different asset allocation, in some cases entirely eliminating an asset class from the portfolio. This implies a precision that just does not exist in the field of financial economics.

	Case 1 (%)	Case 2 (%)	Case 3 (%)	Case 4 (%)
S&P 500 Index	22	0	36	15
U.S. small	9	20	4	15
One-year fixed income	38	40	40	40
EAFE Index	22	36	0	15
International small	9	4	20	15

Investing is not a science. It is foolish to pretend that we know in advance the exact levels for returns, correlations, and standard deviations. Yet that is the underlying assumption of any efficient frontier model. Experienced practitioners know that in order to come up with something intelligent, they need to impose constraints on efficient frontier models. Examples of constraints might be that no asset class can either exceed 30 percent or be less than 10 percent of a portfolio. Another constraint might be that international assets in aggregate cannot exceed 30 or 40 percent of the portfolio. The impact of placing constraints on the model is similar to what a simple commonsense approach without modeling would end up with—a relatively balanced globally diversified portfolio with exposure to all the major asset classes. In other words, don't waste your time with efficient frontier models.

In summary, it is my experience that most investors using efficient frontier models are unaware of their pitfalls. These models are being marketed as solutions to the problem of portfolio construction, but they come without *instructions*. The models are marketed to individuals, not only over the Internet, but also by many large companies to their 401(k) and profit-sharing participants. These corporations may view this offering as a way to fulfill their fiduciary responsibility to educate their plan participants. That is a real problem given the model's pitfalls (unless, of course, they come with the appropriate instructions and disclaimers). Given the problems with efficient frontier models, perhaps investors should be required to show their "driver's license" before being able to use such a model.

◆
Conclusion

Knowledge makes obsolete the inequities that ignorance and prejudice justify. —Errold F. Moody Jr., Financial Planner

About half of all shares of stock outstanding are still owned by individual investors. Many of them continue to manage their affairs as they always have—and as their fathers did. Their portfolios are badly diversified, they seize on the latest market gossip, and they have no idea how to measure whether they are doing well or poorly at the game; they are the noisiest of the noise traders. Others, perhaps out of inertia, fear, or stubborn unwillingness to pay capital gains taxes on old holdings, sit tight and do nothing.
—Peter Bernstein, *Capital Ideas*

Hopefully the evidence presented has convinced you that the stock markets of the world are highly efficient. Furthermore, even when markets are not perfectly efficient, the evidence demonstrates that the costs of trying to exploit any anomaly or inefficiency have proven to be greater than the likely benefit. This makes active management the loser's game—a game that while it is not impossible to win, the odds of doing so are so low that you are better off simply not playing. Many investors take this as bad news since their efforts to outperform the market are not only likely to prove nonproductive, they are highly likely to prove counterproductive after expenses, especially after taxes.

251

Investors taking that viewpoint have the wrong perspective. While it is true that active management is likely to prove counterproductive, that does not exclude investors from having a positive investment experience. In fact, there is great news imbedded in the EMH, if one takes the proper perspective. The EMH states that the current price of any security is likely to be the correct price—otherwise the market would quote a different price. A second major tenet of the EMH is that risk and expected return are related. These two tenets provide investors with great news. First, they do not have to know anything about a particular stock, sector, or the economy in general. The reason is that the market has already incorporated everything that is publicly knowable about the stock, sector, or economy into current prices. Thus unless you have inside information or believe that you can somehow interpret the data better than all the other professionals (and nonprofessionals), there is no likely way to create abnormal (above market) profits. With this recognition, investors can stop spending (wasting) their valuable time researching companies, studying economic reports, spending time on Internet chat boards, reading financial publications that tell you which mutual funds or stocks to buy, and watching CNBC or other financial programs. The market has already done your work for you! It is highly unlikely that your efforts will add value. Instead, investors can now spend their time on the really important things in their life. Instead of watching CNBC, they can spend time with their family. Instead of reading *MONEY* magazine, they can read a good book. Instead of spending time on the Internet, they might go fishing or whitewater rafting (my particular hobby). That is likely to be a far more rewarding experience, financially and otherwise. This is why passive investing is not only the winning investment strategy; it is also the winner's game in life.

The other piece of good news for investors is that to have a good investment experience all they need are three things: First, a belief in the capitalist system—the providers of capital must be rewarded with expected returns commensurate with the perceived risks they take for providing their capital or they will cease to do so—riskier asset classes must provide greater expected returns or no one would invest in them. Second, have the foresight and knowledge to build a diversified portfolio of passive asset class/ index funds that meet your unique ability, willingness, and need to take risk. Third, have the discipline to stay the course by regularly rebalancing your portfolio—eliminating any style drift that market movements may have caused by restoring your portfolio's asset allocation to its targets. These are the only three things you need to do in order to have a good investment experience.

As evidence that the EMH provides the formula for the winning investment strategy—passive asset class investing—I submit the following: Over the last seventy-five years, investors who simply invested passively in the total U.S. stock market would have doubled their investments approximately every seven years. And they could have done so without any knowledge of individual companies, sectors, or the markets. They could have accomplished that amazing feat by simply believing both in the capitalist system and also that risk and reward were related, and by having the discipline to stay the course.

I hope that you have enjoyed the journey through the fourteen truths you must know to be a successful investor. I also hope that you are now a much more knowledgeable investor and that the knowledge gained will help provide you with the patience and discipline needed to provide the greatest chance of achieving your financial goals. You should now be armed with the knowledge needed to both recognize "investment propaganda" when you see or hear it and to also "tune out" the random noise of the market.

Hopefully you have learned that while the world is rapidly

changing for investors, "this time it's different" are the four most dangerous words in the English language. The reason is that while much has changed, nothing has changed the fundamental precepts of economics (risk and ex-ante reward must be related) or the mathematics of investing.

The basic principles of investing never change. Passive investors will continue to outperform active investors with about the same predictability that one expects from spawning salmon, migrating whales, and the swallows of Capistrano. The following eleven simple steps, designed to help you be a more successful investor, are from the conclusion of my previous book, *Rational Investing in Irrational Times*. They are designed to help you avoid making the mistakes that even smart investors make. As Ted Cadsby stated: "While investors can be irrational, and markets move in exaggerated ways in the short term, a long-term and disciplined approach to investing can overcome both of these problems."[1] I urge you to pay careful attention and implement the steps. By doing so you will be far more likely to achieve your financial goals.

1. Listen carefully to the words of Gary Belsky and Thomas Gilovich:

   Any individual who is not professionally occupied in the financial services industry (and even most of those who are) and who in any way attempt to actively manage an investment portfolio is probably suffering from overconfidence. That is, anyone who has confidence enough in his or her abilities and knowledge to invest in a particular stock or bond (or actively managed mutual fund or real estate investment trust or limited partnership) is most likely fooling himself.

Most such people—probably you—have no business at all trying to pick investments, except perhaps as sport. Such people—again, probably you—should probably divide their money among several index funds and turn off CNBC.[2]

2. Unless it is for entertainment value, turn off CNBC (or at least hit the mute button), cancel your subscriptions to financial trade publications, and don't visit Internet chat boards that tout great funds, great stocks, or new and interesting investment strategies. If you need or enjoy the excitement of active investing, set up an entertainment account with 5 to 10 percent of your assets and go ahead and *"play the market."* The odds are you will underperform, but you won't go broke.

3. With help from the tables provided in truth 14, determine your unique risk tolerance, need to take risk, investment horizon, and cash-flow needs.

4. Build a globally diversified portfolio of passive asset class/index funds and/or ETFs consisting of multiple asset classes. For the equity portion, you should strongly consider including such risky asset classes as small-cap stocks, value stocks, real estate, international stocks, and even emerging markets. Too many investors confuse indexing with the exclusive use of an S&P 500 Index fund or a Total Stock Market fund. As Peter Bernstein stated: "If I am going to own an S&P 500 index fund, which I used to think was the answer to all maidens' prayers, I'm buying a very undiversified portfolio in which the greatest weights are the stocks that have gone up the most. Is that really how I want to invest?"[3] Nobel Prize winner William Sharpe agrees with Bernstein. Author Jonathan Burton paraphrases Sharpe as stating that "while it's all right to tilt a portfolio in a specific

direction—say, small stocks over large, or growth over value—investors should temper their enthusiasm."[4]

5. Write and sign an IPS (investment policy statement) and rebalancing table. Review it annually to remind yourself why you adopted your strategy and to see if personal circumstances have caused changes to your original assumptions.

6. Using guidelines established in your IPS, regularly rebalance your portfolio to its targeted asset allocation. Checking your portfolio on a quarterly basis is more than sufficient. Checking it any more often is only likely to cause you to take actions you would probably be better off not taking. Also, remember to rebalance any time you have funds available to invest.

7. Allocate your most tax-efficient asset classes to your taxable accounts, and your least tax-efficient asset classes to your tax-deferred accounts. Whenever possible, use tax-managed funds or ETFs for taxable accounts.

8. Tax manage your portfolio by harvesting losses throughout the year, not just at year-end.

9. Save as much as you can as early as you can.

10. Understand the true cost of major expenditures (see Mistake 32 of *Rational Investing in Irrational Times* for an explanation of this important point).

11. Enjoy your life.

If you follow this advice, you will avoid the investment mistakes that even the smartest people make. Your tuition will have been only the cost of this book. On the other hand, you could choose to play the game of picking stocks, timing the market, and investing in actively managed funds. If you follow that path, consider the following caution: Every few years the market hands out tuition bills that are much more expensive than the cost of this book. The bursting of the NASDAQ bubble in 2000 was the equivalent of a doctoral degree—and the tuition for doctoral degrees is very expensive.

For those interested in learning more about MPT and the EMH, consider reading my first three books. I hope that the knowledge you gain from them will help you avoid what Richard Thaler cautions us against, and what I will conclude with: "If you are prepared to do something stupid repeatedly, there are many professionals happy to take your money."[5]

APPENDIX A

◆

The Enron Debacle:
Lessons to Be Learned

In December 2000, with its stock trading at a peak of eighty-five, Enron had a market capitalization of over $60 billion, making it one of the largest U.S. companies. Less than one year later, with the stock trading at well under one, the company declared bankruptcy—at the time the largest case in U.S. history (shortly to be surpassed by WorldCom's bankruptcy). Over $60 billion in shareholder wealth was lost, and billions more of losses are likely to be incurred by creditors. The company had $31 billion in debt on its balance sheet, with billions more in counter-party risk off the balance sheet—a result of trading activity. What lessons can be learned from this debacle?

1. *Never confuse the highly likely with the certain.* No matter how great you might think a company might be, it might turn out to be a very bad investment. History's trash bin is filled with once great "sure things," including once Nifty Fifty companies such as Polaroid.

2. *Never have too many eggs in one basket.* This is a corollary to the first point. Unless there is no risk (as with U.S. Treasury bills), an individual should create a diversified portfolio, not concentrating his eggs in one basket.

3. *Don't make the mistake of overconfidence.* Two very common errors made by individual investors are to be overconfident of

the likelihood of success of their employer and to be overconfident of their stock-picking skills. They may believe that because they work for the company, they know better than the market the company's future. They may also "know" that there is little risk, so why diversify? A very common practice is for employees to place a high percentage of their 401(k) or profit-sharing plan assets into the stock of their employer (too many eggs in one basket). It is likely that many Enron employees lost a large percentage of their net worth when the firm declared bankruptcy. At the same time they may have lost their jobs.

4. *Diversify all your assets, including your intellectual assets (earning power).* This means considering your employment as part of your asset allocation. If your employer does poorly, your ability to earn income could be dramatically impacted. Allocating your financial assets to the stock of your employer is like "doubling up" your bet. Diversification is the prudent strategy.

5. *Don't confuse the familiar with the safe.* Just because you work for a company and know something about it doesn't mean either that it is a safe investment or, just as importantly, that the market doesn't also have access to the same information, and thus that information is already incorporated into the price of the stock.

6. *Active management is not likely to protect you.* Among the ten largest shareholders in Enron (and the percent of the fund in Enron shares), was Alliance Premier Growth (4.1 percent), Fidelity Magellan (0.2 percent), AIM Value (1 percent), Putnam Investors (1.7 percent), Morgan Stanley Dividend Growth (0.9 percent), and four Janus funds—Janus Fund (2.9 percent), Janus Twenty (2.8 percent), Janus Mercury (3.6 percent), and Janus Growth and Income (2.7 percent). Note that while the

reporting dates varied (based on the latest available information from Morningstar), none was later than September 30, 2001. Among the "true believers" in Enron were the following funds and the respective percent of the fund's assets in Enron (again reporting dates varied, but none were later than September 30, 2001): Rydex Utility (8 percent), Fidelity Select Natural Gas (5.7 percent), Dessauer Global Equity (5.6 percent), Merrill Lynch Focus Twenty (5.8 percent), AIM Global Technology (5.3 percent), Janus 2 (4.7 percent), Janus Special Situations (4.6 percent), Stein Roe Focus (4.2 percent), Alliance Premier Growth (4.1 percent), and Merrill Lynch Growth (4.1 percent). Obviously all the intensive research these firms performed did not protect them, or their investors, from massive losses. It is particularly noteworthy to point out the Janus family of funds, whose commercials tout their superior research efforts and skills. Janus's flagship fund was the largest absolute holder of Enron, holding over 16 million shares. On April 30, 2001, the last time it reported individual fund holdings, eleven Janus funds collectively owned more than 5 percent of Enron. As of September 30, 2001, Janus still owned more than 5 percent of Enron. Another touter of their superior stock-picking skills is the Fidelity family of funds. As of September 30, 2001, together they owned 154 million shares.[1] So much for the value of research. The market is a great humbler.

Hopefully the Enron debacle will provide investors with a lesson that will help prevent them from making any of the six mistakes described above.

APPENDIX B

◆

More Investment Truths You Must Know to Be a Successful Investor

- While it is true that intelligent investors are unlikely to be able to buy undervalued (mispriced) stocks because the markets are highly efficient, it is also true that for the same reason ignorant investors are unlikely to buy overvalued (mispriced) stocks. Ignorant investors are not likely to be exploited because the current market price is always the best estimate of the correct price. In other words, there is not one price for intelligent investors and another for the not-so-smart investors. Everyone gets the same price. Any difference in performance is highly likely to be due to the differences in costs and the exposure of the portfolio to the risk factors of size and value.

- The more you pursue performance, the less likely you are to achieve it because of the trading costs you incur.

- The more attention you pay to the market's daily action, the worse your investment results are likely to be. Paying attention to the noise of the market will only tempt you to take action when inaction is far more likely to be the winning strategy.

- By chasing yesterday's winners, investors act in a convex manner, buying high and selling low. Studies have shown that this causes them to underperform the very funds they invest in by 5 to 10 percent per annum. They should instead be investing in a concave manner, buying low (yesterday's losers) and selling high (yesterday's winners). Simple disciplined rebalancing forces the winner's strategy of concave investing.

- Almost all of the returns from the market come from only about 7 percent of the trading months. The other 93 percent of the months, on average, provide virtually no return. Since such a high percentage of total returns comes in such short periods that are impossible to predict, the only likely way to capture all the returns is to be there all the time, waiting patiently like a deer hunter.

- Despite the advantage of both holding more cash reserves and being able to move to cash easily, active managers have performed worse in bear markets then they do in bull markets.

- Asset classes, such as emerging markets, are risky in isolation. However, when added to a portfolio, risky assets may actually reduce overall portfolio risk (due to low correlation). Thus an asset class should only be considered in terms of its impact on the risk of the entire portfolio.

- Diversification, while reducing portfolio risk, creates another kind of risk, tracking-error regret. If the investor measures performance against a single benchmark like the S&P 500 Index, there will almost certainly be periods of underperformance, even very long periods. However, that does not change the fact that over the long term, portfolio risk is reduced. Tracking-error regret may cause investors to abandon a well thought-out strategy—because they confuse strategy (ex-ante decisions) and outcome (ex-post results)

- While bear markets are tough to endure and may even cause lots of stomach acid, they are good for investors who have long investment horizons. The reason is that investors who have the discipline not to panic now have opportunity to buy at lower prices when expected returns are greater. On the other hand, bear markets are not good for investors in the withdrawal stage.

- Investors who can most afford to take risk (high-net-worth individuals) are the very ones who have the least need to take risk. And the need to take risk should be the overriding determinant of the equity to fixed-income allocation decision.

- It takes far less time to become a licensed stockbroker than it does to become a plumber. And in the few short months it takes, the majority of training received is in sales techniques, not on the principles of investing.

APPENDIX C

◆

Investment Vehicle Recommendations

Note that funds with an asterisk are TM (tax managed) and, therefore, are strongly recommended for taxable accounts. Two asterisks mean the fund is appropriate for only nontaxable accounts.

Domestic Equities

Large Cap

Bridgeway Ultra Large 35*
DFA Large Cap
Dreyfus Basic
Fidelity Spartan
SSgA S&P 500
USAA S&P 500
Vanguard 500 Index
DFA Enhanced U.S. Large**
iShares S&P 500 Index
Vanguard Total Stock Market
Vanguard Total Stock VIPERS
Fidelity Spartan Total Market
iShares Russell 1000
iShares Russell 3000

International Equities

Large Cap

DFA International Large
Fidelity Spartan International
Vanguard Developed Foreign Markets
Vanguard Europe
Vanguard Pacific
Vanguard TM International*
Vanguard Total International
iShares MSCI EAFE
iShares S&P Europe 350 Index
iShares S&P TOPIX 150 (Japan)
iShares MSCI Pacific ex-Japan

Domestic Equities

Large-Cap Value
DFA Large Cap Value
DFA TM U.S. Marketwide Value*
Vanguard Large Value
iShares Russell 400 Value
iShares Russell 3000 Value
StreetTRACKS DJ Large Value

Small Cap
Bridgeway Ultra Small Cap*
DFA U.S. Small Cap
DFA TM U.S. Small Cap*
DFA Micro Cap
Vanguard Small Cap
Vanguard TM Small Cap*
iShares S&P 600

Small-Cap Value
DFA Small Value
DFA TM Small Value*
Vanguard Small Cap Value
iShares S&P 600 Value
StreetTRACKS DJ U.S. Small Value

Real Estate
DFA Real Estate**
Vanguard REIT**
StreetTRACKS Wilshire REIT**

International Equities

Large-Cap Value
DFA International Large Value
DFA TM International Large Value*

Small Cap
DFA International Small Company

Small-Cap Value
DFA International Small Cap Value

Emerging Markets
DFA Emerging Markets
DFA Emerging Markets Small Cap
DFA Emerging Markets Value
Vanguard Emerging Market

Domestic Equities

Fixed Income: Taxable
DFA 2-Year

DFA Global Bond
iShares 1–3 Year Treasury Index
iShares 7–10 Year Treasury Index
TIAA-CREF Fixed Income Annuities
Vanguard Short-Term Treasury
Vanguard Short-Term Bond Index
Vanguard Intermediate-Term Index
Vanguard TIPS**
I bonds

International Equities

Fixed Income: Tax-Exempt
DFA Short-Term Municipal Bond
Portfolio
Vanguard Limited-Term Tax-Free
Vanguard Intermediate-Term Tax-Free

Investors need to be aware that the DFA funds are only available through approved financial advisors. There are several hundred such advisors around the country.

APPENDIX D

◆

The Home Financing Decision: To Borrow or Not

One of the most frequently asked questions I receive from both investors and advisors is related to the financing of noninvestment residential property (a home, be it the primary residence or a vacation home). For investors with the sufficient assets to have alternatives, the question is: Do I use my investment assets to keep the mortgage to a minimum or to pay down an existing mortgage, or do I borrow the maximum? As is the case with many questions related to investing, there is no right answer. However, it is important that the following issues are considered.

- A mortgage should be considered as negative exposure to fixed-income assets and should be treated as such in the asset-allocation picture. So if you are holding a $200,000 mortgage and have $200,000 in fixed-income assets, your exposure to fixed income is zero, not $200,000. This is a very common error.

- An investor cannot beat the risk-free rate of return on a mortgage if the fixed-income asset is to be held in a taxable account. Even with tax-free municipal bonds it is not likely to be able to earn much/any higher returns, especially after considering that there are two risks in municipal bond investing (and none in paying off the mortgage)—credit risk and the risk that the tax exemption on municipal bonds will be eliminated. As always, it is important to never make the mistake of treating even the highly unlikely as impossible. Alternatively, if fixed-income assets can be held in tax-deferred or tax-free accounts, depending on the investments chosen and the assumed tax rate, there might be an advantage to borrowing. In doing the calculation, remember that with an IRA, or other tax-deferred account, the taxes on income are only deferred. There is one more complication. An investor should place the least tax-efficient assets into tax-deferred accounts. Thus if fixed income "crowds out" tax-inefficient asset classes such as real estate, this would be an inefficient use of a tax-deferred account (as fixed income can be held efficiently in taxable accounts in the form of municipal bonds).

- If a home is financed with a fixed-rate mortgage, that mortgage effectively is a short (negative) bond position and should be considered so when looking at your overall portfolio. The fixed rate on the mortgage does provide inflation protection. A fixed-rate mortgage also has a "put" feature. If interest rates decline, the put (putting the mortgage back to the lender by paying it off) allows the borrower to refinance the mortgage at the then current rate. This provides protection against falling interest rates (for those on fixed incomes) and deflation. Of course, the interest rate paid is reflective of the cost of the option feature. If a home were financed with an adjustable-rate mortgage, the risk picture would be considerably different, as the rate on the mortgage would move up or down as interest rates changed.

- Having no or little mortgage provides a high comfort level for investors. This is the "sleep well" issue. With little or no debt, an investor is likely to be more comfortable accepting the economic-cycle risk inherent in equity investing. Thus he/she may be more likely to stay disciplined during the inevitable bear markets. This is important because the discipline to stay the course with an asset allocation is in all likelihood the greatest determinant of returns in the long run (more so than the asset allocation itself).

- With little or no debt, an investor may feel more comfortable taking the greater economic-cycle risk inherent in value- and small-cap stocks. This allows for higher expected returns within the equity allocation. Alternatively, the greater expected returns can be used to lower the equity allocation needed to achieve the same expected rate of return on the portfolio.

- If an investor does borrow, the calculation of the estimated return on any assets invested must consider any advisory fees that will be incurred. This raises the issue of a conflict of interest for even fee-only advisors. Many investment firms aggressively push home equity and other types of loans. Many of them have even entered the mortgage business. The idea is to not only make money from the mortgage origination but to also profit by charging fees on the assets under management or to profit from commissions generated. The investor should be sure that the advisor is providing the advice that is best for the investor, and not what generates the greatest income for the advisor.

- The principal reason to hold a mortgage is if the investor has a *high need to take risk* and he/she estimates a large equity premium. The relatively low after-tax cost of the mortgage compared with the possibility of large relative returns from tax-efficient equity investing can make the mortgage an attractive alternative. As an example, assume a mortgage rate of 8 percent. The after-tax cost for a high-bracket individual is probably under 5 percent. A highly diversified equity portfolio might be expected to return, say, 10 percent, and do so in a highly tax-efficient manner (assuming the use of tax-managed funds). That large differential can be very tempting. However, it does, of course, mean the assumption of all of the risks of equity investing. It is worth repeating that those risks are real and should not be underestimated. Also note that since the equity risk premium is not constant, there are times when it may be more attractive to borrow and invest in equities (when the equity risk premium is high, like in 1975 after the two-year bear market) than at other times (when the equity risk premium is low, like in 2000, after the multiyear bull market).

In summary, there is no right answer. It ultimately comes down to the investor's marginal "utility of wealth." The marginal utility of wealth is a measure of the value to the investor of the incremental expected greater return relative to the incremental risk accepted. The greater the marginal utility of wealth, the more equity one should hold (and thus have as big a mortgage as possible) and vice versa. The bottom line is that the ultimate decision should be based heavily on the marginal utility of wealth question, and the "eat well" vs. "sleep well" considerations.

Other Debt-Related Issues

- Credit card debt is generally the most expensive form of credit, and the interest is not tax deductible (as is the case with mortgage-related debt). A good rule of thumb is the first *investment* individuals should make is to pay down any credit card debt. This type debt should be paid off prior to making any extra mortgage payments. Also, credit card debt should be paid off prior to committing funds to equity investing. And unless the debt is expected to be outstanding for a very short time, equities held in taxable accounts should be sold to pay off credit card debt.

- Nonsubsidized car loans are similar to credit card debt. Thus the same rules of thumb apply.

- In almost all cases I believe individuals should not use margin to buy equities. The basic issue is that equity investors using margin earn lower returns (due to the cost of the margin) yet have the same risk. They also run the risk of margin calls they may not be able to meet. Thus we can conclude that the use of margin for investing purposes is an inefficient use of one's capital. The rewards are simply not commensurate with the risk (this issue is explored more fully in my previous book *Rational Investing in Irrational Times,* Mistake 40). Only an investor with a very high marginal utility of wealth and a very high tolerance for risk should use margin to increase the equity allocation beyond 100 percent—with an equity allocation below 100 percent, the prudent way to increase the expected return of a portfolio is to increase the exposure to the riskier asset classes of small and value stocks. In this case the investor is fully compensated for the incremental risk in terms of higher expected returns.

Notes

Truth 1

1. Mark Carhart, "On Persistence in Mutual Fund Performance," *Journal of Finance* (March 1997).
2. William Sharpe, "The Arithmetic of Active Management," *The Financial Analysts' Journal* (January/February 1991): pp. 7–9.
3. W. Scott Simon, *Index Mutual Funds,* pp. 206–9.
4. "Untangling Emerging Markets," *New York Times,* January 24, 1999.
5. Datastream.
6. *New York Times,* January 24, 1999.
7. Bridge/Dimensional Fund Advisors.
8. *New York Times,* January 24, 1999.
9. *Wall Street Journal,* March 5, 2003.
10. *St. Louis Post-Dispatch,* August 12, 1997.
11. *New York Times,* July 11, 1999.
12. John Bogle, *Common Sense on Mutual Funds,* p. 286.
13. Russ Wermers, "Mutual Fund Performance: An Empirical Decomposition into Stock-Picking Talent, Style, Transaction Costs, and Expenses," *Journal of Finance* (August 2000).
14. John Bogle, *John Bogle on Investing,* p. 89.
15. Adele Kohler, "Market Uncertainty and the Role of Indexing," *SSgA Essays & Presentations,* November 30, 2001.
16. Richard E. Evans and Burton G. Malkiel, *The Index Fund Solution.*

17. Lipper Analytical Services.
18. *Business Week* (February 22, 1999).
19. William Sherden, *Fortune Sellers,* p. 104.
20. Lipper Analytical Services.
21. *The Index Insider,* January 2001.
22. *Wall Street Journal,* March 11, 1998.
23. Burton G. Malkiel and Aleksander Radisich, "The Growth of Index Funds and the Pricing of Equity Securities," *The Journal of Portfolio Management* (Winter 2001).

Truth 2

1. Deborah Lipstadt, *Denying the Holocaust,* p. 25.
2. *Wall Street Journal,* April 29, 1997.
3. Dean LeBaron and Romesh Vaitilingam, *The Ultimate Investor,* p. 200.
4. *Fortune* (October 11, 1999).
5. *Wall Street Journal,* December 22, 1998.
6. *In the Vanguard* (Autumn 2000).
7. Christopher R. Blake and Matthew R. Morey, "Morningstar Ratings and Mutual Fund Performance," *Journal of Financial and Quantitative Analysis* (September 2000).
8. Diane Del Guerico and Paula A. Tkac, "Star Power: The Effect of Morningstar Ratings on Mutual Fund Flows," Federal Reserve Bank of Atlanta, Working Paper 2001–15.
9. Prem C. Jain and Joanna Shuang Wu, "Truth in Mutual Fund Advertising: Evidence on Future Performance and Fund Flows," *Journal of Finance* 55 (2000): pp. 937–58.
10. John Bogle, "The Stock Market Universe—Stars, Comets, and the Sun," speech before the Financial Analysts of Philadelphia, February 15, 2001.
11. *New York Times,* May 19, 2002.
12. *InvestmentNews* (March 29, 1999).

13. *New York Times,* April 4, 1999.

14. Blake and Morey, "Morningstar Ratings and Mutual Fund Performance." www.cqa.org/files_spring_2001/growth.pdf.

15. Amy C. Arnott, "Beyond the Stars: The New Category Rating," *Morningstar Mutual Funds* (December 1996).

16. *Journal of Financial Planning* (September 2000).

17. *Fortune* (July 8, 2002).

18. Smith Barney Consulting Group, "Why Top Performance Is a Poor Indicator of Future Performance," 1997.

19. www.dfaus.com.

20. *Fortune* (March 15, 1999).

21. *Fortune* (October 11, 1999).

22. FutureMetrics Inc., Dimensional Fund Advisors.

23. Andrew Metrick, "Performance Evaluation with Transactions Data: The Stock Selection of Investment Newsletters," *Journal of Finance* (October 1999).

24. William E. Fender and Brian P. Cunningham, "What's the Chance of That Happening?" *The CPA Journal* (March 2000).

25. Paul Farrell, CBS.MarketWatch.com, "Warning: Fund Stats Offer Little Help," April 19, 2002.

26. *New York Times,* October 10, 1999.

27. *New York Times,* July 11, 1999.

28. DFA Advisor Research Letter, July 1998.

29. *Wall Street Journal,* April 17, 2002.

30. W. Scott Simon, *Index Mutual Funds,* pp. 206–9.

31. Jon Christopherson, Zhuanxin Ding, and Paul Greenwood, "The Perils of Success," *Journal of Portfolio Management* (Winter 2002).

32. John Bogle, "Three Challenges of Investing," speech at Client Conference, Boston, Massachusetts, October 21, 2001.

33. William Bernstein, *The Four Pillars of Investing.*
34. *Wall Street Journal,* January 3, 2002.
35. Jonathan Clements, *25 Myths You've Got to Avoid,* p. 86.
36. Christopher R. Blake, Edwin J. Elton, and Martin Gruber, "The Performance of Bond Mutual Funds," *Journal of Business* (July 1993).
37. Christopher R. Blake, Edwin J. Elton, and Martin Gruber, "Fundamental Economic Variables, Expected Returns and Bond Fund Performance," *Journal of Finance* (September 1995).
38. James Philpot, Douglas Hearth, James N. Rimbey, and Craig T. Schuman, "Active Management, Fund Size and Bond Mutual Fund Returns," *Financial Review* (May 1998).
39. John Bogle, *Bogle on Mutual Funds.*
40. William Reichenstein, "Bond Fund Returns and Expenses: A Study of Bond Market Efficiency," *Journal of Investing* (Winter 1999).
41. Richard Fortin, Stuart Michelson, and James Jordan-Wagner, "Does Mutual Fund Manager Tenure Matter?" *Journal of Financial Planning* (August 1999).
42. James D. Peterson, Paul Pietranico, Mark W. Riepe, and Robin Vroom, "Explaining the Future Performance of Domestic Bond Mutual Funds," *Journal of Fixed Income Investing* (June 2000).
43. Christopher R. Blake, Edwin J. Elton, and Martin Gruber, "The Performance of Bond Mutual Funds," *Journal of Business* (July 1993).
44. "Yo: Bond Index Funds Wield Better Yields," *InvestmentNews* (January 25, 1999).
45. "Just How Bad Are Economists at Predicting Interest Rates?" *Journal of Investing* (Summer 1997).
46. *Journal of Applied Economics* (Spring 1996).

Truth 3

1. FutureMetrics Inc., Dimensional Fund Advisors.
2. T. Daniel Coggin and Charles A. Trzcinka, "A Panel Study of U.S. Equity Pension Fund Manager Style Performance," *Journal of Investing* (Summer 2000).
3. *Pensions & Investments* (June 26, 2000).
4. *Wall Street Journal,* August 24, 1995.
5. *Pensions & Investments* (August 9, 1999).
6. *Pensions & Investments* (September 16, 2002).
7. *U.S. News & World Report* (April 22, 2002).
8. Forbes.com, June 1, 2001.
9. *Dow Jones Asset Management,* November–December 1998.

Truth 4

1. Derek DeCloet, "Shift in CIBC Focus Puts Whizz in Closet," *Financial Post,* December 5, 2001.
2. Ibid.
3. *Business Week* (July 14, 1997).
4. *Fortune* (February 5, 2001).
5. Howard Kurtz, *The Fortune Tellers,* pp. 68–70.
6. Benjamin Cole, *The Pied Pipers of Wall Street,* p. 83.
7. Roni Michaely and Kent Womack, "Conflict of Interest and the Credibility of Underwriter Analyst Recommendations," *The Review of Financial Studies* (1999).
8. Patricia M. Dechow, Richard Sloan, and Amy Hutton, "The Relation Between Analysts' Long-Term Earnings Forecasts and Stock Price Performance Following Equity Offerings," *Contemporary Accounting Research* 17, no. 1 (Spring 2000).
9. *Forbes* (January 22, 2001).
10. Benjamin Cole, *The Pied Pipers of Wall Street,* p. 81.
11. *Fortune* (April 26, 1999).

12. Ibid.
13. *Barron's* on-line, June 2, 1997.

Truth 5

1. Nai-fu Chen and Feng Zhang, "Risk and Return of Value Stocks," *Journal of Business* (October 1998).
2. Lu Zhang, "The Value Premium," University of Rochester Simon School of Business Working Paper No. FR 02-19. http://papers.ssrn.com/, November 2002.
3. Joao Gomes, Leonid Kogan, and Lu Zhang, "Equilibrium Cross-Section of Returns." http://papers.ssrn.com/, March 2001.
4. Gerald R. Jensen and Jeffrey M. Mercer, "Monetary Policy and the Cross-Section of Expected Stock Returns," *Journal of Financial Research* (Spring 2002).

Truth 6

1. *SmartMoney* (June 2001).
2. *Fortune* (August 16, 1999).
3. Ibid.
4. Ibid.
5. Ruben Trevino and Fiona Robertson, "P/E Ratios and Stock Market Returns," *Journal of Financial Planning* (February 2002).
6. Clifford S. Asness, *Financial Advisor,* March 2002.
7. Kursat Aydogan and Guner Gursory, "P/E and Price-to-Book Ratios as Predictors of Stock Returns in Emerging Equity Markets" (August 2000).

Truth 7

1. Quoted in Ben Warwick, *Searching for Alpha,* p. 17.
2. Jonathan Clements, *25 Myths You've Got to Avoid,* p. 54.

Truth 8

1. William Goetzmann and Alok Kumar, "Equity Portfolio Diversification," Yale ICF Working Paper, Nos. 00–59.
2. *New York Times,* March 30, 1997.
3. *Wall Street Journal,* September 14, 1998.
4. *Wall Street Journal,* April 6, 1998.
5. Brad Barber and Terrance Odean, "Trading Is Hazardous to Your Wealth: The Common Stock Investment Performance of Individual Investors," *Journal of Finance* (April 2000).
6. Brad Barber and Terrance Odean, "Boys Will Be Boys: Gender, Overconfidence and Common Stock Investment," *Quarterly Journal of Economics* (February 2001).
7. *Wall Street Journal,* October 20, 1998.
8. *Bloomberg Wealth Manager* (May/June 1999).
9. Brad Barber and Terrance Odean, "Do Investors Trade Too Much?" *American Economic Review* (December 1999).
10. Goetzmann and Kumar.
11. Brad Barber and Terrance Odean, "The Internet and the Investor," *The Journal of Economic Perspectives* (Winter 2001).
12. DALBAR, Inc. (www.dalbarinc. com).
13. James H. Smalhout, "Too Close to Your Money?" *Bloomberg Personal Finance* (November 1997).
14. Werner DeBondt, "A Portrait of the Individual Investor," *European Economic Review* 42 (1998): pp. 831–44.
15. Goetzmann and Kumar.
16. Ibid.
17. *Financial Advisor* (March 2001).
18. J. L. Evans and S. H. Archer, "Diversification and the Reduction of Dispersion: An Empirical Analysis," *Journal of Finance* (December 1968).

19. Lawrence Fisher and James Lorie, "Some Studies of Variability of Returns on Investments in Common Stocks," *Journal of Business* 43, no. 2 (April 1970).
20. *Wall Street Journal,* January 29, 2001.
21. Ronald J. Surz and Mitchell Price, "The Truth About Diversification by the Numbers," *Journal of Investing* (Winter 2000).
22. *Bloomberg Wealth Manager* (July/August 2000).
23. Ibid.
24. *Wall Street Journal,* January 8, 2001.
25. *In the Vanguard* (Winter 2001).
26. Eugene F. Fama and Kenneth R. French, "The Cross-section of Expected Stock Returns," *Journal of Finance* (June 1992).

Truth 9

1. Richard Harris, "The Accuracy, Bias and Efficiency of Analysts' Long Run Earnings Growth Forecasts," *Journal of Business Finance and Accounting* (June/July 1999).
2. W. Scott Bauman, C. Mitchell Conover, and Robert E. Miller, "Investor Overreaction in International Stock Markets," *Journal of Portfolio Management* (Summer 1999).
3. Eugene F. Fama and Kenneth R. French, "Forecasting Profitability and Earnings," The Center for Research in Security Prices, Working Paper 456, February 1999.
4. A. C. Raynor and I. M. D. Little, *Higgledy Piggledy Growth Again.*
5. J. Lintner and R. Glauber, "Higgledy Piggledy Growth Again in America," unpublished paper presented to the Seminar on the Analysis of Security Prices, University of Chicago, May 1967.
6. R. Fuller, L. Huberts, and M. Levinson, "Returns to E/P Strategies, Higgledy Piggledy Growth, Analysts' Forecasts Errors, and Omitted Risk Factors," *Journal of Portfolio Management* (Winter 1993): Exhibit G.

7. *Fortune* (February 5, 2001).

8. Jason Zweig, "A Matter of Expectations," Money.com, January 1, 2001.

9. Louis K. C. Chan, Jason Karceski, and Josef Lakonishok, "The Level and Persistence of Growth Rates," *Journal of Finance* 58, no. 2 (Spring 2003): pp. 643–84.

10. *Milwaukee Journal Sentinel* (on-line version), June 3, 2000.

Truth 10

1. William Sherden, *The Fortune Sellers.*

2. *Forbes* (December 26, 1988): p. 94.

3. *Industry Week* (April 20, 1992): p. 76.

4. Burton G. Malkiel, *A Random Walk Down Wall Street,* p. 179.

5. *Wall Street Journal,* December 11, 2000.

6. *Wall Street Journal,* December 10, 2001.

7. *Wall Street Journal,* November 19, 2001.

8. *Financial World* (November 1980).

9. David Dreman, *Contrarian Investment Strategies,* p. 91.

10. *Fortune* (June 11, 2001).

11. *Business Week* (December 31, 2001).

12. Brad Barber, Reuven Lehavy, Maureen McNichols, and Brett Trueman, "Can Investors Profit from the Prophets? Security Analyst Recommendations and Stock Returns," *Journal of Finance* (April 2001).

13. *Financial Analysts Journal* 54: pp. 50–69.

14. *Wall Street Journal,* January 24, 2001.

15. *MONEY* (June 1998).

16. Benjamin Cole, *The Pied Pipers of Wall Street,* p. 93.

17. Patrick McGeehan, "Experts' Top Choices, Gone Awry," *New York Times,* October 7, 2001.

18. Adam Shell, "Experts' Stock Picks Lag Market," *USA Today,* July 9, 2001.

19. *Wall Street Journal,* February 25, 1997.
20. *Fortune* (June 10, 2002).
21. *Business Week* (March 9, 1998).
22. Ibid.
23. W. Scott Simon, *Index Mutual Funds.*
24. Howard Kurtz, *The Fortune Tellers,* p. 35.
25. Sherden, *The Fortune Sellers.*
26. Ibid.
27. Ralph Wanger, *A Zebra in Lion Country.*
28. *Fortune* (May 12, 1997).
29. *Wall Street Journal,* January 13, 1998.
30. *St. Louis Post-Dispatch,* October 4, 1997.
31. Peter Lynch, *One Up on Wall Street,* p. 60.

Truth 11
1. Ted Lux, *Exposing the Wheel Spin on Wall Street.*
2. "The Tax Bind of Bond Funds," SmartMoney.com, June 13, 2001.
3. *New York Times,* February 25, 2001.
4. Robert D. Arnott and Robert H. Jeffrey, "Is Your Alpha Big Enough to Cover Its Taxes?" *Journal of Portfolio Management* (Spring 1993).
5. "Ranking Mutual Funds on an After-Tax Basis," Stanford University Center for Economic Policy Research Discussion Paper 344.
6. Richard Evans, *The Index Fund Solution,* p. 59.
7. James Garland, "The Tax Attraction of Tax-Managed Index Funds," *Journal of Investing* (Spring 1997).
8. Arnott and Jeffrey.
9. *Wall Street Journal,* June 10, 1997.
10. Schwab Center for Investment Research, "How Tax Efficient Are Tax-Managed Funds?" vol. I, issue II, October 1998.

11. State Street Research, *Advisor News* 2, no. 2 (Fall 1998).
12. Robert D. Arnott, Andrew L. Berkin, and Jia Ye, "How Well Have Taxable Investors Been Served in the 1980s and 1990s?" *Journal of Portfolio Management* (Summer 2000).
13. KPMG, *Tax-Managed Mutual Funds and the Taxable Investor.*
14. *Barron's,* June 15, 1998.
15. Money.com, February 1999.
16. *Barron's,* April 6, 1998.
17. *Wall Street Journal,* December 22, 1998.

Truth 12
1. Robert Shiller, *Irrational Exuberance.*
2. Edward Chancellor, *Devil Take the Hindmost,* p. 18.
3. A. E. Murphy, *Richard Cantillon,* p. 171.
4. Edward Chancellor, *Devil Take the Hindmost,* p. 69.
5. Ibid., p. 170.
6. Ibid., p. 168.
7. Medberry, *Men and Mysteries,* p. 205.
8. Richard Thaler, *Advances in Behavioral Finance,* p. 167.
9. Ibid., p. 209.
10. *Wall Street Journal,* April 4, 2000.
11. *Wall Street Journal,* November 27, 2000.
12. Matthew Goldstein, *On the Street,* "Where's the Little Guy?" SmartMoney.com, December 8, 2000.
13. Warren Buffett, *1996 Annual Report of Berkshire Hathaway.*

Truth 13
1. Gur Huberman, *Familiarity Breeds Investment,* September 1999.
2. Kenneth R. French and James M. Poterba, "Investor Diversi-

fication and International Equity Markets," *American Economic Review* 81, no. 2: pp. 222–26.

3. Ibid.
4. Debra Glassman and Leigh Riddick, "What Explains Home Asset Bias and How Should It Be Measured?" University of Washington Working Paper.
5. Hersh Shefrin and Meir Statman, "Behavioral Portfolio Theory," 1997 unpublished paper.
6. F. Heath and A. Tversky, "Preference and Belief: Ambiguity and Competence in Choice Under Uncertainty," *Journal of Risk and Uncertainty* 4: pp. 4–28.
7. David Laster, *Journal of Investing* (Fall 1998).
8. David Blitzer, *Outpacing the Pros,* p. 114.
9. www.globalfindata.com.
10. Dimensional Fund Advisors, www.panagora.com/research/2001crowell/2001cp_5.pdf.

Truth 14

1. Dale L. Domian, Terry S. Maness, and William Reichenstein, "Rewards to Extending Maturity," *Journal of Portfolio Management* (Spring 1998).
2. David Plecha, Dimensional Fund Advisors, "Fixed Income Investing," Working Paper, July 2002.
3. Ibid.

Conclusion

1. Ted Cadsby, *The 10 Biggest Investment Mistakes Canadians Make,* p. 10.
2. Gary Belsky and Thomas Gilovich, *Why Smart People Make Big Money Mistakes,* p. 162.
3. Quoted in Jonathan Burton, *Investment Titans,* p. 218.

4. Ibid., p. 237.

5. Richard Thaler, *The Winner's Curse,* p. 5.

Appendix A

1. *San Francisco Chronicle,* December 3, 2001.

Glossary

Active management The attempt to uncover securities the market has either under- or overvalued; also the attempt to time investment decisions in order to be more heavily invested when the market is rising and less so when the market is falling.

Alpha A measure of performance against a benchmark. *Positive alpha* represents outperformance; *negative alpha* represents underperformance.

Arbitrage The process by which investors exploit the price difference between two exactly alike securities by simultaneously buying one at a lower price and selling the other at a higher price (thereby avoiding risk). This action locks in a risk-free profit for the arbitrageur (person engaging in the arbitrage) and eventually brings the prices back into equilibrium.

Asset allocation The process of determining what percentage of assets should be dedicated to which specific asset classes.

Asset class A group of assets with similar risk and reward characteristics. Cash, debt instruments, real estate, and equities are examples of asset classes. Within a general asset class, such as equities, there are more specific classes such as large and small companies and domestic and international companies.

Barra Indices The Barra Indices divide the three major S&P Indices (400 for mid cap, 500 for large cap, and 600 for small cap) into growth and value categories. The top 50 percent of stocks as ranked by book-to-market value are considered value stocks and the bottom 50 percent are considered growth stocks. This creates both value and growth indices for all three S&P Indices.

Basis point One one-hundredth of 1 percent, or 0.0001.

Benchmark An appropriate standard against which actively managed funds can be judged. Actively managed large-cap growth funds should be judged against a large-cap growth index such as the S&P 500, while small-cap managers should be judged against a small-cap index such as the Russell 2000.

Bid-offer spread The bid is the price at which you can sell a security, and the offer is the price you must pay to buy a security. The spread is the difference between the two prices and represents the cost of a round-trip trade (purchase and sale), excluding commissions.

Book-to-market value (BtM) The ratio of the book value per share to the market price per share, or book value divided by market capitalization.

Book value An accounting term for the equity of a company. Equity is equal to assets less liabilities; it is often expressed in per-share terms. Book value per share is equal to equity divided by the number of shares.

Call An option contract that gives the holder the right, but not the obligation, to buy a security at a predetermined price on a specific date (*European call*) or during a specific period (*American call*).

Churning Excessive trading in a client's account by a broker seeking to maximize commissions, regardless of the client's best interests. Churning is a violation of NASD rules and is illegal.

Closet index fund An actively managed fund whose holdings so closely resemble the holdings of an index fund that investors

are unknowingly paying very large fees for minimal differentiation.

Coefficient of correlation A statistical term describing how
closely related the price movement of different securities or
asset classes is; the higher the coefficient, the more prices
move in the same direction.

Concave investing Specifically the opposite of convex investing. Investors follow a strategy of purchasing yesterday's
underperformers (buying low) and selling yesterday's outperformers (selling high).

Convex investing The tendency for individual investors to buy
yesterday's top-performing stocks and mutual funds (buying
high) and sell yesterday's underperformers (selling low).

Correlation In mathematics, correlation is the measure of the
linear relationship between two variables. Values can range
from $+1.00$ (perfect correlation) to -1.00 (perfect negative
correlation). An example of a strong positive correlation would
be stocks of two oil companies. A strong negative correlation
might exist between an oil company (that benefits from rising
oil prices) and an airline company (that would benefit from a
fall in oil prices).

CPI Consumer price index.

CRSP Center for Research in Security Prices.

Data mining A technique for building predictive models of the
real world by discerning patterns in masses of data.

Diamond An exchange-traded fund that replicates the Dow
Jones Industrial Index.

Distressed stocks Stocks with high book-to-market values
and/or low price-to-earnings ratios. Distressed stocks are generally considered to be value stocks.

DJIA Dow Jones Industrial Average.

EAFE Index The Europe, Australasia, and Far East Index, similar to the S&P 500 Index in that it consists of the stocks of the large companies from the EAFE countries. The stocks within the index are weighted by market capitalization.

Efficient market A state in which trading systems fail to produce returns in excess of the market's overall rate of return because everything currently knowable about a company is already incorporated into the stock price. The next piece of available information will be random as to whether it will be better or worse than the market expects. An efficient market is also one in which the trading costs are low.

Efficient markets hypothesis (EMH) A hypothesis explaining how markets work. *See* efficient market.

Emerging markets The capital markets of less developed countries that are beginning to develop characteristics of developed countries, such as higher per-capita income. Countries typically included in this category would be Brazil, Mexico, Thailand, and Korea.

Ex-ante Before the fact.

Exchange-traded fund (ETF) For practical purposes these act like open-ended, no-load mutual funds. Like mutual funds, they can be created to represent virtually any index or asset class. However, they are not actually mutual funds. Instead, these new vehicles represent a cross between an exchange-listed stock and an open-ended, no-load mutual fund. Like stocks (but unlike mutual funds), they trade throughout the day.

Expense ratio The operating expenses of a fund expressed as a percentage of total assets. These expenses are subtracted from the investment performance of a fund in order to determine the net return to shareholders.

Ex-post After the fact.

5%/25% rule Numerical formula used to determine the need to rebalance a portfolio.

Flipping The practice of selling shares that were allotted to an investor in an IPO almost as soon as the shares begin to publicly trade.

Fundamental security analysis The attempt to uncover mispriced securities by focusing on predicting future earnings.

Futures contract An agreement to purchase or sell a specific collection of securities or a physical commodity at a specified price and time in the future. For example, an S&P 500 futures contract represents ownership interest in the S&P 500 Index at a specified price for delivery on a specific date on a particular exchange.

Growth stock A stock trading, relative to the overall market, at a high price-to-earnings ratio (or at a relatively low book-to-market ratio) because the market anticipates rapid earnings growth relative to the overall market.

Hedge fund A fund that generally has the ability to invest in a wide variety of asset classes. These funds often use leverage in an attempt to increase returns.

I bond A bond that provides both a fixed rate of return and an inflation-protection component. The principal value of the bond increases by the total of the fixed rate and the inflation component. The income is deferred for federal and state and local income tax purposes until funds are withdrawn from the account holding the bond.

Index fund A passively managed fund that seeks to replicate the performance of a particular index (such as the Wilshire 5000, the S&P 500, or the Russell 2000) by buying all the securities in that index in direct proportion to their weight by market capitalization within that index and holding them.

Initial public offering (IPO) The first offering of a company's stock to the public.

Institutional fund A mutual fund that is not available to individual investors. Typical clients are pension and profit-sharing plans and endowment funds.

Institutional-style fund A mutual fund that is available to individual investors, under certain conditions, such as through registered investment advisors. These advisors require their clients to commit to the same type of disciplined, long-term, buy-and-hold strategy that is typical of institutional investors.

Leverage The use of debt to increase the amount of assets that can be acquired, for example, to buy stock. Leverage increases the riskiness of a portfolio.

Loser's game A game in which, while it is not impossible to win, the odds of winning are so low that it does not pay to play.

Market capitalization The market price per share times the number of shares.

Market-cap weighting The ownership of individual stocks determined by their percentage of market capitalization relative to all market capitalization of all stocks within an index or other benchmark. An index fund's holdings are market-cap weighted, not equally weighted.

Micro cap The smallest stocks by market capitalization: The ninth and tenth CRSP deciles. Other definitions used are the smallest 5 percent of stocks and stocks with a market capitalization of less than about $200 million.

Modern portfolio theory (MPT) A body of academic work founded on the following concepts. First, markets are too efficient to allow returns in excess of the market's overall rate of return to be achieved through trading systems. Active management is therefore counterproductive. Second, asset classes can be expected to achieve, over sustained periods, returns that are commensurate with their level of risk. Riskier asset classes, such as small companies and value companies, will produce higher returns as compensation for their higher risk. Third, diversification across asset classes can increase returns and reduce risk. For any given level of risk, a portfolio can be constructed that will produce the highest expected return. Finally, there is no right portfolio for every investor. Each investor must choose an asset allocation that results in a portfolio with an acceptable level of risk.

Mortgage-backed security (MBS) A financial instrument representing an interest in assets that are mortgage related (either commercial or residential).

MPT Modern portfolio theory.

NAIC National Association of Investment Clubs.

NASD The National Association of Securities Dealers.

NASDQ or NASDAQ The National Association of Securities Dealers (Automated) Quotations. A computerized marketplace in which securities are traded, frequently called the "over-the-counter market."

NASDAQ-100 Index The one hundred largest capitalization stocks on that exchange.

NAV Net asset value.

No-load A mutual fund that does not impose any charge for purchases or sales.

Nominal returns Returns that have not been adjusted for the negative impact of inflation.

NYSE New York Stock Exchange.

Out of sample Data from a study covering different time periods or different geographic regions from those of the original study.

Passive asset class funds Funds that buy and hold all securities within a particular asset class. The weighting of each security within the fund is typically equal to its weighting, by market capitalization, within the asset class. Each security is then typically held until it no longer fits the definition of the asset class to which the fund is seeking exposure. For example, a small company might grow into a large company and then no longer fit within the small company asset class. Fund managers may also use common sense and research to implement screens to eliminate certain securities from consideration (in an attempt to improve risk-adjusted returns). To be considered a passive fund, however, those screens cannot be based on any technical or fundamental security analysis. Examples of passive screens would be: minimum market capitalization, minimum number of years of operating history, and minimum number of market makers in the company stock.

Passive management A buy-and-hold investment strategy, specifically contrary to active management. Characteristics of the passive management approach include: lower portfolio turnover, lower operating expenses and transactions costs, greater tax efficiency, fully invested at all times, and a long-term perspective.

P/E ratio The ratio of price-to-earnings. Stocks with high price-to-earnings ratios are considered growth stocks; stocks with low P/E ratios are considered value stocks.

Prudent Investor Rule A doctrine imbedded within the American legal code stating that a person responsible for the management of someone else's assets must manage those assets in a manner appropriate to the financial circumstance and tolerance for risk of the investor.

Put An option contract that gives the holder the right, but not the obligation, to sell a security at a predetermined price on a specific date (*European put*) or during a specific period (*American put*).

Qubes (QQQ) An exchange-traded fund that tracks the NASDAQ-100 Index.

Real returns Returns that reflect purchasing power as they are adjusted for the negative impact of inflation.

Rebalancing The process of restoring a portfolio to its original asset allocation. Rebalancing can be accomplished either through adding newly investable funds or by selling portions of the best-performing asset classes and using the proceeds to purchase additional amounts of the underperforming asset classes.

Registered investment advisor A designation representing that a financial consultant's firm is registered with the appropriate state regulators and that the RIA representatives for that firm have passed the required exams.

REIT Real estate investment trust, a trust available to investors through the purchase of shares in it.

Retail funds Mutual funds that are sold to the general public, as opposed to institutional investors.

Risk premium The higher *expected,* not guaranteed, return for accepting the possibility of a negative outcome.

ROA Return on assets.

Russell 1000 The largest one thousand companies within the Russell Index.

Russell 2000 The smallest two thousand of the largest three thousand stocks within the Russell Index. Generally used as a benchmark for small-cap stocks.

S&P 400 Index A market-cap-weighted index of four hundred mid-cap stocks.

S&P 500 Index A market-cap-weighted index of five hundred of the largest U.S. stocks designed to cover a broad and representative sampling of industries.

S&P 600 Index A market-cap-weighted index of six hundred small-cap stocks.

SEC Securities and Exchange Commission.

Sector Fund A fund that restricts its investments to a single industry or sector of the economy (e.g., health care, technology).

Sharpe Ratio A measure of the return earned above the rate of return earned on riskless short-term U.S. treasury bills relative to the risk taken, with risk being defined as standard deviation of returns. Example: The return earned on an asset was 10 percent. The rate of one-month Treasury bills was 4 percent. The standard deviation was 20 percent. The Sharpe Ratio would be equal to 10 percent minus 4 percent (6 percent) divided by 20 percent, or 0.3.

Short selling Borrowing a security for the purpose of immediately selling it; with the expectation that the investor will be able to buy the security back at a later date, at a lower price.

Spiders (SPDR) Exchange-traded funds that replicate the various S&P Indices.

Standard deviation A measure of volatility or risk. For example, given a portfolio with a 12 percent annualized return and an 11 percent standard deviation, an investor can expect that in thirteen out of twenty annual periods (about two-thirds of the time) the return on that portfolio will fall within one standard deviation, or between 1 percent (12 percent − 11 percent) and 23 percent (12 percent + 11 percent). The remaining one-third of the time an investor should expect that the annual return will fall outside the 1–23 percent range. Two standard deviations (11 percent × 2) would account for 95 percent (nineteen out of twenty) of the periods. The range of expected returns would be between −10 percent (12 percent − 22 percent) and 34 percent (12 percent + 22 percent). The greater the standard deviation, the greater the volatility of a portfolio. Standard deviation can be measured for varying time periods, e.g., you can have a monthly standard deviation or an annualized standard deviation measuring the volatility for a given time frame.

Style drift The moving away from the original asset allocation of a portfolio, either by the purchase of securities outside the particular asset class a fund represents or by not rebalancing to adjust for significant differences in performance of the various asset classes within a portfolio.

Tactical asset allocation (TAA) Attempt to outperform a benchmark by actively shifting the portfolio's exposure to various asset classes (the portfolio's asset allocation).

Three-factor model Differences in stock returns are best explained by company size (market capitalization) and price (book-to-market [BtM] ratio) characteristics. Taken together, research has shown that the three factors on average explain more than 96 percent of the performance of diversified stock portfolios.

TIPS (Treasury Inflation-Protected Security) A bond that receives a fixed stated rate of return, but also increases its principal by the changes in the consumer price index. Its fixed-interest payment is calculated on the inflated principal, which is eventually repaid at maturity.

Tracking error The amount by which the performance of a fund differs from the appropriate index or benchmark. More generally, when referring to a whole portfolio, the amount by which the performance of the portfolio differs from a widely accepted benchmark such as the S&P 500 Index or the Wilshire 5000 Index.

Turnover The trading activity of a fund as it sells securities from a portfolio and replaces them with new ones. Assume that a fund began the year with a portfolio of $100 million in various securities. If the fund sold $50 million of the original securities and replaced them with $50 million of new securities, it would have a turnover rate of 50 percent.

Value stocks Companies that have relatively low price-to-earnings ratios or relatively high book-to-market ratios. These are considered the opposite of growth stocks.

Variable annuity An investment product with an insurance component. Taxes are deferred until funds are withdrawn.

WEBS World Equity Benchmark Securities are exchange-traded funds that track various foreign country indices such as the United Kingdom, German, and French equivalents of the S&P 500 Index.

Winner's game A game in which the odds of winning are reasonably high, and the prize of winning is commensurate with the risk of playing.

Suggested Reading

The following books are highly recommended for those wishing to expand their knowledge of the subjects covered in this book:

- Gary Belsky and Thomas Gilovich, *Why Smart People Make Big Money Mistakes.*

- Peter Bernstein, *Capital Ideas* and *Against the Gods.*

- William Bernstein, *The Intelligent Asset Allocator* and *The Four Pillars of Investing.*

- John Bogle, *Common Sense on Mutual Funds.*

- Charles Ellis, *Winning the Loser's Game.*

- Richard Ferri, *All About Index Funds.*

- Martin Fridson, *Investment Illusions.*

- Howard Kurtz, *The Fortune Tellers.*

- Burton G. Malkiel, *A Random Walk Down Wall Street.*

- Bill Schultheis, *The Coffeehouse Investor.*

- William Sharpe, *Portfolio Theory and Capital Markets.*

- Hersh Shefrin, *Beyond Greed and Fear.*

- William Sherden, *The Fortune Sellers.*

- Jeremy Siegel, *Stocks for the Long Run.*

- W. Scott Simon, *Index Mutual Funds.*

- Nassim Nicholas Taleb, *Fooled by Randomness.*

- Bruce J. Temkin, Don Phillips, and Deborah Thomas, *The Terrible Truth About Investing.*

- Ben Warwick, *Searching for Alpha.*

For those interested in learning more about the history of financial follies, there are three excellent books. The first is Charles MacKay's *Extraordinary Popular Delusions and the Madness of Crowds* (1841). His book is as relevant today as it was when it was first published more than 160 years ago. The others are *Devil Take the Hindmost,* by Edward Chancellor, and *Irrational Exuberance,* by Robert Shiller.

Acknowledgments

N o book is ever the work of one individual. This book is no exception. I thank my partners at Buckingham Asset Management and BAM Advisor Services, Susan Shackelford-Davis, Paul Forman, Steve Funk, Bob Gellman, Ed Goldberg, Joe Hempen, Mont Levy, Irv Rothenberg, Bert Schweizer III, and Stuart Zimmerman, for their support and encouragement. I would also like to thank Rick Hill, Jared Kizer, Vladimir Masek, and especially Wendy Cook for their contributions. Vladimir, thank you very much for your valuable insights and editorial suggestions. Any errors are certainly mine.

My appreciation is expressed to Truman "Mac" Talley, who has been my editor for over five years for all four of my books. His many contributions to each of these efforts have been incalculable. I would be remiss if I did not note the contributions of my agent, Sam Fleishman. I cannot imagine a better relationship between author and agent.

I also thank the people at DFA, especially Weston Wellington. I have learned much from DFA and Wes. He seems to always be able to explain difficult concepts in an easy and often humorous way.

I would also be remiss if I did not thank the many friends I have made on the Web sites www.indexfunds.com and Vanguard Diehards (www.diehards.org). I have learned much from them through our long discussions.

ACKNOWLEDGMENTS

I also thank Dan Solin, an attorney specializing in securities cases. He provided me with valuable insights and information.

Finally, I thank my family: Jodi, Jennifer, and Jacquelyn, thanks for allowing me to monopolize our computer for the fourth time now. I especially thank the love of my life, my wife, Mona. She showed tremendous patience in reading and rereading numerous drafts. I also thank her for her tremendous support and understanding for the lost weekends and the many nights that I sat at the computer well into the early morning hours. She has always provided whatever support was needed, and then some.

Index

INDEX

INDEX

INDEX

Kahneman, Daniel, 63
Keim, Donald, 167
Keirstead, Karl, 167–68
Kerschner, Edward, 161, 169
Keynes, John Maynard, 200
Knight, Frank, 83
knowledge
  information confused with, 131–35
Kodak, 205
Kogan, Leonid, 92
KPMG Peat Marwick, 185–87
Krimmel, John R., 61
Kritzman, Mark P., 64
Kumar, Alok, 125, 128, 130
Kumar, Ashok, 76
Kurtz, Howard, 173

large caps companies
  role of in portfolio, 239
Laster, David, 207–8
Lee, Dwight, 51–52
Legg Mason Value Trust, 43, 46
Lehman Bond Index, 31
Lehman Brothers, 161
Lettau, Martin, 137
"Level and Persistence of Growth Rates,
  The" (study), 150–52
Lilly, Richard, 77
Linder Large-Cap Fund, 43–44
Lintner, John, 148
Lipper Analytical Services study, 12
Lipper Inc., 9
Little, I. M. D., 147–48
location decision
  and portfolio, 242–43
Lux, Ted, 177
Lynch, Peter, 42–43, 174–75

MacKay, Charles, *xi*
Madhavan, Ananth, 167
Magellan Fund, 42–43
Magnan, Robert, 73–74
Malkiel, Burton G., 16–17, 18, 30, 137,
  200
"Managing the Asset Mix: Decisions and
  Consequences" (Arnott), 1
Management of Investment Decisions
  (Trone/ Allbright/Taylor), 23, 54
market strategist
  case against, 160–62
  value of forecasts, 157–75

markets
  efficiency of, 4–8
  fashions and, 198–200
Markman, Robert, 61–62
Markowitz, Harry, 246
Mayo, Mike, 75–76
mean reverting, 143–56
media
  conflict of interest, 79–84
men vs. women
  and investor overconfidence, 127–28
Mencken, H. L., 64
Mensa Investment Club, 129
Mercer, Jeffrey M., 92
Merck, 149, 217
Merrill Lynch, 7, 161
  "We're Bullish on America," 194
Merrill Lynch Canada, 69
Merrill Lynch Focus Twenty, 261
Merrill Lynch Growth, 261
Metrick, Andrew, 32
MFS Research, 170
Michaely, Roni, 77
Michelson, Stuart, 49–50
Microsoft, 8, 149
mid cap companies
  role of in portfolio, 239–41
Miller, Bill, 43, 44, 46
Miller, Merton, 82
MONEY magazine, 37, 79, 80–81, 134,
  169, 188
MoniResearch, 172
Montgomery Asset Management, 7, 127
Moody, Errold F., Jr., 251
Morey, Matthew, 27–28
Morgan Stanley, 7, 19–20, 37–38, 161
Morgan Stanley Capital International
  (MSCI) country indices, 209
Morgan Stanley Competitive Edge Best
  Ideas, 170
Morgan Stanley Dividend Growth, 260
Morningstar
  database, 6, 187, 261
  FundInvestor newsletter, 12, 168
  rating system, 25–30, 33–34
  studies, 9, 180
municipal bonds
  role of in portfolio, 229–30

NASA (National Association of
  Securities Dealers), 71–75

307

INDEX